Also by
Jeffrey Moussaieff Masson

Against Therapy:
Emotional Tyranny and the Myth of Psychological Healing

The Assault on Truth:
Freud's Suppression of the Seduction Theory

The Complete Letters of Sigmund Freud
to Wilhelm Fliess, 1887–1904

The Oceanic Feeling:
The Origins of Religious Sentiment in Ancient India

(with M.V. Patwardhan)
Śāntarasa and Abhinavagupta's Philosophy of Aesthetics

Aesthetic Rapture:
The Rasādhyāya of the Nāṭyaśāstra

(with D. D. Kosambi)
Love's Enchanted World: The Avimāraka of Bhāsa

(with W. S. Merwin)
The Peacock's Egg: Love Poems from Ancient India

A DARK SCIENCE

A DARK SCIENCE

Women, Sexuality,

and Psychiatry in the

Nineteenth Century

Jeffrey Moussaieff Masson

TRANSLATIONS BY

JEFFREY MOUSSAIEFF MASSON

AND MARIANNE LORING

PREFACE BY

CATHARINE A. MACKINNON

THE NOONDAY PRESS

FARRAR, STRAUS AND GIROUX

NEW YORK

Library of Congress Cataloging-in-Publication Data
A Dark science.
Translated from works originally published 1880–1900
in French and German.
Bibliography: p.
Includes index.
1. Psychiatry—Europe—19th century—Miscellanea.
2. Women—Mental health—Europe—History—19th century—
Case studies. 3. Women—Europe—Sexual behavior—
History—19th century. 4. Sexually abused children—
Mental health—Europe—History—19th century—Case
studies. 5. Adult child abuse victims—Mental health—
Europe—History—19th century—Case studies. I. Masson,
J. Moussaieff (Jeffrey Moussaieff).
[DNLM: 1. Child Abuse—collected works. 2. Psychiatry—
collected works. 3. Sex Offenses—collected works.
4. Women—psychology—collected works.
WM 100 D219 1880–1900a]
RC339.E85D37   1986   616.89   86-25683
Published simultaneously in Canada by Collins Publishers, Toronto
Printed in the United States of America
First edition, 1986
First paperback edition, 1988

Acknowledgments

Without the existence of the Lane Medical Library at Stanford University and its fine collection of nineteenth-century journals, this book could not have been written. First, I am grateful to Catharine MacKinnon both for her preface and for her inspiring work. I am indebted also to Dr. Leopold Dickstein, who was very helpful with the German medical terminology; Sue Doell, Leonard Frank, and Diana Russell made excellent suggestions concerning the introduction. Marianne Loring, who has dedicated her considerable skills to improving the quality of these translations, deserves special mention for her unfailing commitment to meticulous scholarship. I wish also to thank Barbara Williams, my editor at Farrar, Straus and Giroux, whose insight, patience, and resourcefulness have improved this book immeasurably; and Roger Straus, who offered his usual unflagging support. And, finally, I wish to express my delight at having two such wonderful children, Simone and Karima, in my life.

For Denise

Contents

Preface

Me dueles, Papá, me dueles.
["You're hurting me, Daddy,
you're hurting me."]

A two-and-a-half-year-old child recently overheard
in a suburban Los Angles shopping mall

Reading these texts is a lot like reading pornography. You feel you have come upon a secret codebook you were not meant to see but which has both obscured and determined your life. The sexual atrocities advanced here by doctors as promoting mental health during the nineteenth century might be beyond belief were they not also practiced during the Inquisition as liturgical justice, by the Third Reich as racial purity and medical experimentation, by the juntas of Latin America and Greece to maintain political power, and today by pornographers in the United States and worldwide as sexual entertainment. Women should study these medical articles for the same reasons they should study pornography: to see what is behind the ways they are seen and treated and to find out what men really think of them.

Behind psychotherapy's guise of treatment, just as surely as beneath pornography's protestations of liberation, lies the sexual sadism that is at the core of misogyny, here in its medical form. Women's bodies are dirty, women's minds are polluted by their bodies, women's sexuality is diseased, sex is evil because women are sex. Because men have social power over

women—power as lawyers and employers and fathers and priests
and teachers and policemen and pimps and writers and policy-
makers as well as doctors (our bodies in their hands)—what
men think of women is what is done.

Like pornography, these articles trade in half-truths. As
lawyer Gerry Spence puts it, "The real weaponry . . . is the
half-truth. It's like a half brick . . . you can throw a half brick
twice as far as a whole brick."[1] The resulting accounts have
all the credibility of truth and all the clout of lies. Both in
pornography and in these psychiatric accounts, it is very difficult to separate the simulated from the actual—what did *not*
happen that the text says did, from what *did* happen that the
text says did not. The diagnoses are not true because their
etiology, in which mind is diseased because body is diseased
because body is female, is not true. The dead-meat-causes-
flies approach to mental distress is not true. That anything at
all was wrong with these women and girls—beyond perhaps
having symptoms of venereal infection due to (undiagnosed)
sexual assault—may also be untrue. The doctors' claims of
healing by their savage methods are also, doubtless, not
true.

But, as with pornography, what these men write about doing
to these women *is* true. They did slice off these women's
clitorises; they did cut into them and remove their ovaries;
they did cut into them and not remove their ovaries but say
they did; they did tie them to their beds and listen to their
struggles and screams; they did rape them with red-hot irons.
The acts that psychiatry calls treatment, pornography (in its
one demystification) calls sex. In both, the acts are presented
as being for her own good and ultimately consensual, the
victim grateful in the end.

[1] Gerry Spence, *Trial by Fire: The True Story of a Woman's Ordeal at the Hands of
the Law* (New York: William Morrow, 1986), p. 374.

And, as with pornography, what these men say they thought, they thought. They thought that personality is genetically determined, that women and children lie about sexual abuse, that a woman's mind is sexed because her body is sexed, that a woman's qualities can be read by whether the look on her face is arousing. Thus, a woman's distress over what may well have been violation is attributed to "moral defect" and "baseness of character" by Schrenck-Notzing, to "precocious perversion" by Fournier, and diagnosed from "her somewhat erotic facial expression" by Flechsig.

Originally a challenger of this nineteenth-century tradition, Freud at first believed that adult women who told him they were sexually abused as children were telling the truth. When he revised his view and decided that the women were not, he became tradition's heir. The standard clinical practice, rooted prior to Freud but previously thought to be based on his work, has been to analyze reports of childhood sexual abuse as mentally telling but empirically false. Jeffrey Masson has argued that Freud changed his mind for reasons that were ultimately obscure but appeared far more personal, ideological, and professionally pressured than clinically based. In *The Assault on Truth*, Masson revealingly traces the documentary trail Freud left of his decision to disbelieve his patients, raising anew the possibility—never abandoned by many women—that Freud's patients and millions of anguished women since were simply recounting something that happened to them: something they did not want that hurt them in a way they could not get over.

Either such events happened or they did not. It is a study in comparative credibility that even after Freud changed his mind on the subject, and even after his reasons were revealed as dubious, the fact that Freud had *once* believed these women apparently gave them more credibility than anything has before or since. In a brief moment of institutional free-fall, the psychoanalytic establishment found itself confronting the possibility that the women had been telling the truth all along. If its rabid reaction to this possibility is any measure, psychoanalysis *must* believe not only that Freud was an objective scientist and right but also that childhood sexual abuse did not happen (at least not to Freud's patients) and does not happen now (at least not very often). Masson's book was more than iconoclastic; it threatened the ground on which psychoanalysis stands: more than Freud's credibility, women's lack of it. The truth about women did not matter to Freud. And neither the truth about women nor the truth about Freud now appears to matter to the Freudians.

When Freud changed his mind and declared that women were not telling the truth about what had happened to them, he attributed their accounts to "fantasy." This was regarded as a theoretical breakthrough. What we—those of us who believe that women and children do not secretly desire and imagine sexual abuse—now know is that "fantasy" in the psychoanalytic sense is not what women, in reality, imagine or desire any more than "fantasy" in the pornographic sense is. Both the psychoanalytic and the pornographic "fantasy" worlds are what men imagine women imagine and desire, because they are what men (raised on pornography) imagine and desire about women. As one doctor in this collection put it, pre-Freud: "Hysterics [meaning women] and children with a lively imagination" falsely allege sexual abuse. Once one realizes that the abuse is real, it is the doctors' elaborate alibis for the perpetrators, and their fantastic theoretical reconstructions of the victims' accounts, that require the "lively imagination." The fantasy theory is the fantasy.

The doctors say that the victims imagine sexual abuse, which is fantasy, not real, and that their sexuality caused it. In fact, it is the doctors who, because of their sexuality, imagine that sexual abuse is a fantasy when it is real. The acts these scientific texts recount, like the acts committed against Freud's patients in their childhood, are no less real and no less harmful than the acts committed against women and children in and because of pornography. Indeed, they are the same acts. Today, pornography is legitimized in the same way psychoanalysis is legitimized: it is all in *her* mind. Psychoanalysis, of which these articles are precursors, has been used to legitimize pornography, calling it fantasy; and pornography has been used to legitimize psychoanalysis, to show what women really are. Pornography presents itself as the answer to Freud's query: *this* is what women want.

Perhaps the process of theory-building occurred like this: Men heard accounts of child abuse, felt aroused by the account, and attributed their arousal to the child who is now a woman. Freud's contribution was the formal theory of fantasy and the unconscious. (The unconscious is where you put what you do not want to own up to; the analyst is supposed to be an expert on it.) Perhaps men respond sexually when women give an account of sexual violation, in the same way that men respond to pornography, which is (among other things) an account of the sexual violation of a woman. Seen in this way, therapy—and court testimony in sexual abuse cases—is live oral pornography. Psychoanalysis attributes the connection between the experience of abuse (hers) and the experience of arousal (his) to the fantasy of the girl child. When he hears it, he is aroused, so she must be aroused. When he does it, he likes it, so it cannot be abusive to her. Because he wants to do it, she must want it done.

This peculiar process, definitely psychosexual and in need of analysis, did not originate with Freud, these readings show. Freud and his contemporaries appear to have shared a mass sexual hallucination that became a theory that became a practice that became a scientific truth because men wanted it that way. They would no doubt protest that what they did was not "sexual," just as genital assault on a child with a waxing brush was, according to Fournier, a mere "simulation of rape," and sexual murders are, to some, "violence, not sex." Consider the lengths to which the psychiatrist in the following twentieth-century case goes to insist that the described killings by Peter Sutcliffe, tried for the brutal rapes and murders of thirteen women, are not sexual.[2] To Dr. Milne, the fact that Sutcliffe systematically killed first prostitutes ("Prostitutes should be exterminated . . . They corrupt men"), then just any woman because she was a woman ("I realized she wasn't a prostitute but at that time I wasn't bothered. I just wanted to kill a woman"), apparently indicated nothing sexual about the killings. Dr. Milne testified that there was no suggestion that Sutcliffe's habit of stabbing his victims through the same hole over and over "had a specific sexual symbolism." Mr. Ognall, the prosecutor, asked: "You take the view . . . there is no underlying sexual component in his attacks?" Dr. Milne: "In simple terms, although his victims were female and it might be thought to provide the suggestion that he must be a sexual killer, I am of the opinion that he is not primarily a sexual killer." Mr. Ognall then held up a seven-inch sharpened screwdriver which had been used to attack Josephine Whitaker. "There is absolutely no doubt that this wicked agent was introduced deep into the vagina with almost no injury to the external parts. That indicates the most fiendish cruelty deliberately done for sexual satisfaction. Do you agree?" Dr. Milne: "It may be a most vicious and foul thing to do, but not necessarily for sexual satisfaction." Mr. Ognall reminded the jury of how Sutcliffe had stabbed Jacqueline Hill through the breast. "Unless I'm very naïve . . . that betrays a specific, clear sexual element in his killing." Dr. Milne: "If you interpret it that

---

[2] Gordon Burn, ". . . *somebody's husband, somebody's son": The Story of Peter Sutcliffe* (London: William Heinemann Ltd., 1984), pp. 253–57. Emphasis added.

way, it does suggest that there may be a possible sexual component . . ." He still did not think that Sutcliffe was a sexual
sadist. Mr. Ognall described the killing of Helen Rytka, whom
Sutcliffe had hit with a hammer. When she was near death,
he had had sex with her. "Could you think of anything more
obscenely abnormal?" Dr. Milne: "I entirely agree with you,
but I still think that this was a use of sexual behavior for entirely
the wrong reason—to avoid detection, quieten her and get
away . . . *It was what the girl expected.*" After reading the
articles in this anthology, one wonders that Dr. Milne did not
consider Sutcliffe's acts to be therapy.

Just as Sutcliffe did what he did as sex, Zambaco enjoyed
doing what he did to the two little girls he treated. He enjoyed
writing what he wrote about them, as many of his male readers
enjoy reading it—sexually. Is Zambaco the soul of a scientist
playing at pornographer, or the soul of a pornographer playing
at science? Alas, there is no such distinction. In a precise
parallel to Sade's classic of pornography, *120 Days of Sodom*,
Zambaco's sexual sadism moves from observation and examination through treatment, including aversive conditioning and
restraints, to surgery and cauterization; Sade moves from ob-
jectification and molestation through rape, battery, bondage,
and discipline, to maiming and burning. Unlike Sade, Zambaco's sadomasochistic march toward death, the ultimate erotic
act—death is death whether in pornography or in medicine—
was stopped because his charges were removed from his care.
Both men used children. Both men did what they wrote. But
Sade had to buy or steal the access for which Zambaco was
presumably paid.

The motion beneath Zambaco's account is the motion beneath many an exalted text: the motion of erection. Pornography was the exclusive possession of the elite until mass media
democratized it. In the nineteenth century, men were looking
at pornography, writing theology; looking at pornography, writ-

ing literature; looking at pornography, writing laws and designing our political institutions. Who is to say they were not also looking at pornography and writing and practicing science and medicine? The world of Freudian psychology, in which everyday objects are infused with sexual meanings, is very like the world of pornography, in which everyday life is transformed into an erotic spectacle for men and a chamber of horrors for women.

When women and children refuse to confirm their abusers' beliefs that they are secretly having a wonderful time, it is said that they lie, congenitally. The psychoanalytic belief in "the mendaciousness of children" seems to be grounded in the specific belief that children lie about sex. In these documents, as in much law today, mothers—women—are said to instigate the lies or inflate fragments of stories into full accusations.[3] Women lie about sex for money, we are told, and often use children to do it. In these articles, as in pornography, children are used like women, as it were smell like women, in powerlessness, in sex.

Now as then, courtrooms have often been the setting for dramas of credibility on questions of sexual abuse. As a corrective for the child's likely lies, Motet, in these pages, urges a legal methodology that simply assumes the child lies. He then invents his own facts and designs a psychological construction of the child's facts which is far more bizarre than the child's—which at least comes from someone who was there. Without skipping a beat since the nineteenth century, public defenders in sexual assault cases are still routinely instructed that when a child "tells a credible story . . . [t]he theory of defense is that there was no abuse, and that the child, without appreciating the consequences, has adopted and incorporated the suspicions of one or more adults . . . The *unspoken* theory

[3] See Phyllis Chesler, *Mothers on Trial* (New York: McGraw-Hill, 1986).

of defense may be that . . . while the defendant may be guilty of indecent assault and battery, he's not a rapist."[4] If the defendant did the acts but did not force himself on the child, there was sex but no abuse; that is, the child wanted it. The defense instructions suggest phrasing questions to express uncertainty: "These things which you say happened"; to show how easily led and eager to please the child is: "Mummy was mad and kept asking what happened even when you said nothing . . . Finally you said yes, and she was happy . . ."; to suggest that the story was manipulated or coached by the prosecutor: "You came to court . . . sat in that chair and practiced your story . . . They told you when your answers were wrong and told you the right answers"; and to establish that the child got words like "penis" from an adult: "Mummy told you that a ding-dong is a penis . . . Some parts of the story were hard to tell . . . Mummy helped you with those words too." Always Mummy. Defense lawyers are instructed to "attack the assumption that the child could only know about sex as a result of first-hand experience": "Establish that she has seen her brother's penis, anybody other than your client's; that the family gets cable TV; that a friend was molested . . . that she has seen *Hustler* or a similar magazine or book." Now exposure of a child to pornography, which can be a part of or a form of sexual assault, has become a defense to a charge of sexual assault. Whenever children accuse adults of sexual abuse, whether or not a picture was taken, both the media and the defense lawyers often impugn the credibility of children because they are children. They take the view that abusive acts are not violations because the acts are sex. Where do you suppose they got an idea like that?

[4] All the quotations in this paragraph are from "Crossexamination of a Child," distributed by the Committee for Public Counsel of the Commonwealth of Massachusetts, appearing in duplicated materials prepared for the Bar Advocacy Program, Westford Regency Inn, Westford, Massachusetts, May 2, 1986. Emphasis in original.

Reading that a nineteenth-century woman could be eviscerated because she was upset, one could conceive a certain gratitude to Freud for getting the psychiatrists' hands off women's bodies, or at least directing their attention elsewhere. But the theory of women's minds he put in the doctors' hands is just as predetermined, just as hierarchical, just as asocial, just as sexualized, just as gendered, just as medicalized, and therefore just as damaging. Many scientists of the psyche continue to this day to deny the simple reality of sexual abuse and its formative role in fracturing women's minds, something which surely calls out to be healed as well as stopped. Trained to ignore the facts of systematic sexual abuse, few healers of the mind seem to have noticed the striking psychological similarities between its survivors and survivors of other horrors and systems of torture. For survivors of sexual abuse, as with survivors of Hiroshima for example, "all feelings [cease] to be on the surface because one [can]not exist and at the same time live with such feelings of abhorrence, disgust, and terror."[5] Survivors of sexual abuse, like survivors of the Holocaust, picture a world which is "characterized by . . . the destruction of the basic landmarks on which the world of human beings in our civilization is based, i.e. basic trust in human worth, basic confidence, basic hope."[6] With sexually abused girls, who grow into over a third of all women,[7] the simple reality of the experience is denied or considered victim-precipitated. The Holocaust and Hiroshima are not considered not to have occurred because their survivors exhibit these sequelae. But

[5] William Niederland, "Post-traumatic Symptomology," in H. Krystal, ed., *Massive Psychic Trauma* (New York: International Universities Press, 1968), p. 67—discussing Robert Lifton's theory of "psychological closure."
[6] Gustav Bychowski, "Permanent Character Changes as an Aftereffect of Persecution" in Krystal, ed., *supra* note 7, p. 81.
[7] Diana E. H. Russell, in *The Secret Trauma: Incest in the Lives of Women and Girls* (New York: Basic Books, 1986), p. 70, documents 43% of girls as victims of incestuous and/or extrafamilial sexual abuse involving sexual contact.

because the trauma of sexual torture induces attitudes and behaviors which in women are considered normally feminine—such as passivity and dependence and fearfulness and fawning and masochism and promiscuity—the sexual abuse of women is essentially seen not to have occurred, because of its impact on its victims.

Sexual abuse of women, like other mass persecutions, happens to each victim as a member of a group. Yet, unlike most other persecutions, it happens to each victim in utter isolation. Like other political atrocities, sexual abuse is a collective experience; all women are targeted for it and live with the terror of this knowledge. But unlike other political atrocities, each act of violation is experienced alone. Unlike any other catastrophe, natural or political, it is often attributed to the secret desire of the victim and the affection of the perpetrator. Although a politics of the experience of sexual abuse has begun to emerge, its inner world, with its effect on all women whether or not it happens to them, is as yet a silent one, its psychology unwritten. Some psychologists are now working with individual victims of rape, battery, sexual harassment, pornography, and prostitution, as well as incest and other childhood sexual abuse, with existing psychological tools. The exposure of the foundations of contemporary psychology in these nineteenth-century readings suggests, however, that a full recognition of the reality of sexual abuse will have to produce a new paradigm of the psyche.[8]

Women and girls had to be treated in certain ways for these texts to be written. And because these texts were written, women and girls will be treated in certain ways. These articles are

[8] In this project, other sources I have found helpful include the work of Phyllis Chesler, including *Women and Madness* (New York: Doubleday, 1972); Alice Miller, including *For Your Own Good: Hidden Cruelty in Child-Rearing and the Roots of Violence* (New York: Farrar, Straus and Giroux, 1983) and *Thou Shalt Not Be Aware: Society's Betrayal of the Child* (New York: Farrar, Straus and Giroux, 1984); and Klaus Theweleit, *Männerphantasien* (1977).

authoritative instructions on method, procedure, and tech-
nique. If she cries, tie her down. If she screams, burn her.
She wants it; it will make her well. Like pornography, the
approaches and procedures recounted and recommended and
eroticized have been done, and will be done, to countless other
women and girls *because of these texts.* To step into these pages
is to step into a world the pornographers have made and discover that you are in your doctor's office and the "image" is
you. No, the patient did not orgasm while having her clitoris
sliced off without anesthesia. No, she was not sexually aroused
by the pain or by being sexually examined in front of an
audience of male doctors. No, she did not combine abstinence
with nymphomania. But yes, Dr. Braun did examine her sexually in front of a crowd of giggling medical spectators; yes,
he did slice off her clitoris; and, yes, he did fantasize about
her sexuality and call it diagnosis. These articles, as writer
John Stoltenberg said of pornography, "lie about women but
tell the truth about men."[9]

Catharine A. MacKinnon

---

[9] John Stoltenberg, "The Forbidden Language of Sex," speech to American Writers'
Congress (New York: October 10, 1981). This insight refers to Andrea Dworkin,
Pornography: Men Possessing Women (New York: Perigee, 1981), who said that por-
nography tells lies about women.

A DARK SCIENCE

Introduction

This is a book of readings, selected and translated from French and German medical journals that appeared between 1865 and 1900. These readings—all from standard, reputable professional journals—illustrate how men in positions of power over women's lives, especially their sexual lives, misused that power to warp, damage, inhibit, and even destroy the women's sexual (and sometimes emotional and physical) selves. They are shockingly brutal, offensive, and pornographic. It is, to paraphrase a title from Doris Lessing, not a very nice story. But it is also a true story—perhaps even *the* true story.

These articles, moreover, are not mere curiosities from bygone days. In some fundamental sense, they represent the unspoken content of much of modern psychiatry. What I mean by this is that these nineteenth-century doctors display openly, deliberately, and without embarrassment an attitude that many modern psychotherapists (including psychologists, psychoanalysts, social workers, sex therapists, and so on) would be ashamed to acknowledge but which I believe accurately represents their approach to therapy. If the origins of this approach are examined, serious questions can be raised about modern psychiatric practice. That is, if we can fully expose the root, perhaps the plant will die.

For this exposure to succeed, it seems to me that what is required is more than a narrative account. Nothing has the same force as a historical document. Much of what follows makes for painful, almost unbearable reading. But for millions of women, these documents constructed and reinforced the nightmare world in which they lived. We cannot begin to understand that world, or free ourselves from the long shadow it cast, until we examine, firsthand, the foundations on which it was built.

The reader may well wonder why I selected these particular articles for this volume from among the many thousands on these topics that were published in the nineteenth century. How did I find them? What criteria did I use?

In a previous book, *The Assault on Truth: Freud's Suppression of the Seduction Theory*, I came to certain conclusions concerning Sigmund Freud's ideas about the sexual abuse of children (inappropriately named the "seduction theory"). I concluded that when Freud rejected the reality of sexual assaults on children, he retreated to the position held by traditional psychiatry in the nineteenth century. The changes that psychoanalysis introduced into society in general were far less fundamental than they would have been had Freud stood by his initial heretical and revolutionary hypothesis. On the surface, Freud remained to some extent in opposition to traditional psychiatry (e.g., in his tenaciously held view that psychoanalysis was not exclusively a branch of medicine, that society was ruled by unconscious forces few understood, etc.), but in fact he achieved an accommodation with that tradition. I was intrigued by the "deep structure," to borrow a term from linguistics, of this accommodation. What permitted Freud to make it, and what enabled so many psychiatrists to accept it?

I believed that I had found the answer in Freud's renunciation of the seduction theory. What had been a deeply disturbing, even threatening account of external reality was turned into a theory about the power of internal fantasy, one that was far less threatening to the fabric of society.

It was logical to assume that Freud was not the first person to consider the topic of the sexual abuse of children. Yet in the entire vast body of writings about Freud and his ideas, I could not find a single reference to a literature on child abuse predating Freud. It was with some sense of discovery, therefore, that I happened upon just such a literature in France when I was researching Freud's early ties with French medicine in the 1880s. Naturally, this material formed a central part of my book. But it occurred to me that, in *The Assault on Truth*, I did not emphasize its importance strongly enough. The existence of this material could not help but alter our understanding of the issue of reality vs. fantasy, whether one believed (as I do) that Freud had failed to solve one of the great riddles of our time when he claimed that accounts by women of sexual abuse in childhood were often imagined, or whether one believed (as do almost all psychiatrists) that Freud's vision offers a satisfactory explanation.

In reaching these conclusions about Freud's attitudes toward sexual abuse, I was satisfied that I had conducted my research as thoroughly as I possibly could. But I wanted to know more about the contours and dimensions of the debate surrounding the sexual abuse of children—and especially surrounding the larger issue of which this was an essential part, the sexuality of women—that had preceded Freud and shaped his thinking so strongly. In this area, I had to admit that my knowledge was far from complete. For my understanding of Freud's dilemma, I was able to track down a large number of relevant books and articles in French and German. Given my limited goal of finding new sources for Freud's shift in thinking about "seduction," this was no doubt sufficient. However, if I wished to carry my research beyond Freud, if I really wished to understand the background of Freud's thinking, then further reading was my next task.

I decided to select what I ascertained to be the major psychiatric, pediatric, and gynecological journals in French and German—thirty-four in all—limiting myself more or less to the period from 1880 to 1900 (which in many ways corresponds to the rise of the importance of psychiatry in European medicine). I finally selected about one thousand volumes. In two years, with the steady assistance of Marianne Loring, I was able to go through some seven hundred and fifty of them.[1] At the same time, I had the very strong sense that to complete my search, it would be necessary to seek out not only published material but unpublished as well, for I knew that when it came to case histories, what got into print was always a less truthful, less frightening, less honest account of a real event. If I could gain access to an extensive collection of real, unsanitized, unfictionalized case histories from the same period, my research would benefit enormously. Did such a collection exist? Fortunately, it did, in the astonishingly complete archives of the Sanatorium Bellevue in Kreuzlingen, Switzerland, which had belonged for generations to the Binswanger family. I was very kindly given access to this unique material during a two-week stay there, and we were able to read all the private medical case histories of female patients in the asylum between 1880 and 1900. This came to some three hundred cases. We made notes on and copies of those we found most interesting. In the end the material was not included in this book, though it formed an important element of the research for it.

With this reading behind me, I felt I was in a better position to understand the background of Freud's thinking about sexual abuse. I came to understand that the theoretical position a psychiatrist took about the sexual abuse of children was a sure indication of his view of women's sexuality. Those psychiatrists who believed that children imagined sexual assaults also believed that these female children grew into "hysterical" women, whose emotional lives would be dominated by these and similar "fantasies."[2] These same women formed the mainstay of psychiatric practice in the nineteenth century. What writings best outlined this process, which I saw as the essence of nineteenth-century psychiatric beliefs? This was a question I kept very much in mind as I read through the journals, and it influenced my final selections. I chose to translate those articles I thought illustrated most graphically what I believe to be the fallacies and contradictions underlying nineteenth-century gynecology and psychiatry.

It is important to stress that the ideas expressed in the articles to follow are not out of the ordinary. They were not published in fringe publications disdained by the luminaries of the medical profession at the time. Indeed, some of the authors of these articles (e.g., Fournier, Hegar, Flechsig) were luminaries themselves, holding university chairs or heading university clinics. Few of these articles called forth any dissent from the medical profession. However, that there were some men (even if very few) who spoke out against abuse tells us something about how, eventually, that abuse can be ended. I would have included more such dissent in this anthology had I been able to find it. Here, only Jasinski and Israel stand out as imperfect examples of physicians whose conscience was touched by what they observed around them.

We cannot know how women, the object of all this writing, felt about what was written. It is safe to hypothesize that they did not read it, for the journals in which it was published were read only by doctors, and women were scarcely among their ranks. Women were the victims of the views expressed in the articles, but they were never afforded the opportunity to corroborate, criticize, or in any way comment on them. No doubt if they had, the dissenting literature would have been vastly augmented and would have improved in quality. Although Sigmund Freud was the first man in history to acknowledge (in writing) the significance of the sexual abuse of children, it is evident that many women, silenced by fear, were aware of this abuse before and after Freud. If they talked to other women, no doubt they would often be believed. If they spoke to men, they would, in almost every case, be disbelieved. I am not aware of a single account of sexual abuse by a woman published during the nineteenth century. Who in the nineteenth century would permit its publication? It was not until the rise of the women's movement in the 1970s that such cases could be openly discussed.[3]

Are doctors of divinity blind, or are they hypocrites? I suppose some are the one, and some the other; but I think if they felt the interest in the poor and lowly, that they ought to feel, they would not be so *easily* blinded. A clergyman who goest to the south, for the first time, has usually some feeling, however vague, that slavery is wrong. The slaveholder suspects this and plays his game accordingly. He makes himself as agreeable as possible; talks on theology, and other kindred topics. The reverend gentleman is asked to invoke a blessing on a table loaded with luxuries. After dinner he walks round the premises, and sees the beautiful groves and flowering vines, and the comfortable huts of favored household slaves. The southerner invites him to talk with these slaves. He asks them if they want to be free, and they say, "O, no, massa." This is sufficient to satisfy him. He comes home to publish a "South-Side View of Slavery," and to complain of the exaggerations of abolitionists. He assures people that he has been to the south and seen slavery for himself; that it is a beautiful "patriarchal institution"; that the slaves don't want their freedom; that they have hallelujah meetings, and other religious privileges.

What does *he* know of the half-starved wretches toiling from dawn till dark on the plantations? of mothers shrieking for their children, torn from their arms by slave-traders? of young girls dragged down into moral filth? of pools of blood around the whipping post? of hounds trained to tear human flesh? of men screwed into cotton gins to die? The slaveholder showed him none of these things, and the slaves dared not tell of them if he had asked them.

[Linda Brent, *Incidents in the Life of a Slave Girl,* 1861]

When we are confronted with cruelty, in accounts of what happened during the First and Second World Wars, for example, we often escape fully imaginative reflection on the events by noting that such cruelty is generally found on both sides of a war. But this is precisely the kind of defense mechanism that leads to the strange phenomenon of "blaming the victim,"[4] which seems to surface every time there is an outrage beyond our capacity to understand. The fact that six million Jews were murdered by the Germans seems to unleash a peculiar kind of fury in some of those who hear about it. Hannah Arendt, in her book *Eichmann in Jerusalem,* blamed the Jews for their own destruction: "Wherever Jews lived, there were recognized Jewish leaders, and this leadership, almost without exception, cooperated in one way or another, for one reason or another, with the Nazis. The whole truth was that if the Jewish people had really been unorganized and leaderless, there would have been chaos and plenty of misery but the total number of victims would hardly have been between four and a half and six million people."[5] The anger in this passage is palpable.

Arendt is not alone. In the three-volume "definitive" edition of *The Destruction of the European Jews,* Raul Hilberg, the noted Holocaust scholar, writes about the period in Warsaw in 1939 when the Jews were forced to wear the yellow star, and states with acid anger: "The Jews took to the stars immediately. In Warsaw, for example, the sale of armbands became a regular business. There were ordinary armbands of cloth and fancy plastic armbands that were washable."[6] Arendt herself cited this particular passage as evidence of "the sordid details" of Jewish "cooperation." But this movement away from the source of the cruelty to the object of the cruelty is an index of the feelings of a troubled and anguished person. It is no longer part of the search for truth but a reflex action, an unloading of feeling. This is evident enough if one stops to think about the comments themselves. Hannah Arendt sounds like God on Judgment Day. How can she possibly know how many victims there would have been had things been otherwise? Never mind whether her claim of cooperation is correct or not: how can her conclusions be taken as anything other than a cry of pain and frustration? Similarly, what kind of statement has Hilberg made? He built his reputation on a masterly command of primary sources, which, until recently, consisted of Nazi records and propaganda. But how could a Nazi source tell us how the Jews reacted to the forced wearing of the yellow star? It could tell us that they were forced to wear it, but could not possibly fathom the emotions of the wearer. Only those who lived through it could do that. Hilberg's source is not a Jew. His account is taken from the anti-Semitic Nazi newspaper *Die Krakauer Zeitung*.[7] But if we relied on such sources for information, no doubt we, too, would arrive at a rather peculiar idea of Jewish conduct during the Second World War. Or rather, not so peculiar: our idea of the Jew would then correspond exactly to that of the Nazi caricature.

This mechanism of shifting one's attention from the perpetrator of a crime to the victim, and then absorbing oneself in the conduct of the victim, is one that seems to me central to nineteenth-century psychiatry in its attitudes toward women and children. What we see in the articles in this book is an openly stated position: The victim must be to blame. If a child claims to have been raped, a great deal of attention is paid to the possibility that this is a false accusation. If the rape is actually proven, then the attention shifts to what the child did to create the opportunity in the first place.

In the wake of the many press reports in the last few years about large-scale sexual-abuse trials—the McMartin case in Los Angeles, for example—a number of articles have appeared in which the public is cautioned not to fall into the trap of mass "hysteria" over the trials, which might lead to the false conviction of innocent citizens. Comparisons with the Salem witch trials are invoked.[8] We arc advised not to allow our emotions to run away with our reason, and not to make irresponsible and unlikely accusations or to be unduly suspicious. But it is not altogether ironic that the word "hysteria" is frequently associated, in the popular imagination and in psychoanalytic tradition, with women. And child abuse, many feel, is a woman's issue. No doubt they are right, if they mean that women, primarily, are the ones who take it seriously, though it affects children of both sexes. The woman who is legitimately concerned about child abuse is said to be "obsessed" with it. I note, however, that accusations of hysteria are rarely followed by a sober presentation of statistics. The reason behind this silence is not difficult to understand: there are no such "sobering" statistics. All the statistics—whether they come from feminists, or the *Los Angeles Times,* or the government—are frightening in their implications: one in three women, before the age of eighteen, will be the victim of sexual assault. If we add to this figure rape and sexual harassment, there is hardly a woman growing up in our society who, at some time in her life, will not be subjected to unwanted sexual aggression.[9] How can it not be a problem that concerns all of us? How can the adjective "hysterical" enter the picture at all, unless as a carryover from the nineteenth century?

Psychiatrists, especially since Freud, use the word in a more refined manner, but it hardly loses any of its pejorative undertones. A "hysterical personality disorder" is still a supposedly serious disorder, serious enough to find its place in the *Diagnostic and Statistical Manual of Mental Disorders* (the *DSM* III, which was published by the American Psychiatric Association in 1980), where it is called a Histrionic Personality Disorder.[10] The authors of the manual write that "individuals with this disorder are lively and dramatic and are always drawing attention to themselves. They are prone to exaggeration and often act out a role, such as the 'victim' or the 'princess,' without being aware of it . . . Such individuals are typically attractive and seductive . . . Flights into romantic fantasy are common. The disorder is apparently common, and diagnosed far more frequently in females than in males." This is little more than an example of name-calling at a particularly primitive level. But it is extremely dangerous, for often it is precisely the woman who has been battered or the woman who has been raped (not to mention incestuously assaulted) to whom this pseudo-scientific label has been attached, and whose real complaints are dismissed as nothing more than what the profession calls "acting out the role of victim." The psychiatrist prides himself on penetrating the "disguise," whereas in fact all he has done is to avoid and deny the reality of the woman's situation, relying upon psychiatric nomenclature to cloak his ignorance.

A blatant example of this, which has been vigorously combatted by feminists,[11] is the very recent decision of the American Psychiatric Association to add a new illness, Masochistic Personality Disorder, to the official diagnostic canon. One of the criteria reads as follows: "Remains in relationships in which others exploit, abuse, or take advantage of him or her, despite opportunities to alter the situation." It is quite clear that female victims of incestuous assault and women who are battered by their husbands are the target of this diagnosis, and on the basis of their suffering are to be labeled as mentally ill as well. The proposal was successfully challenged by the Committee on Women of the American Psychiatric Association. But in my opinion, the victory was a hollow one, for all that was achieved was a compromise: the term "masochistic personality" would be abandoned in favor of "self-defeating personality." I see no improvement, just a refinement and a further exercise in name-calling.

Comparisons between modern child-abuse scandals and the seventeenth-century Salem witch trials usually cite the role children played as accusers in both situations. As a result of children's testimony, many innocent adults were burned at the stake. But like the earlier remarks I cited about Jewish cooperation during the Second World War, this comparison is the result of historical ignorance, frustration, and loose thinking. If we examine the records in Salem, the "children" who made the accusations were mostly in their late teens—they were manipulated not by their fantasies but by adult males into accusing not just any other adult but almost always adult women (when it was a man, then it was a man whom other men wanted out of the way or a man who refused to shun a wife accused of witchcraft). [12] And when it came to burning, only a small number of male "witches" were burned. The rest were women. When we consider the larger phenomenon of witch burning in Europe, we know that for every man who was burned at the stake as a witch, thousands and thousands of women were burned. The parallel, then, with the accusations of child abuse simply does not hold. By and large, *men* did not burn at the stake because of what a child said. (Probably more children were burned as witches' accomplices than men as witches.) *Women* burned at the stake, accused by men, tortured by men, tried by men, and executed by men. [13] If men are now being accused of child abuse on a gigantic scale, it is simply ludicrous for other men to point to the Salem witch trials as a parallel to the alleged abusers' "innocent" suffering.

Moreover, it should be pointed out that modern studies of witchcraft by men stress the "real guilt" of the women: either they were witches (though without supernatural powers), or they were "hysterics" in the tradition of Charcot's early studies of witchcraft and hysteria, or they were socially "marginal" women who were a burden to society.[14] Yet another example of the shifting of guilt from criminal to victim, and of the unrestricted violence that men have unleashed against women throughout history.

Certain unexamined assumptions take on the force of moral truth when they are attested to by an expert. Thus, Jean Piaget's study of lying in his influential book *The Moral Judgment of the Child* has played a crucial role in the field of child psychology since it was written in 1932. Consider these oft-quoted lines:

Everyone knows, thanks to the fine work done by Stern and his followers, that until the age of 7–8 the child finds systematic difficulty in sticking to the truth. Without actually lying for the sake of lying, *i.e.*, without attempting to deceive anyone, and without even being definitely conscious of what he is doing, he distorts reality in accordance with his desires and his romancing. To him a proposition has value less as a statement than as a wish, and the stories, testimony and explanations given by a child should be regarded as the expression of his feelings rather than of beliefs that may be true or false.[15]

Many people believe that children can tell the truth only at certain developmental stages. But these "stages" could well be a figment of adult imagination rather than psychological reality. Too often, adults speak for children, ascribe motives, interpret behavior, or even invent solutions to problems that are entirely foreign to a child. An extreme example comes from an article by James Henderson, professor of psychiatry at the University of Toronto Medical School, entitled "Is Incest Harmful?", published in the *Canadian Journal of Psychiatry*: "Some experienced clinicians and scholars have come to view incestuous behavior in families as a dysfunctional albeit sometimes relatively stable attempted solution to or at least modus vivendi with already existing pain in the form of shared feelings of abandonment or fears of personal or family annihilation. A stable but dysfunctional solution given potential catastrophes of this order may well be preferable to no solution at all."[16] Preferable to whom? To the psychiatrist? And who shares the feelings of abandonment? Whose solution are we discussing? Henderson is of course speaking for the adult male, the initiator of incest, but he does not say this. He pretends to be speaking for the female victim as well. His assumption that incest is usually undertaken by mutual consent of both parties is never examined.

Why do we have a tendency to believe that a child is fabricating, lying, fantasizing, or inventing? Because Western psychiatry has maintained this belief since its inception, no doubt appalled by the fact that children so often speak the truth with no artificial concern for its effects on those around them. In reading through nineteenth-century French and German medical journals, especially journals of pediatrics and psychiatry, I was struck by the number of articles about children's unreliability, their tendency to simulate. Equally pervasive was the view that if children really experienced abuse, they deserved it, or in some sense provoked it. A typical "authoritative" view from the nineteenth century is the following comment by the distinguished Belgian psychiatrist Charles Sansom Féré, from the *Archives de neurologie*:

It would not have been without interest to see if the majority of little girls who become the victims of these degenerates are not themselves predisposed to it by belonging to a special category; a large number of these girls are hereditarily tainted and present organic anomalies. Often they are prematurely developed and have a peculiar genital physiognomy which is mirrored by a particular expression in their eyes. This contrasts with the childlike lower part of the face and the rest of the body. It is this look which somehow brings them to the attention of depraved men.[17]

Is this an isolated instance belonging to a bygone age? I think not. Consider the case of the sexual-assault charge dismissed in 1983 against a Wisconsin man who allegedly fondled a ten-year-old girl: Waukesha County circuit judge Roger P. Murphy said in his decision that although the man had intentionally touched the girl, sexual arousal could not have resulted, since she was undeveloped. And in Lancaster, Wisconsin, in 1983, Grant County judge William Rinecke sentenced Ralph Snodgrass, twenty-four, convicted of sexually assaulting the five-year-old daughter of the woman with whom he lived, to only ninety days in jail, because the girl was "an unusually sexually promiscuous young lady. No way do I believe Mr. Snodgrass initiated sexual contact."[18]

Sándor Ferenczi suggested in 1932[19] that children who are sexually abused may sometimes add to their memories of the real event fantasies of further sexual perversions that correspond to the deeper layer of the internal reality as they experience it. A child may add to an already horrendous tale of abuse a bizarre and seemingly impossible detail. I heard of one case where a young girl told the court that her father opened the belly of her horse and sewed her into it. The court then dismissed her accurate account of abuse by claiming that she was unable to distinguish fantasy from reality. But such a fantasy in no way invalidates the account. We cannot know why the child reports such a story. Perhaps she is telling something about the psychological reality of the abuse, how it isolated her from any hope of protection, for example—though this is merely an interpretation, and hence suspect. Fantasies may act in a manner similar to dreams by revealing the emotional truth underlying the physical reality, and the sensitive listener may learn a great deal about an earlier, even forgotten, event by paying careful attention to these dreams and fantasies. Such embroidery should not make us skeptical of the child's ability to distinguish fact from fantasy; it should simply prepare us for a longer, more difficult, and more complex kind of listening. The process of listening to children in all seriousness and humility has begun only very recently.[20]

As an avid reader of modern psychiatric case histories during my analytic training, I was often struck by a certain imbalance. We knew what the *psychiatrist* thought the patient was suffering from (it should be understood that I use the term "patient" for the sake of convenience; in fact, it is borrowed from general medicine to make psychiatry appear more objective than it actually is), but we very rarely heard the voices of the patients themselves. It was very much like the nineteenth century: Medical doctors wrote in detail about their patients, but the story was very one-sided. I had a feeling that a world entirely different from the one presented in the professional journals existed just beyond my ken. The brief time I spent working in a psychiatric institution (as part of my training, an attempt to catch up on the psychiatric experience I lacked as an academic) certainly alerted me to the existence of a "dark underbelly" of psychiatry. I left because a patient begged me not to permit electroshock; when I learned that this so-called treatment was being administered to him by nurses against his will, as punishment for some minor infraction of one of the many trivial and unjust rules in the asylum, I naïvely rushed to the director with my "discovery" of abuse, only to learn that he and the psychiatrists working under him were completely indifferent to such abuse. I returned to the more rarefied world of psychoanalysis, where, I was persuaded, such barbarities were a matter of the ancient past. How wrong I was is only becoming clear to me today. Psychoanalysis is an integral and essential part of the world inhabited by institutional psychiatrists, who drug, shock, and even lobotomize patients—today, in 1986. One result of the major "anti-psychotic" tranquillizers (such as Thorazine) recently coming into public focus is a condition called tardive dyskinesia, a form of brain damage. Psychiatrists continue to prescribe these drugs in full awareness of the danger of severe brain damage after prolonged use. The more immediate direct effects of these drugs include involuntary muscle movements of the tongue, mouth, jaw, fingers, and other extremities. How sad it is that when we see people on the streets suffering from this artificially induced brain damage we think of the symptoms as a sign of "mental illness" instead of a result of the drugs the patients have been forced to take to cure a disease they never had.

My professional training had left me largely ignorant of a body of literature critical of psychiatry. True, I knew the works of Thomas Szasz, and the anti-psychiatry movement spearheaded by R. D. Laing, but I found these books very unsatisfying. Szasz was not, in my opinion, a serious historian, even though I shared many of his beliefs about psychiatry, and although Laing was justly critical of much of what had happened in British psychiatry, he was substituting his own dubious therapy, leaving intact many of the basic assumptions behind treatment of the so-called mentally ill. "Anti-psychiatry," in Laing's school, was against one form of psychiatry in favor of another, equally undesirable form. It was still psychiatry. Neither Laing nor Szasz struck me as radical enough. Moreover, in their work, psychiatrists were once again speaking for their patients. I soon discovered the more radical professional literature that I was looking for: John Friedberg, in his book *Shock Treatment Is Not Good for Your Brain*,[21] and Peter

Breggin, a psychiatrist who has done a great deal to stop the outrage of what he correctly calls "brain-disabling therapies"— namely, psychiatric drugs, electroshock, and psychosurgery— in his book *Psychiatric Drugs: Hazards to the Brain*.[22] In this book, Breggin points out that even a major advocate of these drugs, the psychiatrist Heinz Lehmann, calls them a "pharmacological substitute for lobotomy." Another outstanding book by Breggin is *Electroshock: Its Brain-Disabling Effects*,[23] a careful, elaborate, scholarly account of the very grave dangers this procedure poses. In his preface, he had the extraordinary fortitude to write: "I did not have the courage to risk my own nascent career by refusing to give electroconvulsive therapy during my hospital training. I have regretted that cowardice for more than a decade." This may well be a unique confession in the annals of medicine. His work against lobotomy helped significantly to discourage the use of this criminal activity.[24]

There can be no doubt that, historically, psychosurgery has been used predominantly against women (and also, to some extent, against children). According to Breggin, whose testimony before Senator Edward Kennedy's Subcommittee on Health in the United States appears in the *Congressional Record*, women are more than twice as likely to be subjected to lobotomy as men: "The fact that she is returned to being a satisfactory housewife and mother is again typical of psychosurgery studies. Not only have the vast majority of patients been women, both in the past and in the current literature, but the two most in-depth prolobotomy studies have already told us psychosurgery is much more effective on women than on men because women can more easily be returned home to function as partially crippled, brain-damaged housewives, while there are no social or occupational roles for partially crippled, brain-damaged men."[25] Also in the *Congressional Record*, Breggin reports on the work of O. J. Andy, professor and director of neurosurgery at the University of Mississippi

School of Medicine, who at the time was operating on hyperactive children. Breggin says: "In a personal letter to me dated May 28, 1971, Andy writes that he has operated on thirty to forty patients ages seven through fifty, the *majority* children. In another personal letter to me, his colleague Jurko writes that the age range begins at *five*. The goal is frankly stated by Jurko—to 'reduce the hyperactivity to levels manageable by parents'! . . . Andy describes the children as suffering from 'some form of hyperactivity, aggression, and emotional instability.' "[26] In his book on electroshock, Breggin also points out that twice as many women as men receive electroshock.

Soon, too, I found the voices I had been looking for from ex-inmates of psychiatric institutions: the brilliant and moving book by Janet and Paul Gotkin, *Too Much Anger, Too Many Tears*,[27] a heartrending account of what life in New York's psychiatric institutions is really like. What had psychiatrists to say about these abuses? When they deigned to recognize them at all, I found a new excuse: Yes, abuses occurred, but they were anomalies, rarities. Thus, the psychiatrist James Mann, reviewing the Gotkins' book in the *American Journal of Psychiatry*, said: "I suppose that it is possible in a world in which anything can happen that Janet had the misfortune to fall upon a selected group of the worst psychiatrists and the worst private and public mental hospitals."[28] Through reading her book and another good book in the same genre, *On Our Own*, by Judi Chamberlin,[29] I found out about the newsletters published by ex-inmates, *Madness Network News*[30] and *Phoenix Rising*, and found the literature I had been searching for. Here were firsthand accounts of electroshock, forced drugging, psychiatric incarceration, and all the myriad forms of humiliation and brutalization that psychiatric patients have always been subjected to, written by people who experienced them rather than by those who administered them. The quality of the writing, the searing anger, and the authenticity of the voices raise many of the pieces high above the level of ordinary reportage. During my reading I came across so many tragic cases it seems invidious to single out any one for retelling. But three in particular could come straight out of the nineteenth century: Ted Chabasinski, in an article written in 1973 for *Rising Up Crazy*, tells how in 1944 he

was sent to the Bellevue children's psychiatric ward, to be officially diagnosed and to be made an experimental animal for Dr. Bender. I was one of the first children to be "treated" with electric shock. I was six years old . . . I spent my seventh birthday this way, and my eight and ninth birthdays locked in a seclusion room at Rockland State Hospital . . . Sometimes there was nothing in the room, nothing at all, and I would lie on the mattress and cry . . . I would curl into a ball, clutching my knees, and rock back and forth on the mattress, trying to comfort myself. And I cried and cried, hoping someone would come . . . And so I spent my childhood waking from nightmare to nightmare in locked rooms with scraps of torn comic books and crusts of bread and my friends the mice, with no one to tell me who I was. And when I was seventeen and the shrinks thought they had destroyed me, they set me free.[31]

Leonard Roy Frank, who has been very active in the movement, managed to get his "medical" files from the "hospital" where he was incarcerated. They form the core of one chapter of John Friedberg's *Shock Treatment Is Not Good for Your Brain*.[32] The documents reveal clearly that Leonard Roy Frank's five major symptoms, in the eyes of the doctors who examined him, were: he was not working; he had grown a large, full beard; he had piercing eyes; he was a vegetarian; and, in the words of the medical examiners, he "lived the life of a beatnik— to a certain extent." When he was taken, involuntarily, to a psychiatric institution, he developed a sixth symptom: he did not recognize that he was ill. Therapy consisted of artificially induced insulin comas and electroconvulsive shocks. The psychoanalyst who diagnosed Frank as a "paranoid schizophrenic" also suggested removing his beard as part of the therapy: "Moreover, I believe that during one of the comas, his beard should be shaved as a therapeutic device to provoke anxiety and create some change in his body image." The doctor who actually gave the shock treatments wrote to Frank's parents: "We have increased the frequency of the shock treatments this week to a total of five treatments, namely one daily, as I wanted to have him a little more confused and clouded at this time if we are to remove the beard so that he would not be too acutely aware and distressed by this procedure."

One of the activists in the Psychiatric Inmates Liberation Movement, a most incisive thinker, is a woman in her twenties who has asked to remain anonymous out of fear that her family would have her recommitted. She showed me the documents she obtained from the psychiatric institution concerning her hospitalization (she would call it, correctly I believe, incarceration). The admitting doctor, who was a young resident in psychiatry, recognized what was happening to this fifteen-year-old girl: she was the victim of incestuous assault by her father. Given his position within the institutional hierarchy, however, the resident dared not express himself openly (sexual abuse was not a popular topic in the early seventies in psychiatric hospitals). He used the normal formula: "This is an adolescent girl struggling to resolve Oedipal difficulties and struggling to separate from her family." Translation: This is an adolescent girl trying desperately to fend off an incestuous, violent father, and get herself to a safe place, away from the scene of a horrendous crime. The resident continued: "The father also has obvious sexual relationships with X." A brave, unambiguous phrase. It was not to remain, however. The attending psychiatrist, who was also the head of the hospital, went through the report and made two key changes: where the resident wrote "obvious," she substituted "somewhat," and where the resident wrote "sexual," it was changed to "sexualized." The resident summarized by saying that the "patient is an adolescent girl with a severe adolescent adjustment reaction with massive anger." She had, he states, to "resolve her neurotic conflict as well as her separation battle with her parents." Considering that he knew she had been sexually assaulted, this is an extraordinary statement, one that effaces the truth of her victimization with a psychological cliché. Is the desire to leave home under these circumstances a neurotic adolescent adjustment reaction or simple courage? The doctor recognized what was really happening to this girl, but was completely unable to admit it publicly. Is this good medicine or bad ethics? When a letter was sent to the committee for admissions at a second institution, the corrections of the psychiatrist replaced the resident's honest account, so that it now reads: "The father also has somewhat sexualized relationships with X." The real sexual abuse was glossed over, forgotten, replaced, and the girl began her odyssey in the nightmare world of institutional psychiatry.

These and other cases dramatically underline the disparity between what the doctor says the patient feels and what the patient really feels. For example, the psychiatrist administering electroshock may say: There is no memory loss. And the patient says: I have lost my memory. It is easy to know whom to believe. One is speaking theoretically and out of a desire to protect his practice, the other is speaking from experience. I have never heard of any psychiatrist who has undergone shock "therapy" himself. I gather that a group of ex-inmates of psychiatric institutions in England have offered a large reward to any psychiatrist willing to undergo shock treatment, but have yet to find any takers.

As far as I know, no prominent child psychiatrist or child psychoanalyst has written about the sexual abuse of children in any sustained fashion. It is as though the topic were not entirely germane to the field of child psychiatry. And if one were to confine one's reading to the standard textbooks in psychiatry, it would seem as though sexual abuse is rare enough to justify this lack of interest. In the 1975 edition of the *Comprehensive Textbook of Psychiatry*, James Henderson estimates that the frequency of all forms of incest is one case per million.[33] Yet we now know, from the more sophisticated random sample surveys done by Diana Russell and others, that the true figure is alarmingly higher.[34] Russell's statistics show that, before the age of fourteen, 28 percent of 930 San Francisco women had experienced unwanted sexual touching or attempted sexual touching, and the figure for sexual abuse before the age of eighteen was an astonishing 38 percent.

When C. Henry Kempe published his original article on physical child abuse in 1962, he noted an atmosphere of denial:

There is reluctance on the part of many physicians to accept the radiologic signs as indications of repetitive trauma and possible abuse. This reluctance stems from the emotional unwillingness of the physician to consider abuse as the cause of the child's difficulty . . . psychiatric knowledge pertaining to the problem of the battered child is meager, and the literature on the subject is almost nonexistent . . . Many physicians find it hard to believe that such an attack could have occurred and they attempt to obliterate such suspicions from their minds, even in the face of obvious circumstantial evidence. The reason for this is not clearly understood.[35]

Physicians writing about the sexual abuse of children confront an even greater wall of disbelief and denial. Thus Suzanne Sgroi, writing in 1978, complained: "Sexual abuse of children is a crime that our society abhors in the abstract, but tolerates in reality . . . Those who try to assist sexually abused children must be prepared to battle against incredulity, hostility, innuendo, and outright harassment. Worst of all, the advocate for the sexually abused child runs the risk of being smothered by indifference and a conspiracy of silence."[36]

Such disbelief has a long and distinguished history in psychiatry in this country. One of the most famous examples comes from Lauretta Bender, in her classic article "The Reaction of Children to Sexual Relations with Adults": "These children undoubtedly do not deserve completely the cloak of innocence with which they have been endowed by moralists, social reformers and legislators . . . A most striking feature was that these children were distinguished as unusually charming and attractive in their outward personalities. Thus it is not remarkable that frequently we considered the possibility that the child might have been the actual seducer rather than the other way round."[37]

The influence of these and many other similar statements on the teaching of psychiatry has been considerable. Consider, for example, the first edition of the Freedman and Kaplan textbook (1967), where Eli Robinson writes about the treatment of incest: "Ideally, younger patients . . . should be referred to residential treatment settings (rather than foster homes, for example). Foster home placement will, in all likelihood, produce attempts to seduce their foster parents, since no effort has been made to deal with the underlying problem. On the other hand, if such patients live with a group of other patients of the same sex and approximately the same age, and proper treatment facilities are available to them, the intensity of their Oedipal strivings may diminish."[38] It is evident that Dr. Robinson considered incest to be a problem centered in the victim. It is as though he were blaming a mugging victim for leaving the house. Total confusion reigns in Dr. Robinson's article: he is under the illusion that the incest satisfies the

Oedipal strivings of the *victim*. The confusion has not been cleared up in the later edition. The new article on incest is by James Henderson. He writes:

Incestuous relationships do not always seem to have a traumatic effect. The father-daughter liaison satisfies instinctual drives in a setting where mutual alliance with an omnipotent adult condones the transgression. Moreover, the act offers the opportunity to test in reality an infantile fantasy whose consequences are found to be gratifying and pleasurable. It has even been suggested that the ego's capacity for sublimation is favored by the pleasure afforded by incest and that such incestuous activity diminishes the subject's chance of psychosis and allows a better adjustment to the external world. There is often found to be little deleterious influence on the subsequent personality of the incestuous daughter. One study found the vast majority of them to be none the worse for the experience—many were married with children and several were respected members of their communities.[39]

Five minutes with a survivor of incest will tell you more about it than fifty years of textbooks on psychiatry. Let me quote from a letter I received recently from a victim of incest:

I have been preoccupied with understanding the act of sexual assault on children for thirty-five years, since the moment I was myself assaulted. I liken the experience to being dropped (at five years old) from an airplane over the middle of the Pacific: whereupon I spent thirty years of my life swimming from one piece of debris to another, alone and vulnerable to attack. All the while I kept myself alive mentally by sheer determination to discover how this could have happened . . . I recall my attacks vividly. My father had divorced and remarried, taking custody of me. My new stepmother's father came to visit and proceeded to attack me twice. He would wait until I was asleep and then I would be awakened by a hand clamped over my mouth . . . and then he proceeded. The violation was as if an atomic bomb had gone off in my head. All I could think about was trying to ascertain whether or not I was dead or alive. I was actually fighting death face to face. I have no trouble understanding how some children actually die during such an attack . . . My "grandfather" was discovered. I'll never forget that day I stood in our kitchen and told my story of what had happened. I had been so close to my father. I could not understand the look on his face, a look he carries to this day. The real horror came when he dismissed me from the kitchen and from his life and love—forever. The old man was sent to a mental hospital for a few months and then released. My father brought him back into the house as an honored guest . . . I sat at the dinner table with him, as I was instructed. I was told I would be small if I objected . . . I had lost the love of my father, I had gained the distaste of my new mother, and this monster was treated like royalty, while I was still being beaten for spilling my milk . . . The twist to this story that may interest you is that my insanity was not completely the result of the attacks. In addition, I was the daughter of a young Freudian psychiatrist who offered my sanity to the altar of the Oedipal "theory" of the beleaguered Freud, and forced my life to exhibit that profile through mental torture and physical abuse. In short, my father denounced me publicly as constitutionally flawed . . . It never occurred to me that the old man should have faced criminal charges for at least assault and battery. I just accepted my life and waited for the day I would find out the truth. Your book confirmed all my suspicions. I was too blocked to see that Freud had been forced to participate in a massive cover-up. I have since been able to restart my life back where it left off. I'm extremely weak, but I'm all right, and very grateful to you.

Given the views of the major textbooks in psychiatry, it is evident that many psychiatrists accept the absurd view that a child initiates, desires, fantasizes, or is in some other sense equally responsible for incest. Consider the effect of the following dialogue in a recent court case in Southern California involving Dr. Phillip L. Kelly, a psychiatrist called by the defense as expert witness in the case of a fifty-eight-year-old man who twice impregnated his eleven-year-old stepdaughter:

PROSECUTOR: Are you telling us that it is natural for a 58-year-old man to have intercourse with an 11-year-old girl?

DR. KELLY: Yes.

PROSECUTOR: You have indicated that you don't think the defendant is a danger at all. Do you think that he is likely to want to have sex with a young woman if that opportunity presents itself? A young woman being someone who might be twelve or something like that?

DR. KELLY: If it were an opportunity in the family situation, it could be possible.

PROSECUTOR: And you don't think that that is a danger?

DR. KELLY: No.

PROSECUTOR: Do you find it significant that the defendant caused the girl to get pregnant when she was, what, eleven years old?

DR. KELLY: It is a piece of data. I don't find it particularly significant.

PROSECUTOR: Do you find it significant that he again got her pregnant and she had an abortion? Do you find it significant that after she had a child he continued to have sex with her, caused her to be pregnant again?

DR. KELLY: It is a piece of data.

PROSECUTOR: Do you find it significant data?

DR. KELLY: Not in terms of making a diagnosis, no.[40]

Psychiatry has hardly distinguished itself by taking a heroic stance against oppression.

Most of the articles in this anthology can be regarded as pornographic. I think an article such as Zambaco's, for instance, exemplifies the saying of the radical feminists that pornography is the theory and rape the practice. Surely these children were raped by Zambaco in ways that are every bit as terrible as the actual act itself. When we see that pornography is not merely harmless fantasizing on paper, but actually documents the most horrible kind of sexual cruelty, we may think twice about our "live and let live" stance. Those who have trouble accepting the realness of the events described in these articles should think again about their belief in the "unrealness" of pornography. These articles from the nineteenth century and a modern pornographic book or magazine serve the same social function: to subjugate women.

I think the recent work by Catharine MacKinnon and Andrea Dworkin[41] is extremely helpful to our understanding of this phenomenon. MacKinnon puts it very well when she writes: "Pornography strips and devastates women of credibility, from our accounts of sexual assault to our everyday reality of sexual subordination. We are deauthoritized and reduced and devalidated and silenced."[42] Or again:

The law of obscenity is to pornography as pornography is to sex: a map that purports to be a mirror, a legitimization and authorization and set of directions and guiding controls that project themselves onto social reality, while purporting merely to reflect the image of what is already there. Pornography presents itself as fantasy or illusion or idea, which can be good or bad as it is accurate or inaccurate, while it actually, *hence accurately*, distributes power. Liberal morality cannot deal with illusions that *constitute* reality because its theory of reality, lacking a substantive critique of the distribution of social power, cannot get behind the empirical world, truth by correspondence. On the surface, both pornography and the law of obscenity are about sex. In fact, it is the status of women that is at stake.[43]

Pornography, in my opinion, is a form of sexual abuse. It is no more a fantasy than physical sexual abuse is a fantasy. For pornography is a prime example of male oppression of women, and we are surely under no obligation to tolerate its persistence. Pornography is an act, one that abuses women. To tolerate pornography under the guise of protecting freedom of expression, or freedom of thought, or freedom of fantasy, is to subscribe to a naïve and erroneous view of fantasy. An article such as Zambaco's brings us back to that sober and terrible reality. Zambaco's view about the sexuality of the two little girls is a fantasy. But it is not a fantasy that was confined to paper: it was acted out and thus was not harmless. Zambaco did not describe what he would have liked to do; he described what he did. His sexual abuse was carried out under the guise of medical treatment, protected by the authority of the physician.

It may surprise some readers to learn that doctors still perform unnecessary experimental surgery on women's reproductive organs. Gena Corea, in her book *The Mother Machine*, writes: "In 1977, hysterectomy became the nation's most commonly performed operation and remains so as I write." She notes that "the majority of doctors present at a 1971 meeting of the American College of Obstetrics and Gynecology registered approval of prophylactic hysterectomy for relief of anxiety, sterilization, or prevention of cancer. Six years later, Dr. James Sammons, the AMA's senior staff physician testifying before a House commerce committee hearing, said that hysterectomy may be acceptable as a treatment for anxiety."[44] Are we still in the nineteenth century? Corea continues: "One survey of thirty-five hospitals in the Los Angeles area in 1948 found that many women had had their uteri removed solely because they complained of backache, experienced some irregular bleeding or had tilted uteri. (Tilted or 'tipped' uteri are, in most cases, perfectly normal.)"

Nawal el Saadawi, an Egyptian physician, writes that when she was six years old she was taken from her bed, with no explanation, when "suddenly the sharp metallic edge dropped between my thighs and there cut off a piece of flesh from my body. I screamed with pain despite the tight hand held over my mouth, for the pain was not just a pain, it was like a searing flame that went through my whole body. After a few moments, I saw a red pool of blood around my hips."[45] What happened to her, female circumcision (that is, the excision of the clitoris and the labia minora), is not uncommon in the Muslim world and in parts of Africa. It is happening today to millions of women.

It seems that the field of violence to children and to women is particularly susceptible to a peculiar kind of research. A perhaps extreme example is the notorious article by Suzanne Steinmetz, "The Battered Husband Syndrome," published in *Victimology*,[46] which begins: "While the horrors of wife-beating are paraded before the public, and crisis lines and shelters are being established, the other side of the coin—husband-beating—is still hidden under a cloak of secrecy." Then she provides some astonishing "statistics": "While husbands were the victims of hostility and attack in 63 percent of all conflict situations, wives were victims in only 39 percent . . . further analysis revealed that in 73 percent [of conflict situations] . . . the wives were more aggressive; in 10 percent husband and wife were equal." Amazing. But even more amazing is the source of these sobering "statistics," a 1963 study of twenty consecutive editions of all comic strips appearing in the nine leading New York City newspapers during October 1950. Comic strips! And this constitutes "insight" and "research." Nor has the article been uninfluential. This was pointed out very well by Elizabeth Pleck, Joseph Pleck, Marilyn Grossman, and

Pauline Bart in their comment on the atrocious methodology of the article:

The "findings" of Dr. Steinmetz have received wide attention in newspaper reports, in family advice columns, and from congresspersons considering legislation about family violence. It may also have led to a reduction in public support for programs to aid battered wives . . . In a UPI story in the *Chicago Daily News* (August 31, 1977), the headline reads, "Study Backs Up Suspicions Husband Is More Battered Spouse." Its first sentence states that "more men than women are victims of domestic violence, according to a study sponsored by the National Institute of Mental Health."

We know that a woman who makes an accusation of rape stands to gain very little. Indeed, she is often made to feel that she is the one who has committed the crime. Consider the following passage from Maya Angelou's moving book *I Know Why the Caged Bird Sings*: "He grabbed my arm and pulled me between his legs. His face was still and looked kind, but he didn't smile or blink his eyes. Nothing. He did nothing, except reach his left hand around to turn on the radio without even looking at it. Over the noise of the music and static he said: 'Now this ain't gonna hurt you much' . . . and then there was the pain. A breaking and entering when even the senses are torn apart."[47] She was hospitalized, and there was a trial:

"What was the defendant wearing?" That was Mr. Freeman's lawyer.

"I don't know."

"You mean to say this man raped you and you don't know what he was wearing?" He snickered as if I had raped Mr. Freeman. "Do you know if you were raped?"

A sound pushed in the air of the court (I was sure it was laughter).

It has been testified to time and again that in court women encounter the same atmosphere that made the rape possible in the first place. Not only has psychiatry not supported the work women have done to combat rape, it has a legacy of support for the other side. Thus Diana Russell tells of the rape victim who recounted that: "The first staff member who saw me was a psychiatrist. His first words were, 'Haven't you really been rushing toward this very thing all of your life?' "[48]

Menachim Amir, in his influential 1971 book, *Patterns in Forcible Rape*, has a chapter entitled "Victim-Precipitated Forcible Rape," which begins with the ominous words: "In a way, the victim is always the cause of the crime" and ends: "Thus, the role played by the victim and its contribution to the perpetration of the offense becomes one of the main interests of the emerging discipline of victimology."[49] John Henry Wigmore's highly influential ten-volume textbook, *Evidence in Trials at Common Law*, still standard in many law schools in the United States, Canada, and England, states:

It is a matter of common knowledge that the bad character of a man for chastity does not even in the remotest degree affect his character for truth, when based upon that alone, while it does that of a woman. It is no compliment to a woman to measure her character for truth by the same standard that you do that of a man's . . . There is, however, at least one situation in which chastity may have a direct connection with veracity, viz. when a woman or young girl testifies as complainant against a man charged with a sexual crime—rape, rape under age, seduction, assault. Modern psychiatrists have amply studied the behavior of errant young girls and women coming before the courts in all sorts of cases. Their psychic complexes are multifarious, distorted partly by inherent defects, partly by diseased derangements or abnormal instincts, partly by bad social environment, partly by temporary physiological or emotional conditions. One form taken by these complexes is that of contriving false charges of sexual offenses by men. The unchaste (let us call it) mentality finds incidental but direct expression in the narration of imaginary sex incidents of which the narrator is the heroine or the victim. On the surface the narration is straightforward and convincing. The real victim, however, too often in such cases is the innocent man . . . No judge should ever let a sex offense charge go to the jury unless the female complainant's social history and mental makeup have been examined and testified to by a qualified physician . . . Every girl who enters a plausible but unproved story of rape should be required to have a psychiatric examination . . . The reason I think that rape in particular belongs in this category is one well known to psychologists, namely, that fantasies of being raped are exceedingly common in women, indeed one may almost say that they are probably universal . . . We who have had extensive criminal experience among the mentally ill, know how frequently sexual assault is charged or claimed with nothing more substantial supporting this belief than an unrealized wish or unconscious, deeply suppressed sex-longing or thwarting.

This is from the 1970 edition![50] It serves as a disturbing reminder that what is represented as the result of careful scientific research is often nothing more than an expression of the prejudices of the time.

Dr. Jasinski of Lemberg

Sudden Death of a Girl

about Thirteen Years Old

as a Result of Intense Emotion*

The teachings of Kant, Schopenhauer, von Hartmann, Frauenstaedt, and other profound thinkers did much to transform the ideas of civilized European nations, and thus brought about, at least partially, a number of desirable changes in lifestyle and world-view—or, at the very least, paved the way for such changes. Moreover, in the field of criminology, which affects social conditions so profoundly, there is now a perceptible salutary trend toward overdue reform. Presently, the criminal justice system is based, as we know, on the principle of free will, and consequently the punishment of the criminal seems a natural and unavoidable conclusion. But now post-Kantian philosophy has convincingly shown that, just as an inexorable law of causality reigns in the physical world, a law of motivation governs the moral sphere. That is, human actions occur as a result of the same compelling force that, to use Schopenhauer's example, determines the course of a bil-

---

* "Plötzlicher Tod eines etwa 13jährigen Mädchens in Folge heftiger Gemüthsbewegung." *Berliner klinische Wochenschrift*, 25 (1888), 685–88. Unfortunately, I could find no biographical information about Dr. Jasinski—not even his first name.

liard ball. Every human act is the result of two factors, motive and character, innate as well as acquired. The anatomical correlate of the inherited predisposition is the brain, which in the case of criminals, especially in the category of the so-called degenerates, almost always shows deviations from the norm. The acquired character, on the other hand, is the result of such diverse influences as upbringing, habits, role models, etc. If, therefore, the deeds of a criminal do not result from his free will but, of necessity, from the structure of his brain, his upbringing, etc., it follows that there must be less emphasis on punishing him than on rendering him harmless to human society. The modern, or criminal-anthropological, school strives toward the same lofty goal.

In order to deal with every criminal in accordance with the security needs of society, his character must be studied—directly as well as indirectly. This is done partly by studying his biography, partly by precise measurements of his skull. Noticeable abnormalities in the structure of the skull will permit us to conclude that there are abnormalities as well in the content of the skull, namely the brain.

There is absolutely no doubt that once the reforms described here are effected, not only will society be more secure, but the criminal justice system will be immensely simplified. As proof, I will cite a phenomenon that occurs almost daily in forensic medicine: a professional thief is caught red-handed and sentenced to a number of years in prison. As soon as he has served his term and obtained his freedom, he commits another burglary, gets caught, and judge and jury once again waste their valuable time in sentencing him anew. This cozy game is often repeated ten to twenty times in the individual's life, and each time all of the sluggish judicial procedures are set in motion. Now, if in the future one were to start with the premise that this habitual thief is not to be punished but merely rendered harmless, perhaps one would realize that one is dealing with an anthropologically degenerate individual. Accordingly, after his first burglary and upon detailed examination of his character, one would immediately sentence him to hard labor for a lengthy period, or simply deport him.

Let us take another frequently occurring phenomenon. A degenerate individual, therefore a danger to society, is apprehended after a murder during a robbery. Because of so-called extenuating circumstances, he is not beheaded but merely sentenced to prison for several years. During his imprisonment he is in contact with other criminals and thus receives a higher education in his métier; that is, a heretofore perhaps unskilled criminal becomes an accomplished one. As such, he is now far more dangerous to society than he was before, and therefore there is all the more reason that he should be rendered harmless. Instead, precisely the opposite happens, for he is thrown into society regardless of the consequences as soon as his punishment is over.

These examples make it clear that the judicial system plays a very questionable role in society. Society has a recognized right to be protected, and the chief role of the judicial system is to provide such protection. But current laws compel the system to do the opposite, to endanger the security of society.

Since crime, as we have seen, is the result of motive and character, these two factors have to be considered during sentencing. It follows that in the future judges and forensic physicians have to be well versed in the study of character, and also in psychology, particularly physiological psychology. Even now, psychological knowledge is indispensable for forensic physicians in cases of injury resulting from the fault of another person. The forensic physician must be able to diagnose and prove damage not just to the body but also to the mind, since man is both mind and body.

Here, we are concerned with the consequences of violent emotion. The major task of the forensic physician is to deter-

mine the force of this emotion, since emotions lie at the core
of the difference between men and animals. The emotions
constantly interact with the body. Thus, all injuries, even if
originally confined to the body, extend their influence to the
mind, and there cause reactions whose effects on the organism
are frequently more damaging than those of the injury itself.
To prove my point, I need only recall the secondary consequences of a railway accident. The primary bodily injury is
often quite minor, and yet the emotional upheaval due to
shock is sometimes so significant and persistent that the victims
remain ill their entire lives and are plagued by various nervous
and psychological ailments.

In our "expert opinions," we physicians are primarily concerned with bodily injuries and their consequences. We pay
little or no attention to the concurrent emotional upset or
upheaval. Thus we are guilty—and that is the reason for my
digression—of the same major error committed by judges in
the criminal cases discussed above; that is, we disregard the
most important factor. I now put aside the important question
of whether, from the judicial standpoint, our expert opinions,
since they are mostly one-dimensional, have full scientific
value and are able to serve as a basis for legal decisions. I only
wish to state that the reason for this one-dimensional view lies
in the fact that the study of the mind and the consequences
of emotional upheavals is not a required part of the curriculum.
In the textbooks of forensic medicine, this subject is treated
like a stepchild. While whole volumes are devoted to other
topics of interest to forensic medicine, such as forensic psychopathology, the consequences of violent emotional upset
are for the most part discussed very briefly, indeed are barely
allotted a few pages.

Accordingly, it is necessary to be familiar with the fields of
study dealing with the emotions in order to trace and identify
all the consequences of a harmful event not only in the body

but also in the mind. The most important of these fields, in addition to the ones already discussed, are psychophysics, comparative ethnography, and positive philosophy. One may object that the latter could be of no use to the forensic physician. However, I intend to show that for several reasons it is important for him to have a good background in philosophy. First, philosophy, as is well known, is that science which sheds the clearest light on emotional life. Its guidance helps us negotiate the wild miasma of feelings and impressions which arise in the human mind when it is extremely excited and when an emotional storm is raging. Furthermore, each of the many disciplines which examine mankind, on which the forensic physician must base his opinion, considers him from its own specific point of view; that is, from a bias. The forensic physician, however, needs an overview, so that he can consider the claims of the different disciplines and consolidate them into a unified whole. Only philosophy offers that all-encompassing viewpoint. Moreover, "reality" does not always reflect the full emotional range of events; nor is its sequence always reliable. It is often necessary for the forensic physician to supplement the actual facts, to organize them, to uncover the relationship of various seemingly unrelated details and in this manner to construct a clear and precise picture of the entire mental process. All this can of course be achieved only by a forensic physician well trained in philosophy. Finally, the expert opinion of the forensic physician must distinguish itself by its maturity and objectivity. Such an opinion can be rendered only by those whose intellectual horizons have been widened and illuminated by philosophy.

Now that I have related what I consider essential for understanding the event referred to in the title of this essay, I shall turn to the event itself. In brief it is as follows: In a local coeducational primary school, the teacher, a brutal individual given to sudden fits of temper, yanked a student, Marie F., a

Jewish girl about thirteen years old, from her seat, forcibly turned her over his knee, and administered a number of blows to her buttocks with a cane, because she had been somewhat restless. The girl who had been treated so brutally had barely returned to her seat when she sank to the ground and lay dead. In the brief moment after her return to her seat and before her death, she leafed through her schoolbook absentmindedly and a fleeting smile appeared on her face.

The autopsy of the suddenly deceased girl ordered by the court showed extreme and active hyperemia of the brain and its membranes as the only anatomical cause of death. The condition of all other organs, on the other hand, was completely normal, as was the state of her health prior to death.

After the autopsy, the forensic physicians were faced with the question of what had caused the fatal hyperemia of the brain. There is absolutely no answer to the question from a purely physical point of view; that is, from the standpoint of the body alone, for no mechanical insult had been dealt to the skull—particularly none capable of causing lethal hyperemia. Moreover, the behavior of the child after her return to her seat would be incomprehensible to those ignorant of human emotions. Indeed, the indifference with which she turned the pages of her book, and her smile, normally taken as a sign of joy and inner contentment, might even mislead them and make it harder for them to understand the ensuing catastrophe. The forensic physicians in Marie F.'s case found themselves in a precarious position. They stated in their "expert opinions" that her death was a complete mystery, and therefore that it could be nothing but pure coincidence.

Let us now consider Marie F.'s death from the truly scientific point of view, one that provides an overview of the entire human being, mind as well as body. We shall find that not only is there no mystery to this death, but it is so obvious that all the pieces fall into place. Let us try to visualize what happened.

A young girl in the full bloom of youth sits in class and feels happy. Fully conscious of her happiness, she smiles a little and whispers a few words to her neighbor. The teacher notices this. As his actions attest, he is a brutal and inconsiderate individual, and instantly orders the girl to leave her seat so that he can beat her with a cane. It goes without saying that the voice issuing this order must have been enraged, his glance threatening and evil. No doubt this alone sufficed to frighten the poor girl and fill her with dread. Moreover, she knew from her experience of this brutal man that she was about to be caned. She therefore hesitated—justifiably so—to obey the teacher's orders. The teacher was compelled to forcibly drag her from her seat and turn her over his knee. This brutal procedure in itself added to the terror and helped bring about the ensuing catastrophe. The actual physical blows no longer mattered: at the most, they may have brought the measure of emotional shock to overflow.

In addition to fright and terror, there were other emotions which gripped Marie F. Of these I will mention only outrage, disgrace, shame, and humiliation. The sense of outrage was completely justified, since, thanks to the humanitarian views of our time, caning, particularly of girls, is strictly forbidden in our schools. The beating was a flagrant injustice. It was also a violent assault on her modesty, particularly since boys as well as girls were present in the classroom. This could only have increased the girl's shame and humiliation.

Furthermore, let us not forget that Marie F. was of Jewish extraction. It is well known that such girls are especially sensitive, that their feelings are very delicate, that they are intellectually as well as physically precocious. Marie F., accordingly, could be considered mature. As such she must have been all the more outraged and indignant at the injustice and humiliation she suffered. Moreover, Marie F. came from a poor home and surely was aware of the religious and social prejudices still held by the majority against poor Jews. Thus, she knew that nobody would offer her any sympathy, no matter how great the injustice. All these depressing feelings and thoughts acted like a storm battering her spirit, and the impact of this storm had a devastating effect on her emotions.

Finally, another important factor must be considered. Inhabitants of a large city expand their mental horizons as they do their physical horizons. City dwellers take many things in stride, and make light of much that would drive a small-town dweller to despair or even suicide. Marie F. had lived all her life in a small town; a town, one might say, that the world had passed by. Therefore, in her eyes what happened must have seemed the worst thing in the world. She knew that news of her disgrace and humiliation would immediately spread all over town. She thought of herself as forever dishonored, and that dreadful thought must have added not a little to her emotional upheaval.

Professor Maschka, in his book *Forensic Medicine*, made the following statement about violent emotional upheaval: "It is known that violent emotions—for instance, fear, fright, anger, even joy—can in some cases deeply disturb the human organism and even threaten its very existence."*

One can generalize that the consequences of violent emotions are as diverse as their causes: terror, for example, virtually paralyzes people, for it renders them momentarily speechless, breathless, and motionless. Outrage over unjust and contemptuous treatment is revealed by continuous changes in skin color; that is, the faces of affected people fluctuate between pale white and red. These signs of inner turmoil become no-

---

* *Handbuch der gerichtlichen Medicin*, vol. 1, part 2 (1882), p. 811.

ticeable when those people find it necessary to suppress their indignation. Such moral suppression is found, for instance, in the attitudes of subordinates toward their superiors. When anger is suddenly aroused, the face reddens; a wild look comes to the eyes, which shine and seem to send off sparks; the vein on the forehead swells, sometimes threatening to burst. An excess of sorrow and nagging despair can turn hair white overnight and lead to insanity, as history has documented. Violent fright often causes jaundice; sudden terror, on the other hand, causes convulsions, epilepsy, temporary loss of speech, even unconsciousness. Others experience violent headaches, which can escalate into meningitis, or develop some form of nerve fever; others collapse, lifeless, as if struck by lightning. This happens during or very shortly after emotional upset. An autopsy discloses either nothing unusual in the brain [technical footnote omitted] or an advanced case of hyperemia of the brain and its membranes. In the case of older persons suffering from arteriosclerosis, hyperemia leads to a stroke, as the final link in the chain. In the case of younger persons like Marie F., death ensues without a stroke.

Death from emotional shock, as experience has shown, is a rare event for young and healthy persons; the question of why it happened to Marie F. calls for an answer. I have already partly responded to this question by listing the factors that contributed to her exceptional emotional turmoil. A second question that could be raised here is why she did not immediately expire under the blows of her teacher. The answer is that, according to the laws of psychophysics, a certain amount of time has to elapse between the emotional shock and the death resulting from it, to give hyperemia of the brain time to take over.

After her return to her seat, Marie F. seemed to busy herself with her book. This behavior was very natural and appropriate under the circumstances. She lowered her head and stared fixedly at the book, for, overwhelmed by feelings of shame and humiliation, she could not face her classmates with tearful eyes. Also, her classmates were probably secretly jubilant over the shame and injustice that had been inflicted on her; taking delight in the distress of others is as much a part of human nature as compassion.

Finally, let us analyze the child's final smile. As we know, the psychological explanation of smiling differs, depending on the cause. If we experience something pleasant, our smile reveals joy, or at least contentment; otherwise it can, depending on the situation, express scorn, derision, contempt, disdain, or even emotional pain. Marie F.'s fleeting smile permits two interpretations: on the one hand, she wanted to belittle what had happened to her in front of her classmates and thus put a damper on their pleasure at her pain; at the same time, her smile can be regarded as a sign of loathing and contempt for her teacher. He wronged her in several respects. To recapitulate, first he cavalierly acted in defiance of the rule against caning, probably because Marie F. was nothing but a poor Jewish girl. Second, he took advantage of his physical strength and assaulted the delicate and defenseless girl; that is, he maltreated her brutally. In addition, he offended her modesty in the most outrageous manner. All this must have awakened in Marie F., not a desire for revenge, since she felt she was much too weak for this, but a sense of loathing and contempt for her tormentor. Those feelings could not be expressed in any way other than a smile. It was no sign of joy. On the contrary, as she smiled, raging within was a storm of the most painful feelings. The battle must have been a terrible one, and the emotional torment it generated must have greatly surpassed the measure of what any human can be expected to bear. Only thus—overcome by unbearable emotional torment—was it possible for Marie F., in spite of her youth and health, to sink lifeless to the ground.

Paul Flechsig

On the Gynecological

Treatment of Hysteria*

CASE 1: *Hysteria magna; castration*

This case concerns A.L., thirty-two years old, unmarried, hereditarily tainted, since both father and mother died of brain disease (cerebral apoplexy—possibly *dementia paralytica*). At age nineteen, her menses ceased for about a year. At the same time, she suffered great irritability and excitability; after that, her menstrual periods were mostly irregular and she had a tendency toward constipation. At age twenty-four she suffered from "breast cramps" for several months. Since her twenty-eighth year, when her mother died, she has suffered almost incessantly from nervous disturbances and psychological abnormalities: severe and constant depression, much talking in her sleep, at the same time complaints relating to her inner sexual organs (particularly pain), because of which she now frequently seeks medical help. She formed an attachment to the young doctor who was treating her without any real reciprocation on his part. As a result, she developed a noticeable romantic interest in her male relatives, although this interest

* "Zur gynäkologischen Behandlung der Hysterie." *Neurologisches Centralblatt*, 19/20, 1884.

was within the boundaries of good taste. Starting at about age twenty-nine, she began to suffer major hysterical convulsions (see below), which continued with only short interruptions until her admission to our clinic. She was placed in a hospital run by the Lutheran Sisters. She did not improve there. She then returned to her relatives (eight months before her admission here) and again consulted several outstanding gynecologists, but without success. One of the latter diagnosed a fairly large, fluctuating, parametrial cystic mass (no indication on which side). Her general cramps were developing into more localized ailments, such as trismus, singultus, and globus. Furthermore, she was subject to laughing and crying fits, vomiting, tympanites, urinary retention combined with a painful urge to urinate, severe pain in the lower abdomen, which became unbearable during menstruation, headaches, and, from time to time, hemianesthesia on the left side (once she thought she had lost her arm and leg); also, a sense of heaviness with "paralysis-like weakness" in her left extremities, aphasia, and, on one occasion, bleeding from the nose and ears.

In the years prior to her admission to our clinic, her psychological anomalies had steadily increased in intensity, variety, and duration. She suspected the men around her (doctors, relatives, etc.) of committing indecent acts on her person, or of trying to do so. She expressed other feelings of persecution as well. She was depressed much of the time, suffered from anxiety, wished to die, wanted to commit suicide, and even made a halfhearted attempt to do so. Later, religious sentiments developed. She spoke frequently of Jesus, who would heal her. At times she was very agitated, screamed and sang at the top of her voice, so that her housemates asked that she be removed. These states of agitation stemmed partly from hallucinations. She saw herself surrounded by wild animals, saw people attack her with a knife, heard water running, and also spoke of a lion who lay by her door to protect her. Her sense of reality seemed to be seriously affected by this, and she occasionally committed senseless acts. For instance, she cut off her hair and was pleased to have "made this sacrifice for my sister." Her alertness and her capacity for useful work diminished more and more. In the end she no longer did any work at all—except for one time when she got up very early and participated energetically in the household chores, but only because of a hallucination, a dream. She claims to have seen a figure in white, seated on her bed, who told her she was now well—but her zeal for work lasted only a few hours. Her memory became weaker, especially concerning recent events. She seemed to have poor judgment; her speech was mostly senseless drivel. Because of the increasing frequency of her states of agitation—that is, her screaming, singing, etc.— she was brought to the mental asylum on April 3, 1883.

Present status: The patient is of average height and weight. Aside from her sexual organs, all internal organs are healthy, with the exception of the lungs, which appear enlarged. [The rest of this paragraph, giving detailed physiological measurements, is omitted here.] As for her psychological state, only a minor degree of feeble-mindedness can be observed, because the patient strays easily from her topic and talks about a lot of unimportant things, displaying a childish smile and speaking in a slow, clumsy manner.

The next day [April 4] she spoke of sexual assaults that she claimed were made on her; of Christ, who would release her from her suffering, etc. On the third day, toward evening, she had an attack lasting three-quarters of an hour. She suddenly fell to the floor, arms extended (as though nailed to a crucifix). They could not be bent, even with great force. She suffered from trismus, her eyes wide open and fixed on the people surrounding her. Her conjunctival and pupillary reflexes were normal . . . When the attack was over, the patient began to speak in a stilted tone and in broken German: "I nothing bad did, I knows you, you looks different," etc. . . .

From a psychological point of view, the patient exhibited a chronic depression varying in intensity during the first month of her stay in the clinic. She wept a great deal, had presentiments of death, anxiety attacks accompanied by precordial pressure, and was intractable most of the time. Early in May, her mood reversed itself; first there was a laughing fit, followed a few days later by absolute mania; joyous singing, an urgent need to jump about, exuberance, flight of ideas, erotic mannerisms—all this went on sporadically for a few weeks. From mid-May to mid-June her mood was mostly one of indifference. There were many attacks of abdominal pain and fainting. From the middle of June her mood became angry; she was rude, she testily complained about the doctors, she claimed to have been slandered, maligned, and mistreated by them (hallucinations?). She screamed for hours on end, especially at night. She called to her lover, recited biblical verses and songs, wished to die, etc. As a result, she often had to be put in isolation. In between she staggered about like a drunk, with strangely distorted features, totally confused and uttering nonsensical gibberish. At the end of June, her behavior became normal, though her continuous childish, irrelevant chatter made her permanently hoarse. This continued until the day of her operation.

Other nervous disturbances that were discovered in the clinic include singultus, vomiting, chills accompanied by pale, cold extremities, pain in back of her head, double vision in the left eye, a painful need to urinate combined with urinary retention (often on a nearly empty bladder), and frequent constipation.

A manual examination of the (virginal) sexual organs revealed a thick, scarred strand of tissue near the left broad ligament; the left ovary seemed displaced downward, and the uterus seemed situated too far toward the left. Otherwise, the uterus and ovaries showed no palpable abnormalities.

Menstrual periods were irregular during her stay in the clinic and were always accompanied by severe abdominal pain. Prior to the onset of bleeding, hysterical attacks occurred with greater frequency in one form or another; yet neither these attacks nor the increases in abdominal pain were exclusively connected with menstruation. They could also occur independently.

In view of the fact that, in the past, the patient had been treated for an extensive parametrial cystic mass, and in view of the conclusions reached during a pelvic examination, the following diagnosis was made: chronic parametritis, resulting in shrinking, scarring, and secondary displacement of the left ovary, possibly including the uterus and the right broad ligament. (The patient herself frequently stated that it felt as though she had a band running across her pelvis which expanded and contracted like a rubber band.)

The first question that arose from this diagnosis was whether the pathology of her sexual organs had caused her nervous anomalies. For a portion of the latter—particularly the severe pain, the difficulties in urination, etc.—this was undoubtedly the case. The occurrence of pain in the lower abdomen and the hemiparesis and hemianesthesia on whichever side had the more severe pain made it very likely that the brain was at least partly connected with the pelvic affections. Accordingly, therapy had a twofold task: removal of the source of irritation in the lower abdomen and reduction of the intensified excitability of the central nervous system. As we have seen, we could not alleviate the latter until we had dealt with the former. (Mild cold-water treatments, lengthy tepid baths, morphine, chilling the patient's spine according to the Chapman method, general faradization, potassium bromide, antihysteric sedative medication, etc., were used without lasting success.) The efforts made by gynecologists, some of them outstanding authorities in their field, have largely been unsuccessful, even though they did manage to bring about some resorption of the parametrial cystic mass. However, the paroxysms of pain remained constant. New measures had to be taken. The question that arose was: What is the real cause of the pain? One could not be certain that its origin lay exclusively in the ovaries, since "ovarialgia" can result from other parts of the internal sexual organs. Yet one must assign a certain role to the ovaries, since the paroxysms of pain occurred regularly some time before the onset of the menses. Therefore, the expectation seemed justified that extirpation of the ovaries could eliminate at least the premenstrual increase in pain, and perhaps also the pain possibly resulting from the displacement of the left ovary. If this sexual illness were not eliminated, it can be presumed that the patient would be a permanent invalid, unable to enjoy life in any manner. On the basis of these considerations, castration was resorted to on July 10 . . .

The healing of the surgical wound progressed smoothly: her axillary temperature rose to 38.2 C. only once. The dressing was removed on the twelfth day to reveal a linear scar. The patient was given an elastic body binder and got out of bed the first time for a short while toward the end of the second week.

As far as the postoperative condition of her nervous system was concerned, the patient acted in a completely normal manner during the first four days. She was calm and contented, and did not complain of pain. Her paralysis was completely gone. Never since her admission to the clinic had the patient exhibited such normal behavior. Yet toward the end of the first week, morbid manifestations began to resurface.

She complained of severe abdominal pains, "which are totally different from before," of a painful urge to urinate, and of urinary retention. A moderate cystitis proved to be the cause.

At the same time, on the fifth and sixth days, there was a moderate discharge of blood from the vagina. Toward evening, hallucinations lasting several hours recurred. In a somewhat hazy state, she spoke of little horses, fire, and other visions (perhaps visual hallucinations). At the same time, she appeared calm . . . Beginning on October 18, she again began to manifest transitory mental anomalies. Her mood was mercurial; for hours she could be in high spirits, sing, gesticulate, talk volubly, jump about, etc., without any obvious reason; at other times she was depressed, spoke of suicide, was obstreperous, rude, etc. In between, the periods of normal behavior lengthened.

Once each during the months of October, November, and December she briefly manifested states of agitation as intense as those observed before the surgery. She screamed, incessantly called for her lover, sang songs, prayed, cursed, etc. The first two attacks were halted by chloroform. However, the third time, on December 6, all attempts to calm her failed (cold showers, chloroform, ethyl bromide, etc.). She was therefore placed in isolation and, since she threatened suicide, stripped naked and covered with blankets that could not be torn off. The next day she calmed down completely. She remembered everything about the events preceding her isolation and said the reason for her behavior was that it gave her pleasure to torment others. After this, there were never any further nervous disturbances, either repeat performances or new variations. She occupied herself busily, became contented and calm, and left the clinic at the end of December 1883 in a totally normal condition. Her reports, which she gave us regularly, at our request, repeatedly stressed that she feels "newborn," and that until now (the second half of September 1884) there have been no recurrences of hysteria. During a visit in July 1884 she gave the impression of complete normalcy in all respects, especially in her mental agility and good judgment.

Discussion: In view of the course of the illness just described, the question arises: What role did castration play in the cure? It is immediately obvious that there was no change for the better until after the operation. How can we explain this? Did the surgery have a mostly psychological impact or did it in fact remove the major physical cause of the symptoms? In support of the first interpretation, one could cite a recent article describing a case of severe hysteria that was completely cured by sham castration.* On the other hand, there are a number of reports of severe hysterical symptoms disappearing instantly after psychological treatments of various kinds had been applied. It would be premature to include our case in this latter category. Severe hysteria can arise in many ways—through psychological trauma, diseases of the reproductive system, or disease of other internal organs. We can judge the relative success of various therapeutic methods only by comparing their effects in cases of like nature and etiology. Then the question arises: Are there recorded cases of severe, long-standing hysteria accompanied by similar ailments of the sexual organs (parametric induration, atrophy of the ovaries, and small cyst degeneration of the ovaries) which were cured exclusively by psychological means, without removal of the ovaries? I must declare that there is no proof of such a case and I doubt that the aforementioned sham castration by Dr. Israel belongs in this category. There are not sufficient similarities to our situation; its postoperative course was totally different. In Dr. Israel's case, symptoms resembling peritonitis lingered for a week after the sham operation. After that there was a complete cure (of unknown duration). In our case, normal behavior returned after the operation, but later on the patient had a serious relapse. Whereas her non-psychological disturbances

---

* Israel, Berliner medicinische Gesellschaft. Meeting of January 14, 1880. I know about it from Erlenmeyer's *Centralblatt*, 3, p. 53.

gradually diminished, after peaking briefly, her recurring psychological disturbances climaxed on a critical level. Moreover, in our case, there can be no question of any psychological interference, as in Israel's case, for our patient before and after the surgery was totally in the dark as to the nature of the operation. We deliberately avoided upsetting her with any discussion of the subject. In addition, in our case, our observations during the operation as well as a number of postoperative symptoms point to the fact that pathology of the sexual organs did indeed contribute to the hysterical symptoms. It would be a distortion of the facts if one did not connect the severe pain in the area of the left ovary with the degeneration and pulling of adhesions on that ovary. The fact that the pain recurred after the surgery does not prove anything to the contrary. This pain resulted from fresh inflammatory outbreaks in the pelvic organs; at first it was confined to the urinary bladder—or to its surrounding tissues, where there probably was hyperemia due to congestion (bleeding on the fifth and sixth postoperative days). The resulting pain had a very different character than before. At that point small exudates appeared on the peduncles. We know this from repeated elevations of temperature and the persistence of the usual pelvic pain, including an exquisite sensitivity to touch, that alternated between right and left sides. (We cannot exclude the possibility that the silk sutures left in the body had something to do with this.) These symptoms reached their peak in October 1883. The occurrence of spontaneous paralysis, which abated when vaginal bleeding abated, dramatically illustrates the close connection between the nervous disturbances and the affections of the lower pelvis.

The psychological disturbances that resurfaced in October seem surprising at first glance. Had they been caused exclusively or directly by the illness of the sexual organs—as were the pain, the paralysis, the collapses—one would have expected them to diminish and increase at the same time as the latter. But they increased while the others were receding. For this, in my judgment, a quite simple explanation can be given: While the patient held hope for an early cure until the beginning of October, she was bitterly disappointed by the recurrence of her severe symptoms. Accordingly, even now, a good part of her psychological abnormalities seem deliberate ("it gave her pleasure to torment others"), and that is why a psychological shock such as being placed in isolation naked sufficed to put an end to them on the spot. If this reasoning is correct, it may give a general picture of the relationship between psychological abnormalities and abnormalities of a different nature in the case of some hysterics. The psychological dysfunctions would not rise independently but would result from the latter and therefore develop and recede with them.

[*Case 2 omitted*]

CASE 3: *Hysteroepilepsy; stenosis of the external cervical os; surgical dilatation; patient cured*

This case concerns T.F., eighteen years old, no hereditary taint. She has suffered from convulsions since she started menstruating several years ago (the exact date is unknown). These convulsions occurred frequently before and during bleeding but less frequently during the intervals between periods. At the same time, she suffers from frequent and severe lower back pain, vomiting, urinary retention, etc. She feels perpetually weak, has no appetite, and tends toward constipation. Her sleep is disturbed, and she sometimes suffers from anxiety attacks. She consulted a well-known gynecologist, who diagnosed stenosis of the external cervical os, made repeated attempts at cervical dilatation, and later sent the patient to a spa specializing in mineral waters and baths. Even though the dysmenorrheal symptoms decreased, the convulsions continued and even increased in frequency. The patient was admitted to our mental hospital on October 27, 1883 (not for treatment of mental illness but for treatment of convulsions).

Present status: Somewhat smaller than medium height, the patient is a well-developed girl weighing 54 kilos, with a pale complexion. Except for her genitalia, her organs are normal in every way, with no signs of degeneration. Her nervous symptoms include feelings of pressure and lightning-swift pains in her head, and a tingling in her hands. From the psychological point of view, the only thing out of the ordinary is her somewhat erotic facial expression. Examination with a speculum reveals extreme stenosis of the external cervical os and a copious thin discharge.

A hysteroepileptic attack occurred shortly after admission: it started with jubilant exultations, followed by tonic spasms of the torso and extremities and extreme opisthotonos. Her sensory aspect resembled a moderately deep hypnosis. There continue to be one or more attacks almost daily. They begin like the one described above. Frequently, the tetanic state is followed by a series of clonic spasms. The patient moves her torso violently and rapidly so that she thrusts herself upward in bed. Meanwhile, she rolls her entire body longitudinally and violently. Her sensory perceptions are somewhat dulled, but her intellectual capacity is totally unchanged. The patient attempts to avoid exposing her body during an attack, which occurs most frequently at the sight of men. The patient masturbates and in the company of women frequently speaks of sexual matters in a cynical way. From November 11 to 19, she is given 2.5 grams of sodium bromide three times daily.

On November 17 a surgical dilatation of the external cervical os is performed via a cross-like incision. Several wedge-shaped sections of the cervical canal are extirpated. There is conical dilatation; tamponade with iodoform gauze; antiseptic treatment.

Following this, the patient suffers three more attacks . . . On the last of these dates, a totally pain-free menstrual period begins.

Beginning November 19, the patient suffers frequent lower back pain, pain near the bladder, urinary incontinence, vomiting, constipation, headaches, and dizziness, which diminish slowly and disappear altogether around January 8. Her erotic mannerisms gradually abate. Starting at the end of November, we administer vaginal douches with 1/1000 potassium permanganate and lengthy daily sitz baths.

On December 24, the patient is very depressed, claims to be held in contempt by her doctors and others around her, claims to have overheard insulting remarks about her and speaks of suicide. This depression no doubt is due to a remark made by her father that she was considered to be a "nymphomaniac" in the clinic, that is, to psychological influences having nothing to do with her operation. Her bad mood gradually improves and is gone by January 8. On January 23, the patient is discharged, completely cured. She appears to be in glowing health and has gained four kilos. At last report, she is still well (as of September).

Discussion: I cited the above case only because many psychiatrists reject the gynecological treatment of neurosis. The failure of the first therapeutic method could easily have led to this case being cited as proof of the uselessness of gynecological treatment of erotic hysteria, whereas it actually proves the opposite. Above all, it is necessary to choose the correct method.

GENERAL REMARKS

The discussions held at the gynecological session of the last international medical congress amply demonstrate that, at present, the opinions held by gynecologists about the value of castration in neurosis and psychosis still vary considerably. It seems to me, however, that psychiatrists have not considered the matter at all. Apparently, the evidence gathered is too thin and critical evaluation of negative and positive results too difficult to permit a conclusive judgment. In the case of psychosis in particular, if one can believe the international literature and the discussions at the congress, castration has been performed barely a dozen times. It is remarkable that only two of these cases occurred in Germany. Reports of total cures were made by: Hegar (1), Franzolini, (1, though the period of observation, three and a half weeks, is too brief to permit a definite judgment), Goodell (1). Reports of some improvement: Tauffers (1), Goodell (2). Reports of a plain negative result without further changes for the worse: Ollshausen (1). Reports on changes for the worse of the psychosis after, or as a result of, the operation: Tauffers (1), Lee (1), Priestley (1). So there is a record of a total of ten cases, of which three (or two) were followed by a cure, three by improvement, one by no change, and three by a change for the worse. If one sets aside the cases without decisive success, the good and bad results just about balance each other out. If one were to conclude from this that castration carries a risk of severely damaging the integrity of the brain, particularly in mental patients, the cases related above definitely speak against the operation. I did not observe a single indication of any adverse effect whatsoever on the patients' psyches. Only mentally beneficial effects stand out in my mind. This is quite remarkable and encourages me to place greater weight on the good results than on the bad ones. It appears that, where the latter are concerned, the operation was performed inadvisedly or incorrectly, which is not surprising considering that the reliability of castration as a cure for psychosis and neurosis is still awaiting empirical validation. Since, according to our experience, one must expect a relapse of psychosis after the operation in the majority of cases, the importance of appropriate follow-up treatment comes immediately to mind. In both cases, the duration of the relapse was (by chance?) twenty weeks. Of course, it depends on the individual case whether and with what intensity the relapse occurs. It is obvious that to expect the cessation of all nervous disturbances instantly after the operation, or to look at such success as a criterion for justifying the operation in cases of chronic psychosis or neurosis, is totally unreasonable. Moreover, it will be necessary to determine whether the nervous disturbance is newly occurring—a problem resulting from the way the operation was performed, for example, and therefore possibly avoidable—or a return of the original complaint.

I have no doubt that it will be possible to sharpen the criteria for advising castration in cases of neurosis and psychosis, an essential precaution in an operation that in spite of scientific progress is not without its dangers. We are already off to a good start, as the remarks made at the Copenhagen congress (particularly by Hegar) seem to indicate. It is not realistic to expect an early solution to this problem, because each case, particularly where subtle diseases of the sexual organs or complicated psychological disturbances are present, can properly be evaluated only through cooperation between a gynecologist who is an expert diagnostician and a neuropathologist or a psychiatrist. It is not possible to state whether any specific complex of symptoms requires surgical treatment, especially with psychosis. In the successful cases cited above, we dealt with melancholic, maniacal, slightly paranoid symptoms, as well as with cases of mild retardation—that is, conditions easier to cure than psychosis. It would of course be of the greatest importance to discover whether we could stop the more severe forms of progressive psychological degeneration of hysterics with castration. It is obvious that all cases, as well as all hysterical symptoms, cannot be measured with the same yardstick. Some, I am convinced, are surely connected with diseases of the sexual organs, even if in very different ways. In some cases, the advisability of surgical treatment deserves scrutiny through empirical observation. That alone is decisive.

Biographical Note

Paul Flechsig (1847–1929) was professor of psychiatry at the University of Leipzig, and head of the well-known psychiatric clinic at the university. His reputation was worldwide.

This article is important not only because of the enormous prestige its author enjoyed in European medical circles but also because it played an important role in the famous case of Daniel Paul Schreber, a judge who was placed in the psychiatric hospital headed by Flechsig on the basis of his "delusions." See William Niederland's *The Schreber Case* (New York: Quadrangle Books, 1974) and his "Schreber and Flechsig: A Further Contribution to the 'Kernel of Truth' in Schreber's Delusional System" (*Journal of the American Psychoanalytic Association*, 16 [1968], pp. 740–48).

Freud wrote a famous paper in 1911 about the homosexual origins of paranoid delusions on the basis of Schreber's memoirs. Schreber developed the "delusion" that Flechsig wished to turn him into a woman, to castrate him. Freud attributed these "fantasies" to Schreber's wish to be a woman. William Niederland was the first to expose the fact that Flechsig really did castrate women. What Niederland did not know is that Freud had in his personal library a reprint of this very article. It is exceedingly curious that Freud did not modify his views once he became aware, through this article, that Schreber's fears were grounded in reality. Schreber was not paranoid, he was perceptive. The elaborate categories for different forms of "paranoid schizophrenia" in modern psychiatric and psychological textbooks are nothing more than the refusal to recognize that atrocities such as those performed by Flechsig exist, that they have always existed, and that they form the central core of the reality of every so-called mental patient. Every "paranoia" suggests the presence of a terrible underlying reality.

In the year he died, Flechsig published an autobiography, *Meine myelogenetische Hirnlehre (mit biographischer Einleitung)* (Berlin: Julius Springer, 1929), in which he comments on the operations he performed; "unpleasant consequences," he noted, were often the result.

Démétrius Alexandre Zambaco

Masturbation and Psychological

Problems in Two Little Girls*

It serves no purpose to go back to Hippocrates to identify the dangers of masturbation, but it is impossible to concern oneself with this terrible habit and its disastrous consequences without mentioning Tissot.

Until the last few years, it has been difficult to engage in clandestine relations in the Orient. Not only were there no hospitable institutions for the young which could provide a true safety valve benefiting both family and society, but the government carried out, through the police, a strict surveillance of any building in which some Don Juan might offer an illegal sacrifice to Venus. These energies could have been put to better use elsewhere. The Ottoman authorities arrogated the right to protect the purity of their subjects' morality by forbidding natives or foreigners to enter any house of ill repute where a man might indulge his virile passion, even when done with the greatest respect for convention and discretion. As a matter of fact, the police conducted raids on the slightest sus-

* "Onanisme avec troubles nerveux chez deux petites filles." L'Encéphale, 2 (1882), 88–95; 260–74.

picion and, with great pomp and din, led any man who was caught therein through the streets—day or night. The ladies' man who could not escape this embarrassing public exhibition of his sexual guilt by generously greasing the palm of the chief of police was not spared blows with a blackjack or a rifle butt!

The most powerful embassies could hardly protect their subjects from the brutality of this absurd police force, which assaulted delinquents for obeying nature's demands; whereas the most shameless license was given to those who transgressed the laws of nature, hence the encouragement of pederasty and lesbianism. These people encountered neither judicial penalties nor societal disapproval.

Thus the absence of brothels (until recently) explains why masturbation is much more prevalent here than anywhere else, and why it is practiced up to an advanced age.

I have much to say about male masturbation and its consequences in the Orient. I plan to deal with that later. Today I will discuss a strange case of masturbation in two very young girls. This is a vice I could not totally eradicate in spite of the use of all conceivable methods, sometimes the most violent ones. The moral aberration of these children is so advanced that they use all their ingenuity to invent the most astonishing, unheard-of ways to excite themselves and find satisfaction.

CASE HISTORY

X is ten years old. She is delicate, thin, nervous, very intelligent, old for her age; she meets people and chats with them like a woman; she always has a smile on her lips and a sugary expression on her face—a slight hint of hypocrisy that belies her youth. Her kind and amiable manner makes her liked by everyone. She is proud, vain, capricious. In all games, she is always the leader. She keeps for herself the role of queen, princess, or fairy. She frequently wants to dominate other children. She does not hesitate to use her nails and teeth on those who dare challenge the privileges she allocates to herself. She has great influence over her playmates, whom she occasionally tyrannizes. Nevertheless, they voluntarily bear their yoke in deference to her charismatic graciousness. Everyone is attracted to her because of her caresses and her tenderness. Strange thing! Little boys are her admiring slaves. She is successful at playacting, and above all she enjoys pretending to get married. She "marries" her boyfriends and then sends them off one by one. At this, she demands that they weep and be heartbroken. Jealous, envious, vindictive—her moods change for no reason. Sometimes she rolls on the floor, screaming in fits of rage; sometimes she sinks into melancholy. Sometimes she is wildly merry; sometimes deeply absorbed in daydreams. She is flirtatious and charming; she loves to dress up, and she adores perfume. One fact must not be overlooked: she has indulged in petty thievery since early childhood, and carefully hides away things she likes, even though she could have them for the asking. This tendency to steal was first observed when she was only five years old. She loves to learn and asks endless questions. She has a lively sense of fantasy and loves beauty, but does not like to pray, mocks other children's piety, and makes a face when one speaks to her of God.

At the beginning of 1879, the child began to lose weight even though her appetite remained good. She was very anemic and nervous. She had a leukorrheal vaginal discharge and itching of the anus. I examined the area and found she had pinworms. I prescribed calomel suppositories, iron and potassium bromide. Following this treatment, X appeared to improve. Starting around June of the same year, however, X began to steal continuously: sweets, candy, ribbons, various small objects. Then she was caught in a trap set for her. In spite of being caught in the act, she denied her guilt with imperturbable audacity. She laid claim to outraged innocence.

She grew indignant. Her face became distorted with rage; it was an indescribable scene. From then on, a change took place in her constitution and physical appearance; she looked more and more sickly. It was also observed at this time that she went to the toilet very frequently and remained there for extended periods. Sometimes she was taken away, and one day she was even found asleep in there. It was also observed that X had a great predilection for hiding in the bushes or deep in the forest with certain other children, as far away as possible from nursemaids or teachers. A small area enclosed by hedges was her exclusive domain. She placed a chair in it and allowed only a few favorite little girl friends to join her. She named this spot the "palace of delights." She spent much time in there with a little boy. What went on in that palace of delights? Suspicion had not yet been completely aroused, but it is certain that the children played at engagement and marriage. They actually exchanged rings and promised to wed when they were grown up. Later, an end was put to these inopportune intimacies, and supervision was increased.

In March 1881, X suffered strong pains in the lower abdomen, tenesmus, and had great difficulty in urinating. It was then that I noticed a very distinct irritation in the vulvar area, in which various parts were swollen. I revealed my fears to her parents. X was forced to admit her deeds. She wept a lot and promised to stop. Nevertheless, she continued to waste away. Kindness, advice, admonishment, supervision, nothing had any effect on her. X continued to abuse herself, as she admitted later. At the same time, daily thefts recurred. Her whims, quarrels, and bad moods made her unbearable. Also at this time, her teacher noticed that almost all her movements were lewd in nature. Sometimes she even rubbed herself with both hands, her face revealing her pleasure. Unconcealed touching occurred all the time. Her gait became strange; she walked with legs apart, bending the knees, twisting her hips.

Her bearing was very indecent. Seated in a chair, her posture was revolting. She sat on the edge, opened her legs, bent her body forward, and thus contracted the various parts of her body to bring about sensations of voluptuousness. Kind treatment had no effect on her. Her vice became more and more deep-rooted; it became necessary to change tactics and treat her severely, even with the most cruel brutality.

Corporal punishment was resorted to, in particular the whip. X submitted without protest, but no benefit whatever was achieved. She became contemptible. Her features became animal-like. Frequently, regardless of who was with her, she opened her legs, stiffened, and produced a voluptuous spasm. When she was scolded, she trembled and wept bitterly. She had a terrible fear of the whip, which was administered generously. In spite of this, she abused herself more and more in a thousand ways; with her hands, her feet, or any foreign object she got hold of. She rubbed herself on the corners of furniture, assuming certain postures, stiffening her body, etc., etc. I shall later reveal in detail all the means which her fertile imagination resorted to daily, and the relentlessness with which she continued what she herself called her "horrors."

It was at this time that we decided to tie her hands, then her legs and feet. A remarkable turn of events! Her upper body grew thinner and thinner, whereas her thighs, her hips, and her genitals continued to grow. In front of her teacher, her parents, servants, friends, strangers, she adopted a lascivious posture and indulged her passion in a most indecent manner. Even in the streets, her behavior attracted the attention of people passing by. Thus neither kindness nor severity had the slightest effect.

The whip only made her seem dazed, more deceitful, more perverse, and meaner than ever. It was decided to guard her continually at that point; nevertheless, she found a thousand ways to satisfy herself. When she did not succeed in tricking her guardians, she would fall into the most terrible rage. Her mouth would fill with saliva, she would turn alternately red and pale; she would twist her body and struggle in fury if one tried to hold her. In these moments, she would sob and shout at the top of her voice: "Why do you deprive me of such an innocent pleasure?" and shortly thereafter: "I know it's dirty, but it isn't anybody's business but my own. Leave me my pleasure! Even if it kills me, I don't care. I want to do it, and die. I want to!"

One day she prayed as follows: "Dear God, since my sister claims you are omnipotent, show me a way to do this without sinning."

At this time we had to have recourse to the straitjacket to prevent this child from continuously touching herself. We kept her forearms crossed on her chest, her hands at the level of her shoulders; her legs and feet were spread apart and were tied very tightly to the iron posts of her bed; a beltlike bandage, used as a strap, tied her body to the mattress with knots attached to the bed. In spite of all these precautions, X rivaled the Davenport brothers in finding ingenious ways to unravel the ropes and satisfy her desires. Indeed, in the morning her genitals showed definite traces of having had violent contact with a pointed object. The following night, by pretending to be asleep, we were able to observe her reach her goal after several hours of work and Kabyle-like contortions, frequently interrupted by body spasms. She braced her head, pulled at the straitjacket with her teeth, and managed to get her hands close to her genitals. During the day she had taken the precaution of sticking hairpins into her pillow. Now she pulled them out and straightened them with her teeth, and when they were thus elongated, she held one end between her teeth and managed to touch her genitals with the other. This solved the puzzle for us. Indeed, it often happened that the straitjacket and all the ropes were still in place, yet her genitals were scratched and bleeding, sometimes even deeply wounded.

During the night she almost always succeeded in satisfying herself thus. If she did not, she moaned; her cries were raucous and became more and more savage. She shook her bed wildly and in this state of exaltation had neither restraint nor shame. She gnashed her teeth and insulted everybody; she screamed at the top of her lungs: "I detest my father, I abhor my mother— I beg God to make them die." In a word, she threw a tantrum; her face took on the paleness of a cadaver, her eyes were wild and fiery and appeared to burst from their sockets; drops of cold sweat bejeweled her forehead. These scenes of violence, these manic fits, were soon followed by contrition, by acts of tenderness and repentance; it was in these affectionate and lucid moments that she confessed completely and gave up her secrets. She promised to reform and begged us not to abandon her.

When, during the day, the temptation became ungovernable, she asked, as a way to fight against it, permission to wash her genitals with cold water. But soon these ablutions became too frequent. It did not take us long to discover that the sponges had holes in them where they had been penetrated by her fingers, and that the washings were only a pretext to enable her to satisfy her inclinations and escape punishment. In one of these moments of repentance and calm, X made the following confession:

"I only vaguely remember—it was some years ago, after all—that a maid who stayed with me when I went to bed would lift her skirt and give herself over to prolonged rubbing on her shameful parts. I think I got the idea of touching myself from her. Later on, I had a governess who told me that I should never put my hands there; this prohibition, by being too often repeated, aroused my curiosity, and I told myself that it couldn't hurt to try it once. Long ago I got into the habit of doing this. I would get up early to play with my dolls, I would dress them, then I would mechanically do that. Whenever I got bored, I would play that game, but without any desire, without feeling pleasure. Later I would pretend that I was sick there, and my play would include taking an enema and placing a poultice there. I used anything that fell into my hands—grass, sand, etc.—and I gave myself enemas with little sticks. For years sticking pieces of wood up has always been pleasurable to me.

"But to tell you the truth, to be really happy you must do it with the object you desire at that very moment. Later the urge would come over me at almost regular hours. At first, touching myself two or three times was sufficient. I excited myself especially in front"—the clitoris—"but later I had to rub myself harder and harder. When we lived in our old house"—1877—"I showed my little sister how to do what I was doing." Her little sister was then four years old! "I was bored playing this game by myself. I needed some playmates with my pleasures. But my little sister got no pleasure from it and didn't want to do it. I forced her. She didn't start to feel pleasure until the winter of 1881.

"Y and I did a lot of these horrors. We locked ourselves in a bathroom and we took off all our clothes; then, facing each other, we touched ourselves, either with our hands or with pieces of wood. Later on, I got together with a little boy whom I liked a lot and did the horrors with him. A few months later I showed little V how to do the same thing, and the three of us touched ourselves all together.

"It's horrible to feel a great desire to do it and not be able to. It's enough to drive you crazy. I would be capable of killing anyone who got in our way. During those moments I am seized, as if in a trance; I see nothing, I think of nothing, I fear nothing and no one; nothing matters to me as long as I can do it!

"When I was sad or unhappy for some reason, I did it even more. This is why I abused myself more than ever when they found out I was stealing. It was at this time that I began to put pieces of wood inside me"—vaginal masturbation!—"rubbing with force. Often I used a Jerusalem palm that had been blessed." (It seems that this branch gave her more pleasure than any other foreign body, because she could add the pleasure of moral sacrilege to the pleasures of the senses.)

Finally, after exhausting her supply of rounded objects, she graduated to pointed objects, such as scissors, forks, pins, etc. She had a particular predilection for hairpins. As soon as she saw one, she felt the desire to use it. "Later on," she added, "my habit was noticed, and they wanted to prevent me from doing it. I got into a terrible rage and said that nobody had any right to prevent me from using my fingers and my body as I saw fit. I became enraged at everybody, even at God, who made me miserable by first giving me a taste of happiness. I became evil and wanted to do as much evil as possible. I often thought of the devil, whom I called to my aid. He actually came, I saw him; he made the whole thing easier, because he helped me to feel detached from myself. But the first time he showed himself he came uninvited. It was night. I was in bed. Suddenly the closet door opened wide and the devil appeared. He was big, black, and grinning. His eyes were green. Then all the closets and all the drawers opened and an infinite number of little demons came out of them. It was horrible to watch! I have never forgotten that abominable scene!

"After all this, I repented, confessed, but it was impossible to stop, and so I began again. At night, I often called upon the devil for help. Once, I even felt that he seized my shoulders with his hand. Sometimes I begged him to kill my parents and hurt everybody. If only I could be a demon myself in order to do evil!

"Still, I like to go to church and read the Bible. I feel calm and tranquil during the service"—which did not prevent her from being caught there one day, when it was filled with people, doing the "horrors" with her prayer book.

Conclusive proof that this poor child was falling prey to deviant mental illness is the fact that she did not confine herself to masturbation alone, even with all its variations and refinements. Often, in front of her sister, she would urinate standing up and would then examine the pattern made by the stream of urine. She also touched her excrement and forced her little sister to do the same thing.

Apart from the procedures already mentioned, X could provoke a sensual pleasure spasm by rubbing herself against the edges of furniture, or squeezing her thighs together tightly, or rocking back and forth on a chair. During walks, she took to limping in a certain way, like a bandy-legged person. Or else she would suddenly lift one of her feet high into the air. At other times she would take small mincing steps, then quickly walk on, and suddenly turn sharply to the left.

Finally, she tried, often with success, to stimulate her genitals by stepping on the bent end of a piece of wood found on her walk, causing it to spring up and swing back and forth.

If she saw a hedge she would straddle it and rub herself against it several times. The patience and cunning used by this child are really astonishing! Often she would notice a bush and make a mental note to use it days later.

She would pretend to fall down, or bump into something so she could rub herself against it. Suddenly she would stop and cry out: "Just look at this beautiful flower!" but only to draw attention away from her so that she could quickly kick up her heels against her genitals.

But that is not all! By dint of cunning and shrewdness, X has achieved an end that is astonishing in a young child from a good family, who has been well educated from earliest childhood. The following is certainly a good illustration of her perversion, her instinct for indecency, her neurotic depravity, her moral turpitude: X is being watched with eagle eyes. She is seized with an irresistible desire to do her "horrors." She is tied up, wearing a straitjacket and a "chastity belt" (pubic bandage), her feet are chained, but nonetheless she absolutely must experience that pleasurable sensation, for the thought has come to her and she cannot resist its execution. So she puffs up her neck by contracting it into her shoulders, she holds her breath, she acts as if she had to blow her nose or spit. Then she begins to tighten her anus as at the end of defecation. In short, she alternately contracts and releases the anal sphincters and anal levator muscle by repeating these movements, which I had her demonstrate in front of me. Even the vaginal constrictor itself takes part in these spasmodic contractions, which shake her entire perineum. The vulva expands, and from a distance one can hear a rhythmic dull sound. In fact, the labia majora alternately come together and separate, and as they do so, they make a smacking sound, similar to the noise resulting from suddenly opening the lips after the mouth has been closed. It is like the clicking of the tongue against the palate. This monotonous noise sometimes goes on for hours. The people who are in charge of guarding the child note that it is hateful to hear this sound break into the silence of the night. Often both sisters give themselves over to the same perineal contractions and produce the sound simultaneously. Nevertheless, these children remain otherwise immobile, as if they were glued to their beds, pretending to be asleep. X claims that it takes a long time, sometimes more than an hour, to reach the initial sensual spasm by means of this procedure. If, forewarned of these nocturnal scenes, one administers a good slap to X as soon as she begins, one succeeds in stopping her. But if she is given time to get excited, stopping her before she has achieved satisfaction provokes a terrible storm: she screams, acts as if she were possessed, and is seized by clonic and tonic convulsions.

We have already said that, when X first began to masturbate, nature was not demanding anything at all; that is to say, it was not the genital organs which led to her desire to masturbate. Rather, it was an idea, a cerebral impulse, which led X to excite her sexual organs, still quiescent and insensitive in themselves. I would express my thoughts better if I said that her masturbation, at the beginning, was cerebral masturbation, and it was only later that it became sexual. The clitoris and the vagina, awakened and sensitized by these repeated touchings, gave rise, in their turn, to lascivious thoughts, and so X reached the point in her story where we now find her, continuing her lamentable habits by means of two separate excitations: cerebral and sexual.

In the past, once the cerebral excitation had been produced, it often charged the sexual organs, almost as if by electricity, after which she was no longer able to tame the desire to satisfy her passion. When X, cold (speaking from the body's point of view), suddenly conceived the idea of masturbating, she would stiffen her entire body, especially her legs, with all her might, and would thus induce the physical excitation after the cerebral excitation. Lately, however, her sexual sensitivity is such that a single touch is enough to bring about an orgasm. The more sudden the touching, the quicker the orgasm. In June, as a result of the large number of sexual abuses she has administered to herself, X was seized by a nervous trembling which spread throughout her entire body and which was accompanied by a pain so intense that the child began to scream and then went into a tetanic state lasting for several minutes, during which it was impossible for her to make the slightest movement. She was as stiff and immobile as a frog after violent electrocution.

The great fear that she felt as a result of this made her

behave for several days. As for her general health, X was getting more and more exhausted. She complained of piercing headaches; she experienced the sudden onset of nervous fevers, which would last for several hours; she would feel erratic pains over her whole body and twinges in her genitals; frequently she was taken over by anxiety, feelings of suffocation, and palpitations with a tendency to lipothymia; at times she was seized by extreme agitation and by an irresistible impulse to move about. She would jump from her chair as far as possible and pace from one end of the room to the other; sleep was rare; she claimed to spend two or three nights at a time in total insomnia. She was exhausted, her mind was in a deplorable condition, she was not taken out of her straitjacket except for meals. Nevertheless, during these brief moments of liberty she had but one exclusive thought: to touch her genitals, or else to stick a fork or the handle of her knife into her vagina. One day she was caught red-handed and the fork torn from her hands. She broke into sobs, got up from the table, and screamed at the top of her voice: *"I want to do it! Have pity on me! Let me do it!"* Thus, X's condition was getting progressively worse, and in order to avoid a scandal, she had to be moved to a chalet in the middle of a garden, far away in the country. Her little sister, Y, about six, to whom she had taught her shameful habits, was with her. In addition to servants, two governesses were hired to watch the children day and night and to prevent any furtive activity. Everything there was well organized: the day was scheduled in such a manner that their every minute was occupied and their attention was distracted from their vice. An attempt was made to inspire religious sentiments by prayer and reading pious books.

They took walks twice a day, and various kinds of games made their life pleasant; but it was no use. X's *idée fixe* was to overcome the vigilance of her guardians. While the maid was dressing her, she would quickly touch her genitals or bang her heel against them. When bathing in the ocean, she would use her toes with astonishing dexterity to pick up seashells and little pebbles, which she would then put into her vagina. Or else, when she was being undressed, she would remove a hairpin and hide it in her mouth, waiting for the right moment to use it. She would dunk her head and stay underwater for several seconds in order to rub herself with her hand.

From time to time X has moments of regret, realizes she is on a fatal downward course, sheds tears, promises to change, but these are no different from the oaths of the drunkard. One minute later she invents a new intrigue. Thus, one day she is sorry and cries like a Magdalene upon reading a touching and affectionate letter from her mother which exhorts her to change; but at the same moment she rolls up the very letter that so moved her and slips it skillfully beneath her dress until it touches her genitals. And so it is that she cannot be left alone even to carry out the most urgent calls of nature. It became necessary to place bells on the hands and feet of both children (who had been tied with straitjacket, chains, and ropes as previously described) in order to prevent all movement, any dangerous rubbing. But how could we prevent the contraction of the muscles of the perineum, which brought about an orgasm in spite of all the precautions taken?

Since baths in the ocean overexcited the children's nervous system, they have been replaced by lukewarm and prolonged fresh-water baths. Furthermore, four grams of potassium bromide are given daily to supplement their diet, which includes milk, vegetables, beer, and no red meat.

These lengthy baths and the rest of this regimen made the children weaker. For approximately three months the same condition prevailed, the same scenes of agitation and violence recurred. If one showed X the crucifix, she became even more agitated. Once she bit it and spat on it. She cried that she would rather see the devil, who helps her succeed. The next moment she repented, begged that prayers be said for her and that the Psalms be read to her! Her hallucinations also took place during the day. Once, in the middle of a grammar lesson, she suddenly cried: "Chase him, chase him away, I do not want the devil right now." One day during a walk she suddenly stopped, letting out a terrible scream. Her face took on a look of terror. She rushed into her teacher's arms, screaming: "There he is! He is horrible, and his eyes are glowing! I am going blind, I can no longer see!" Her voice became hoarse, and her facial expression resembled that of a madwoman. One moment she effusively embraced her teacher, the next she beat and bit her; she wanted to leave everything behind and run away. One day she wanted to jump into the street from a second-story window. Sometimes she wants to be caressed and expresses gratitude for affection. At other times she gets angry at the sympathy shown for her suffering. "No one must share in it," she says, "because my suffering is shameful!"

On August 26, seeing what little success was achieved by coercion, by shackles and other means of restraint, by corporal punishment, I ordered a complete release from all that. I attempted to revive her self-esteem by counseling and kindness, to raise her dignity, to appeal to her sense of honor. I brought to her attention the atrocious consequences of her habit; I promised to give her complete freedom of movement if she would be reasonable and obey me. But I made sure to add: "If you do not listen to me, I shall be ferociously cruel. I will burn your genitals with a red-hot iron." X appeared very moved by my expression of sympathy, but did not promise to be good in the future. "I will do my best," she said, "but I am not sure I shall succeed and therefore can make no promises." Strange thing! She did not want to be freed from her bonds. "I have no confidence in myself," she said. "Put my straitjacket back on, tie me up, I beg you." It was necessary to agree to her request, but otherwise the rigid regimen that had been applied until then was abandoned. I insisted that she be left a little to herself, for I noticed that she revolted against all forms of severity, that she got her back up in some way against every instance of brutality, that she countered all corrective measures with some kind of tricky ruse. It was as though she felt greater happiness in reaching her goal when she could triumph over great obstacles!

Her treatment: cold showers; potassium and ammonia bromides, two grams each every twenty-four hours; ferrous wine, various nourishing foods. In the days following, X appeared calmer, from a mental point of view. She had no hallucinations. She admitted giving way to her vice on several occasions, but with greater moderation. As a result of the continous touching and excitation, her sexual parts were so sensitive that when the maid suddenly pulled off the child's nightshirt while getting her dressed, she caused something like an electric shock that made the child's entire body vibrate. X blushed, her breathing became irregular, her skin moist, her face radiant; in a few seconds the voluptuous sensation had reached its peak. "This time it was not my fault," she said. "The pulling on my shirt was too strong. Brisk rubbing in that area produces a reaction I cannot control." In effect X is easy to arouse. The slightest grazing of the sexual organs brings about erethism with lightning speed, a phenomenon clearly visible in her face. Thus when she bends down to pick a flower, she quickly touches her genitals with her hands, and her goal is attained. The same thing happens if she barges into furniture while walking by, or if she hugs someone. It can easily be seen that it was absolutely impossible to obviate all the circumstances under which she could continue her self-abuse.

The nights are filled with recurrences of ordinary abuse; there is constant nervous twitching; her nocturnal crises are often calmed by a few kind words and repeated forehead stroking. The child looks better and appears happy. She does her

lessons with pleasure. She admits with sincerity that she provokes erotic spasms twelve to fifteen times a day. She even
introduced a paintbrush into her vagina. Her genitals are very
inflamed; she has a thick, abundant, greenish-yellow discharge.

On August 29 X looks charming. A striking change in her
has taken place. Her bearing is good. She reacted to the visit
of a relative with grace. She chatted amiably, recited poems,
sang a song. But she touched herself several times after the
visit, was gloomy during her walk, and her voice became hoarse
again. That is a sign of rising nervousness in her. Later, seated
in a chair, she jerks her head and rolls her eyes, looking upward
frequently. She complains that God is unjust toward her, since
He gave her everything to make her happy and now He takes
her happiness away. "I ask Him to let me die," she says. "I
am so afraid of the operation with which the doctor threatened
me! And furthermore, how shameful to be cured by force and
not by my own free will." Veritable chaos reigns in her small
head! Sometimes she says: "You will save me, with God's
help," and her eyes shine with joy; sometimes she fears that
it is too late and that she is definitely lost. Her hallucinations
start again. Her wild gaze spots the terrible head with green
eyes. She imagines that a cloud of devils is descending on the
house and that she is turning into a demon herself!

She thinks she is dead already, that she enters her house
without being seen, and that she hurts everyone in it, which
makes her happy. She is convinced that she is in communication with the devil and has a mysterious relationship with
hell. It must be noted that excessive masturbation inevitably
leads to these very hallucinations and mental disorders.

X has been thinking about marriage for some time. She
already seems to instinctively relish the idea of the enjoyment
of sexual relations.

One day, in order to distract her, someone spoke to her of

the mythological power of fairies to obtain what they desire. "I wish," said she, "that there be as many men as women on earth, so that they all might marry."

"Do you believe that happiness is tied to marriage?" asked her teacher. "There are many happy, useful, unmarried women." X replied, smiling, "I am not a saint!"

Her face is alternately purple, with an insolent expression, or pale, with dull eyes. When she becomes agitated, she paces up and down the room, or balances on one foot or the other. She rants when she speaks, or assumes an affected manner; her features are contorted by spasms; she grimaces or laughs wildly, without rhyme or reason. In this agitated state, X is incapable of doing anything. Reading, conversation, play, everything seems hateful to her! Suddenly her expression becomes cynical; her agitation reaches its zenith. X is overwhelmed by her desire to do it. She wants to hold back or wants others to try to stop her. But she is dominated by one thought: to achieve it. Her ardent glance appears to be searching, her lips draw in and out incessantly, her nostrils tremble. Later she becomes calmer, she seems to recede into herself. "If only I had not been born," she says to her little sister, "we would not be the shame of our family." And Y responds: "Then why did you teach me to do the horrors?" Hurt by this approach, X replies: "If only someone would kill me! What happiness! I could die without suicide."

On September 14, in the afternoon, X suffers a terrible crisis of overexcitement. She walks rapidly, she shouts, she weeps, she grimaces frequently, she grinds her teeth. The teacher tries to manage her, but is kicked. She foams at the mouth, she gasps for breath, and says over and over again: "I don't want to, I don't want to, I can't control myself. I will do the horrors, stop me, hold my hands, tie up my feet." Several moments later she totally collapses. She becomes sweet and gentle again and begs not to be abandoned. "I know I will kill myself," she says. "Save me."

As you can see, the instinct for self-preservation sometimes wins out over the attraction of vice. She explains how she must be tied up in order to efficiently frustrate her efforts. But the inconsistencies do not stop. The next day, on one of her walks, she is seized by a crisis of desire even in the presence of a stranger. In vain an effort is made to reinforce her sense of propriety. She cannot control herself. She strolls indecently in front of the passersby in spite of the admonitions of her teacher. She causes a scandal in the small village where their walk took them. The teacher, aided by a servant, takes her away in a carriage to cut short this scene. Scarcely seated, X throws herself backward in order to produce an erotic sensation. The presence of the servant does not discourage her from this unchaste behavior. On the twenty-eighth she is tormented by remorse and asks the priest to hear her confession. There is nothing more heartrending than the picture before our eyes: while the venerable priest counsels her, she is bathed in tears, her hands are folded, she prays fervently, bowed to the ground, but suddenly a diabolical thought crosses her poor mind, and taking advantage of her bent position, she rubs her private parts with . . . the priest's cassock!

I shall abbreviate as much as possible the story of little Y, X's sister, whom I have mentioned above. She is less intelligent and less attractive than her older sister. Unfortunately, the two children were not separated. Thus the little one copied all the actions of the older one. All techniques invented by X were taken over by Y. Her genitals are so well developed that there are already tufts of hair on the labia majora, even though Y is only six years old. All violent methods used on X were also applied to her. Because of her strong constitution, the whip was applied to her with so much force that her buttocks are striped with angry welts. Nothing succeeds with Y any more than with her sister. A pubic bandage had no effect. The genitals are very inflamed and blood-red. There is a constant thick yellow discharge with a very repulsive odor despite several washings per day. This child, whose sexual desires have been awakened for several months, often prepares herself for excitement with preliminary body movements. Even though her constitution is strong and she looks bright, when she has abused herself a lot she is reduced to such a state of imbecility that she no longer understands what she is told. She then appears very pale and cross-eyed.

Suddenly the idea comes to her that she must satisfy herself. Her eyes shine, her speech becomes slurred, her saliva is abundant. Sometimes tears flow. She often reproaches her sister for teaching her to do the "horrors." This does not stop her from copying her older sister: the same indecent gait, the same maneuvers when she is tied to her bed, the same trickery to deceive her keepers. She receives the same treatment as X, with the same lack of success.

While in London to attend the International Medical Congress, I met Dr. Jules Guérin. I told our eminent colleague about the desperate case of the two children and asked his advice. Dr. Guérin assured me that, when all else had failed, he had cured young girls suffering from masturbation by burning the clitoris with a hot iron.

Back in Constantinople, I had no difficulty convincing the family to accept the advice of the eminent academician. I decided to begin the experiment with little Y.

September 8: The poor child trembles, speaks extremely fast, and yet reasons like a sixteen-year-old. She begs me not to burn her, she is even grateful that I forcefully remove her straitjacket. I notice wounds on the labia minora, running in a perpendicular direction to them. They are proof of violence committed yesterday with a table fork! The opening of the vagina is a brilliant red; it is really painful to see so young a child so perverse. She confesses readily all she has done during my absence. "I am ashamed, sir, to tell you all my horrors," she says. After some hesitation she admits to me that she rubs herself with her hands, her feet, with any object she can put her hands on. At my request, she shows me how she manages to reach her goal in her bed and how she produces the clicks of the vulva simultaneously with her sister for much of the night. We have already described in detail what causes this sound, which can be heard over a distance of several meters. It results from a rhythmic movement of the labia majora and strong contractions of the anus, which shake the entire perineum. "But who could have shown you these infamies?" I asked. "I thought them up myself, sir," she said. "I experience pleasure at every contraction, every squeeze. My sister does the same."

All was ready for the electric cauterization, but the tears, the pleading, the promises of Y so moved me that I preached to her for over an hour. I explained to her that her health would be ruined and her reputation lost if she continued on her present path. But if she didn't keep her word, she would be burned during my next visit. "It is shameful for you to be tied up like an animal in a stable, or like a criminal." We tried cold showers and potassium bromide, but no sooner did I leave than she began again with a vengeance.

September 11: In order to frighten her as much as possible, I prepared a display of red-hot coals; I placed an enormous iron ax on top of it; I blew on it until it turned red. She trembled at the sight of this infernal scene. "You did not keep your promise, so now I will show you that you were wrong— by keeping my promise!" I told her. Then I picked up the enormous red-hot ax, but I only cauterized her clitoris with a tiny stylet, three millimeters in diameter, that had been heated red-hot by an alcohol lamp. "If you do it again," I told her,

"I will burn you with the large iron ax, and I will show no mercy."

September 14: The operation had an immediate salutary effect. Little Y has been good since the cauterization. "The pain is terrible," she said. "I will never do it again." Although completely free of constraint, she was very well behaved on her walk and very calm during the night. But on the afternoon of the fifteenth, her features changed suddenly. Her hands were very agitated, just as they were each time she was getting ready to commit her crime. In the twinkling of an eye, one of her hands disappeared under her skirt and Y turned completely red. Pressed with questions, she admitted that she did it, but tried to justify herself by saying that it was impossible for her to resist the desire that was tormenting her. She was reminded of the scene with the fire and was put under supervision. Toward evening she threw a fit, then cried and sobbed. This is what happens to both sisters when they are seized by an irresistible need to touch themselves and are restrained.

On the fifteenth, she stuffed a piece of wood into her vagina. Later, she bent down toward a small table and managed to touch her genitals with the ornaments on her foot. Yet she has been abusing herself much less since the cauterization. Touching is no longer sufficient to bring about an orgasm. She has to rub, repeatedly and for a long time, at the orifice of the vagina, because her clitoris, far from being excitable, is extremely painful to the touch. Our surveillance of little Y is paying off.

September 16: A new cauterization. I burned her three times on both labia majora, and once on the clitoris, and to punish her for her disobedience I cauterized her buttocks and loins with the dreaded large iron. She swore to me that she will not fail again, and confessed that she feels very guilty because since the first cauterization she has not had as much desire to excite herself: "I see that this method will work, because I have been able to go more than twenty-four hours without doing any horrors."

The day after, she complains of her burns but continues to search for an occasion to touch herself, and only stops as soon as she is threatened with being burned.

X, seeing the punishment inflicted on her sister, has become very sad. She repeats time and again: "If only I could die! I see that I will have to undergo the same torture. What can I do?" She continues her excesses, even though her physical condition is very alarming: she is pale, thin, weak, and the lower part of her body is edematous nearly up to her knees.

Yesterday, when the Angelus was rung, she started to tremble, and her terrified eyes were drowned in tears. She tried to run away, shouting: "The ringing bells remind me of the Last Judgment."

September 19: Third cauterization of little Y, who sobs and screams.

In the next few days, however, Y successfully struggles with her temptations. She has become a child again—she plays with her doll, amuses herself, and laughs lightheartedly. She begs us to tie her hands every time she is not sure of herself. Once, when she succumbed, she was whipped on her already wounded buttocks. Many times she is seen trying hard to control herself. Nevertheless, she does it two or three times in twenty-four hours, though she has, generally, complete freedom of movement. It is very little compared with the thirty or forty times she abused herself daily before the cauterizations. Her governess is delighted with the results we obtained. X, on the other hand, is tearing more and more at the veil of modesty. One night she discovered a way to rub herself against one of the ropes that bound her, until blood came. On another occasion, caught in the act by her governess before she was able to satisfy herself, she threw a terrible tantrum, during which she screamed: "I want to do it—oh, how I want to do it! You

cannot understand how much I want to do it!" Her memory
is getting worse and worse, she can no longer do her lessons;
she still has her hallucinations, and even her arms have been
affected by edema. She acts as indecently as before when she
takes her walks: she jumps into the bushes, kicks her heels
against her genitals, etc. Her urine contains no albumin.

September 23: X repeats: "I deserve to be burned, and I will
be. I will bravely submit to the operation; I won't scream."
From ten at night until two in the morning, she has a terrible
nervous crisis: several times she falls unconscious. Sometimes
she has visual hallucinations, other times she is incoherent
and delirious. "Turn the page," she will say, or: "Who is hitting
me?"

September 25: I apply a button of fire to X's clitoris. She
does not flinch during the operation. For the twenty-four hours
following she behaves herself completely. But after that she
returns to her old habits with a vengeance. In order to prevent
any rubbing, we are obliged to keep her standing, her legs tied
together, or propped against a chair, but one turned upside
down so she cannot rub herself against its edges. She complains
of vague pains in her chest and begins to cough. An examination turns up nothing.

Little Y behaves. The inflammation of her genitals resulting
from her vigorous rubbing has disappeared.

October 12: Little Y begins her horrors again. She howls
like a wild beast when she hears me come; I give her some
violent and extremely painful electric shocks on her genitals
with the Clarke machine. This method, as we might have
expected, does not succeed. On the contrary, according to her
governess, Y was very excited by this procedure and abused
herself even more than on the preceding days.

October 17: X once again has a veritable fit of insanity,
during which she tries to throw herself out the window. Yesterday she rubbed her vagina with a piece of bronze so savagely

that she almost hemorrhaged. I cauterized the clitoris and the entrance to the vagina of both sisters.

After that day, the two little patients were separated and removed from my care. According to the information I have, little Y has been completely cured. As for X, she continues to abuse herself as she did in the past. But she lives far away in the country, deprived of both medical attention and treatment.

REFLECTIONS

The preceding observations have been set down in such a detailed and meticulous manner that it is not necessary to append a long commentary. They alone sufficiently highlight the main points of this interesting case.

Instances of masturbation in little girls of such a young age are rare. We know of only two other documented cases: from Fonssagrives, about a seven-year-old girl whose behavior forced the use of a belt, but with no success, since the child achieved her goal by slipping a long feather underneath her binding till it reached her genitals; and from Deslandes, a three-year-old girl who, in spite of her early precocious activity, was able to abstain from further abuse until her marriage.

We have established that the masturbation of the two young sisters was both clitoral and vaginal.

If we examine the origins of this vicious habit, the very first conditions under which it was contracted, we find two main causes: pinworms, at least in the older child, and negative influence. Indeed, little X did have worms, for which I treated her. Now, much like rashes in the genital area, pinworms in the lower extremity of the rectum can cause the manual excitation of the genitals as the patient tries to relieve the uncontrollable itching. But X already had her curiosity aroused by seeing the maid touch herself when she thought the child was asleep. As for little Y, she was corrupted by her sister when she was four years old, along with several other children.

It is not possible, given their tender age at the time, that our young patients began to abuse themselves to satisfy sexual needs. They did it to imitate others, and to avoid boredom during the hours they were not otherwise occupied. Later, after frequent repetition of this exercise, there was something like a very precocious awakening of the sexual instincts, with a compulsion to satisfy them immediately and at any price. I think one can consider this irresistible desire, this untamable wish, a genuine neurosis. Quite often X struggled with all her might to control this morbid compulsion, but to no avail. In spite of every effort, she was not able to restrain herself, any more than someone suffering from chorea is able to stop moving, or a hysteric is able to forestall an attack. Many was the time that X decided to reform and begged to be tied up and prevented from doing it. The next moment she used all her ingenuity to escape the vigilance of the people appointed to guard her.

At the onset of this vicious habit, any excitement came exclusively from the brain. It was only later, after frequent repetition of the rubbing, that the excitation took hold of the genital apparatus itself.

Little X had many nervous troubles. At times she bore a burden of the most profound melancholy and wished to die. At other times she was seized by a manic animation violent enough to turn a normally sweet and docile child into a wild beast, hitting and biting the very people she respected the most if they opposed the gratification of her desire once the craving had reached its peak.

Soon afterward, a period of depression, calm, and remorse would set in. In particular, I must stress the absolute extinction of any moral sensibility. Indeed, once these two children were possessed with the urge to masturbate, they were not the least concerned with convention or who was present. Without blushing, they would give themselves over to totally shameless acts in front of passersby or servants. If we add to the above the hallucinations that X so often displayed, we can be completely certain that her psychic problems were profound ones.

X's vision had also undergone considerable deterioration. In this regard, I should mention a similar case which I treated while I was practicing medicine in Paris. An unmarried woman of twenty-seven confessed to me that she touched herself very many times every day—she developed almost total progressive amaurosis. Desmarres Sr., to whom I sent the patient without informing him of her habit, recognized the real cause of her increasing loss of vision. He revealed this in a sealed letter that the patient delivered to me. Later the woman, following our advice, renounced masturbation and thus recovered her sight.

I will add only a few words about the therapy used in the case of the two young girls. Medication was completely ineffective; so were sedatives and tonics. Showers and hot baths were unable to bring about serenity. Moral instruction was equally unhelpful. Counseling, prayer, caresses, threats, the most cruel punishments, religion, with its menaces and its promises—nothing could prevent these poor children from giving way to their disastrous excesses!

A pubic belt, a straitjacket, bonds, straps, shackles, the most assiduous surveillance merely stimulated them to invent new ways to masturbate by using guile and ingenuity.

It was only cauterization with a red-hot iron that gave satisfactory results. From the very first operation, we were able to decrease orgasms from forty to fifty per day down to no more than three or four in twenty-four hours. Through this method, little Y was, according to the information that reached me, completely cured. All in all, she was cauterized four times. X was cauterized only once, after which I lost sight of her.

Therefore, the fact that she continues to masturbate does not allow us to judge the efficacy of this method.

It is reasonable to presume that cauterization with a red-hot iron deadens the sensitivity of the clitoris, and that if repeated a certain number of times, it can entirely destroy the clitoris. The second sensitive genital spot, the vulvar orifice, is also deadened by cauterization, and therefore one can easily imagine that children, once their genitals have become less sensitive, would be less likely to touch themselves there.

It is equally probable that, once the clitoris and the vulvar orifice become the site of a more or less intense inflammation following the operation, touching there will be painful instead of a source of pleasure.

Finally, fear at the sight of the instruments of torture, and the images that a red-hot iron produces in the imagination of children, should also be counted among the beneficial effects of electrical cauterization.

We believe, therefore, that in cases similar to those discussed above, one should not hesitate to have recourse at a very early stage to the red-hot iron as a cure for clitoral or vaginal masturbation in little girls.

Biographical Note

Démétrius Alexandre Zambaco-Pacha was born in Constantinople of Greek parents and studied medicine in Paris. He died in 1914, after a career crowned with many honors, among them Commander of the French Legion of Honor. His biography can be found in the *Bulletin de Société Française de dermatologie et syphilis* (No. 25 [1914], pp. 189–92). He wrote a series of books on leprosy and a book entitled *Les Eunuques d'aujord'hui et ceux de jadis* (Paris: Masson, 1911). His book *Les Affections nerveuses syphilitiques* (Paris: J. B. Baillière, 1862) won a special prize from the Académie

Impériale de Médecine. An obituary published in *Paris médecine* (1914, supp., p. 119), says: "A feeling of profound compassion led Zambaco to concern himself with leprosy and with lepers, just as it led him to concern himself with eunuchs."

The article included here did not go unheeded. No less an authority than Richard von Krafft-Ebing, professor of psychiatry at the University of Vienna, cited this case in *Psychopathia Sexualis* (Stuttgart: Ferdinand Enke, 1918, 15th ed., p. 51), under the heading "Paradoxia." He calls it a "disgusting" story, not because of what Zambaco did, but because of what Zambaco saw. Paul Moreau de Tours, in his book *La Folie chez les enfants* (Paris: J. B. Baillière, 1888), mentions "the very instructive case of Zambaco." The case is partially reproduced, too, in Maurice Heine's *Confessions et observations psychosexuelles tirés de la littérature médicale* (Paris: Editions Jena Cres, 1936).

Auguste Motet

False Testimony

Given by Children

*before Courts of Justice**

I have the honor of presenting to the Académie de médecine a study of false testimony given by children before courts of justice. Confining myself to the limits imposed, I nevertheless wish to elaborate on a certain mental state which has not been written about in any detail, though it has not escaped the notice of astute observers.

I do not wish to repeat the study that Bourdin undertook in 1882, which became the subject of an interesting discussion by the Société médico-psychologique.† Bourdin dealt with a far more general topic than I. He started with children's lies and understandably branched out to discuss lying in all age groups. The classification which seemed simplest to him was based on the motive of the liar: (a) the lie as a joke; (b) the lie as an outgrowth of passion; (c) the lie as a means of defense; (d) the lie as a means of attack. The development of this classification led to unusual character studies. The adult

* "Les faux témoignages des enfants devant la justice." *Annales d'hygiène publique et de médecine légale*, 17 (1887), 481–96. [For the little biographical information available on Motet, see *Archives de nécrologie*, 29 (1895), 147.]
† *Annales médico-psychologiques*, 6th series, vol. 9, 1883, pp. 53, 55.

has his place in it as much as or more so than the child. M. Fournet, for his part, found material for a medical-psychological study on "Mental and Moral Morbidity" in children.

That is not the goal that I sought. I wish to show, exclusively from the medical-legal point of view, that it is necessary to be prudent and reserved in the face of depositions given by children. I cannot forget the serious consequences they sometimes entail. I have in mind the words spoken by a man under arrest to the child who had falsely accused him: "I am innocent, but I bear you no ill will, my poor little child, for the misfortune you have brought on me, because you do not realize what you are doing."

If, having studied the circumstances under which mendacious depositions can arise, I am able to attribute the false testimony of children to a pathological process rather than to simple instinctual perversions; if I am able to help the magistrate reduce an accusation to nothing, I have accomplished a useful, humane task, and I have served the interests of justice and truth with honesty.

It is important not to give this statement any interpretation other than the one I give it. I have not said that from now on the testimony of children must be disregarded and that all information they furnish must absolutely be ignored. But I maintain that frequently one must be wary with children and accept their statements only after being convinced that no suspicious elements are part of their testimony.

Since I have cited Bourdin, I shall make my own the phrase that ends his work, and which could serve as an epigraph to mine: "The lie, elevated in the mind of the liar to the level of truth, presents no danger when it comes to petty interests or indifferent matters, but when the lie is placed at the seat of justice, the welfare of the accused is severely affected. The judge gives credence to the child's words, because he thinks him or her truthful. Severe inequities can result from the judge's faith. Let us leave this subject in the shadows. It is up to educators, and especially doctors, to dispel the myth of the infallible truthfulness of children. This is a most noble task."*

I do not believe that this subject must be "left in the shadows." I believe I will have undertaken a "noble task" if I am able to shed some light on it. It is up to the doctor to show that under certain conditions of a "particular mental state," the child may encounter, during a temporary or permanent disturbance of his mental processes, the elements of very complicated lies, which have all the appearance of truth and which are all the more gripping because the child's convictions are deeper and more sincere.

I need not, so I believe, defend myself against the accusation, sometimes brought against us, that we create severe obstacles to criminal investigation with our so-called new procedures. The magistrates who honor us by asking our advice in these delicate matters know that our contribution to their decision is made with the utmost caution and prudence. If today, as we borrow from medicine its methods of investigation and analysis, we rely increasingly on more concrete facts, it is one more consequence of the advancement of science. Were we not to raise doubts which, at times, collapse in the face of facts, we would be guilty of not keeping pace with scientific progress, and would stand in the way of letting science be used in the service of truth.

I know nothing more moving than the tale of a child giving the details of a crime of which he claims to have been either the witness or the victim. The naïveté of his speech, the simplicity of the setting attract interest and invite confidence to a singular degree. Those around the child are easily overwhelmed by emotion intensified by the indignation and pity that the story evokes. It is easy to see how parents, friends,

---

* Loc. cit., p. 384.

neighbors accept without question the child's statement, true
or false. They incessantly add new details and construct a story
much more complex than the original one; the child seizes
on it, makes it his own, reproduces it without variations, and
before the magistrate he makes his accusation with terrible
precision.

Lasègue tells us that at one time he had to intercede in a
serious case. A clothing merchant, accused of sexually assaulting a ten-year-old child, was called before an investigating
magistrate. He protested indignantly, stating that he had not
left his place of business at the hour of the supposed assault.
The deposition of the child was clear and precise. She repeated
every detail, and the parents confirmed her story. The judge,
shaken by the attitude of the merchant, who was a perfectly
honorable man, did not pursue the matter and put an end to
it. But the accused continued the investigation for his own
sake. He wanted to know why the child accused him, and this
is what he found out, with Lasègue's help: the child had played
hooky. She came home long after the usual time. On her
arrival, her anxious mother demanded to know where she had
been. She stammered, the mother pressed her with questions,
she said yes to every one; the mother imagined that she might
have been the victim of a sexual assault. Once on this trail—
we don't really know why she took it—she continued her
questions, and without being aware of it supplied the answers
herself. When the father arrived, it was the mother who, in
the child's presence, told the story she made up. The child
remembered it, she knew it by heart, and willingly let herself
be taken to the rue Vivienne. When asked whether she recognized the house where "the man" took her, she pointed to
the merchant's house. Thus, the story was complete, until the
day when the escapade was reconstructed and reduced to nothing—a fairy tale, which could have had grave consequences.

By chance, I was able to observe four such incidents in a

short period of time. By putting strong pressure on the children who made the accusations—and I found sincere ones among them—I was able to understand their psychological states as well as the conditions under which they acquired their convictions. Now, these psychological states have their parallels: in hysterics, for example, whose lies are often very complicated, part truth and part falsehood. They bear an astonishing resemblance to the fantasies of children. We shall see why.

Here, gentlemen, follows one of the most interesting cases to come under my scrutiny. On the morning of November 19, 1885, Albert Morin, seven and a half, son of a newspaper vendor, receives from his mother the newspapers he must deliver in the neighborhood. He takes care of his job as usual, and does not return home. A search is made for him everywhere, but it is not until evening that a telegram from the police notifies his parents that he was found in Billancourt. Two fishermen pulled him from the river Seine, where he was about to drown.

He says that in the morning a man accosted him in the street and asked if he wanted to come with him. He draws a portrait of the man and describes in detail his clothing and manner. He refused to go along, but the man took him "by force." On the way the child complained that his arm hurt. The man asked him what was wrong. He replied that he had been hurt and had been treated at Berck three months for the injury. Then, after a long walk, they reached the river, and without a word the man pushed him in the water. He cried for help. Two fishermen rescued him. He was carried into a house and placed in front of a fire, and was given dry clothes, etc., etc.

This tale, without variation, was told to several people. The description of the man was so precise that there was no problem locating him: he was a certain C., who worked in a wax museum that had been set up for several weeks on the Boulevard de Rochechouart, close to Albert Morin's home. The child had seen him frequently at the door of the booth, giving his sales pitch.

In spite of his vehement denials, C. was arrested. The police commissioner believed himself to be on the trail of a great crime; he did not doubt the sincerity of the child; he did not for a moment consider that a seven-and-a-half-year-old could make up a long story in which the smallest details appeared accurate. For him, proof positive was furnished when Albert Morin described the clothing of the man who carried him off and added that the man had a lame right leg.

But the investigating magistrate, his curiosity aroused, did not accept these claims without reservations, even after a long interrogation of the child, during which the child repeated his earlier statements. C. offered an alibi and proved it. What, then, was the child's deposition worth? If it was false, in spite of all apparent sincerity, what was one to think about the mental state of a child who had a ready answer to, and seemed absolutely sure of, everything? To solve that problem, I was given the task of examining young Albert.

I saw the child in his home, and even though his mother was so sure of her son's truthfulness that she considered my visit useless and even indiscreet, I was able to obtain from her information of decisive importance.

"The one thing that's certain," she told me, "is that since that affair the little boy has lived in constant fear. He has nightmares every night, he cries out in his dreams about the man. He says the man will throw him in the water or bury him." By probing further, we found out that Albert Morin had been sleeping badly for a long time; he urinated in his bed almost nightly. After we learned about these sleep disturbances, we were able to follow the psychopathological evolution of his delirious conviction.

In spite of scant opportunity to study it in sequence, one

often finds that children's development is as much partially premature as partially arrested. When the precocity is intellectual, it is not unusual to find a remarkable exaltation of the sense of wonder. Fantasy is easily stimulated, and if the individual circumstances and the environment encourage this particular disposition, exaggeration cannot be far behind.

Now, young Morin lives in a milieu as disadvantageous as possible. Every minute, he hears of various upsetting events recounted in the newspapers sold by his mother; he has before him pictures showing scenes of violence; he listens to commentaries, he remembers them and dreams about them. A wax museum comes to his neighborhood; in front of the booth there are wax figures. He stops and stares in fascination. There is a mixture of curiosity and terror when he sees the motionless heads. He often returns to this scene, which both attracts and frightens him.

In the midst of this inanimate world, a man moves, talks, and—strange coincidence—the child hears him say one day to the crowd: "Enter, you will see the head of Morin, who was killed by Madame C.H." The rest matters little to him, for he is Morin and the head that the man will show is his.

Here lies the emotional shock: the impression was made; perplexity and obsession will follow, and make it lasting. And instead of the deep, calm sleep that is normal at his age, frightening dreams will haunt him and fantastic complications will arise, the memory of which will not be completely lost upon awakening. Thus a constant threat of danger is present in his mind. One day, perhaps after a chance encounter with C., the child, overcome by fear, runs off, unthinkingly. He arrives at the banks of the Seine. At that moment, the vision must have disappeared and the child fell into the water—an ordinary mishap. But precisely because he is awake, it is necessary for him to explain his flight and fall. Up until now, the child has been a legitimate actor in the drama improvised by his terror. He confesses all that he dreamed and feared. He accuses the man he recognizes, the one who displayed the head of Morin. The more his fantasy has been stimulated, the longer its incubation period, the more precise are the details of his description. They cannot vary, they have taken root too profoundly. He will add but one thing, and it is not his invention but that of his mother, who inadvertently completed the tale of adventure. The child first said that he fell into the water after slipping on a rock. His mother must have concluded, and convinced her son, that C. had thrown him in the water. That is how these things usually happen. The sympathy for the young "victim" draws a crowd of curious onlookers, for whom the adventure story is repeated verbatim a hundred times and whose convictions far surpass those of the narrator himself.

This setting, these expressions of sympathy, more noisy than enlightened, do not displease the child, who instinctively is proud that he is the center of attention. But basically, what have we here? A very interesting emotional state in a child whose fantasy has been vividly stimulated. The child, under the influence of the terror provoked by a wax-museum show, has previously had sleep disturbances. One day, in a state of automatism similar to a somnambulist's, he puts one of his terrifying dreams into action. His troubled mind invents an adventure whose reality can be believed and which is nothing more than a pathological event, an *autosuggestion*.

At almost the same time, I was called upon to examine a child who was confined to a correctional institution. His complaints created some excitement. He declared that a certain person in the institution, whom he identified clearly, had entered his cell at night, turned him over in his bed, and proceeded to touch him in an obscene manner. He had seen the person, and pointed to the spot in the cell where his black garment had appeared.

The following night he was on his guard. Ill at ease, he slept badly, waking up with a start every few moments; the apparition returned, and the next day he made his accusation, complete with precise details. The real explanation was not difficult to come by. The child had intestinal worms and severe itching of the anus. Erythema intertrigo had been produced by frequent rubbing; therefore, sleep was troubled.

All that was needed to disturb his sleep was for the night guard to shine his lantern into the cell through the bars above the door. The cone-shaped shadow created by the beam of light had been mistaken for black garments by the child. The feeling of itching in the anus was transformed into touching. In this young mind, already perverted by communal life in an institution, a story consisting half of night terrors and half of recollections of obscene conversations took on all the earmarks of a sincere conviction. In a similar process, children accuse each other of wrongdoing and of crimes which have never taken place. There is the story of a child of thirteen who was arrested and charged with throwing one of his little friends in the water. Young Marinier did indeed disappear from May 31 to June 3, 1886, but had not been thrown in the water by Massé. The statements of the latter are absolutely false. One asks whether Massé was not a "hallucinator," whether he was not mentally ill to describe in detail how he had drowned his little friend when nothing of the kind had happened.

One need not look far for the explanation. The children had discussed the disappearance of Marinier, which had caused quite a stir. One of them had told his parents that Massé had gone swimming with Marinier and had pushed him in the water. It is perhaps this child who made up the story.

What is certain is that the grandfather of the vanished child was notified. He looked up young Massé and handled him roughly. Massé was frightened and defended himself without conviction. Many questions were thrown at him, and in this case the questions also supplied the answers: "Where did you throw him? There, it must be there." And the bullied child answered, "Yes." Other people intervened, each offered his own version; in the troubled young mind, an unconscious effort was made to put everything together, and in that young head the cold truth and the notions of those around him appeared to be one and the same.

The child scarcely needed to add anything to this. If one wonders how, in the midst of a made-up tale of this kind, he could give details that made the story sound likely, all one has to do is probe a little further and one will find the answer.

Mixed up in this affair were a picnic basket and a hoe brought along by little Marinier, which Massé supposedly threw into the Marne. Massé learned of this from the policemen. They are the ones who first spoke of it in front of him, and when Marinier's grandfather asked him, "What did you do with the basket? Did you throw it in the water?" he answered, "Yes," as he had to the first question accusing him.

When he was arrested and brought before the investigating magistrate, Massé alternately admitted and denied the deed. If one interrogated him in a certain way, he recited his lesson by rote; if one spoke to him kindly, he said the opposite of what he had just affirmed. In his mind there was a confused medley of truth and lies which made finding a solution to the problem quite difficult. The return of the missing child fortunately simplified everything. Nonetheless, what remained was the phenomenon (more common than one might think) of a child playing a role in an improvised drama which he did not even have to take the trouble to invent.

·   ·   ·

We still remember the desecration of tombs in the Saint-Ouen cemetery last year. The guilty party escaped. One day, the local police received an anonymous letter which denounced a certain D. as the desecrator and a certain X as his accomplice. D. was arrested.

He was a young man of nineteen, of slender build, without any deformities, without anything that would indicate degeneracy. His face showed little intelligence. His flesh was white and soft and he appeared effeminate.

At the police station, he incriminated himself; he gave details which initially appeared very precise but which, if one examines them closely, did not go beyond information supplied by the newspapers. He said it was his friend who defiled the corpse. When questioned closely, he became uneasy, and at the end of the interrogation a strong reversal occurred. His instinct for self-preservation was awakened, and without truly realizing the serious situation his own words placed him in, he retracted. He suddenly suffered a genuine nervous crisis. From that moment on he no longer incriminated himself but energetically denied having written the denunciation that was found unsealed in a post office. Brought before the examining magistrate, his attitude appeared so strange that a psychological examination was called for. We were charged with it, and found in his family background: (1) on the maternal side, a grandmother who suffered a cerebral hemorrhage, and remained hemiplegic on the left side with mental impairment, and a hysterical aunt; (2) his father, whose background is unknown, was debauched, lazy, a drunkard who drank absinthe and was always in a state of alcoholic arousal. His brutality was excessive, and after the death of his consumptive wife, he abandoned his children. The youngest, D., was raised by his grandmother. He never suffered from serious childhood illnesses or from convulsions. He was difficult to raise, did not walk unaided until he was seven years old, and did not speak intelligibly until he was nine. He wet his bed until he was fifteen. Mild-mannered, he attended school until he was thirteen. He learned to read tolerably well, but wrote badly and barely knew how to count. At sixteen he began reading novels. His imagination was excited with great ease. But in the midst of these sentimental exaggerations he preserved a puerile quality which left him with ideas and tastes inferior to those of other young people his age. He did not drink.

He was subject to delirium, with hallucinations lasting several hours. We were able to observe one of his fits: without ever becoming agitated or noisy, his speech was completely incoherent. This neuropathic state, which surely was not epileptic in origin, was similar to hysteria in many respects.

He was absurdly vain and pathologically unstable. This manifested itself in bizarre resolutions, in a tendency to lie, in wild fantasies. He devoured the newspapers and crime reports. As a result of a certain tendency frequently encountered in cases of mental deficiency, he was always ready to assume a role, to put himself on stage. In a manner that was as naïve as it was lacking in foresight, he took pleasure in sending out written, defamatory declarations: once he accused his uncle of setting fire to a house; the next time he accused himself. In a word, he was degenerate and feebleminded. The influence of his father's alcoholism paved the way for his perversions of character, his lies, and his tendency toward vain exaggeration. It is almost unnecessary to continue to demonstrate further that his condition was pathological. D. acted indiscriminately and by his false accusations jeopardized his uncle's peace of mind. Just a bit more and he would have jeopardized his uncle's very freedom. Obviously, he was capable of doing much harm and it seemed necessary for us to prevent this. We ordered his internment in an insane asylum.

It is easy to see how important it is from the medical-legal point of view to be on guard against these false accusations; the most serious complications can arise. What happened in Hungary a few years ago is a striking example.

A young girl from Tiszaeszlar named Esther Solymosi disappeared. What became of her? No one knew. Two and a half months later, boatmen found the young girl's body in the Theiss. The corpse was examined; some recognized it as the body of Esther Solymosi and others didn't.

But religious passions were aroused. In this village, Catholics and Protestants live in a state of hostility with the Jews. The opportunity was seized to make life difficult for the Jews. They were accused of killing Esther in the synagogue; a rumor spread; the day and hour of the crime were supplied. Soon there were abundant details. When the judicial process began, the judge blindly embraced the prevailing passion and hate. His mind was made up before there was any investigation. He allowed his opinion to prevail.* A thirteen-year-old child, Moritz Scharf, son of one of the alleged assassins, was interrogated; the child knew nothing, but bullied and treated roughly, he finally said that his father had enticed the young girl to come to his house, then sent her to the synagogue. Moritz heard a scream; he went out, looked through the keyhole of the temple door, and saw Esther stretched out on the floor. Three men, whom he named, held her arms, legs, and head; the butcher Salomon Schwartz made a deep cut in her neck with a knife and collected her blood in two dishes; what more was done to the body he did not know. He repeated this tale over and over. In vain, the alibis of the accused men were proven. In vain, it was shown that it was impossible to commit such a crime in broad daylight in the busiest area of a large

* *Revue des deux mondes*, August 1, 1883.

village, in a synagogue where light was admitted from a waist-high window through which one could see all that was going on. There was no trace of blood anywhere. In vain, trustworthy persons stated that Esther had been seen more than an hour after the time of her presumed murder. The deposition of the child was taken and the judge who had led the inquiry did not want to give it up. He sequestered his young witness until the day of the hearing, when the child recited, as though it were a lesson learned by heart, the appalling deposition, which he ended up believing himself.

It is to the credit of our country that such things are no longer possible and that examining magistrates are no longer like those who, as described by Voltaire, "fear the power of prejudice." It is to our credit as physicians that we are able to shed light on such delicate matters, frequently so difficult to investigate.

When we deal with children it is important to remember that their young minds are always ready to reach for the ex-traordinary, that fiction appeals to them, and that their ideas take on an independent life of their own; that they are able with astonishing ease to flesh out their fantasies; that this in-stinctive curiosity—this need to know, on the one hand, and the pressure of environmental influence, on the other—pre-disposes them to accept uncritically all that comes to them from whatever source. Soon they no longer know what came from where. They are excused from analytical thought pro-cesses. Memory, the only player on their mental stage, permits them to reproduce a story without variations. But it is precisely through this monotonous repetition that children may be judged. When the expert physician, after several visits, hears in the same words, with the same details succeeding each other in the same fixed order, a story of the most serious events, he can be certain that the child is not telling the truth and is unwittingly substituting ideas acquired during the course of real events in which he may have taken part.

I said that these events have their parallels: A few weeks ago, Dr. Charcot, who kindly offers his advice at the Salpêtrière to those who wish to learn, presented us with a young hysteric. During hypnosis she had been convinced that a sum of fifty francs had been offered to her by one of the assistants. She had been given a receipt for the sum and had lived with that belief.

One day, when she was in an alert state, she was asked how she had obtained an object with which she adorned herself flirtatiously. She said she had gone out one afternoon to the rue de la Paix and had paid twelve francs for the object in question. "You have money, then?" asked Professor Charcot. "Certainly," she replied. "Surely you remember the fifty francs that Monsieur gave me?" "How much have you left?" "About thirty francs." "Can you show them to us?" "Of course, the guard is keeping the money for me." In fact, the guard had thirty-five francs belonging to the patient, for safekeeping. The source of the money was very different from what she believed it to be. It came from her family.

Upon further analysis, what do we find? A suggestion is added to accumulated facts. A likely, but absolutely false, story is built around the suggestion. The patient had not left the Salpêtrière, had not gone to the rue de la Paix, had not bought or paid for the ornament, had not received fifty francs. A confused jumble of memories existed in her mind, impossible to clarify, which she could not sort out and which, arranged in a certain sequence, gave her tale all the earmarks of truth. All that was necessary to distinguish between truth and falsehood was to know that this girl had never left the asylum and that her money had been given to her by her family. The guard's testimony to this effect sufficed.

I told this story because it paves the way for my conclusion: In forensic medicine, if the study of problems as complex as those I have presented compels further reflection, if great obstacles must be overcome, the doctor trained in research of this kind will find in the framework of clinical practice, in meticulous and patient observation, the skills necessary to carry out his mandate with dignity and bring to the judicial process the enlightenment that is expected of him.

Alfred Fournier

Simulation of Sexual Attacks

on Young Children*

1

We will be dealing with sad things and sad people. But public interest demands that we speak of them. This is a duty from which the physician, by profession the witness to such ignominies, must not recoil.

What I have in mind is the simulation of sexual abuse of young children, a simulation inspired by the profit its originator hopes to gain from his criminal plans.

I have two reasons for bringing these facts to your attention.

The first is that the physician naturally finds himself called upon to play a role—and a major one—in these matters. Indeed, it is the physician who is called upon by the courts to judge the nature of the violence committed upon the victim, and it is he who is called upon by the courts to determine whether lesions found on the child should be attributed to sexual or any other kind of abuse.

The second reason is that it is in the general public interest,

* "Simulation d'attentats vénériens sur de jeunes enfants." Annales d'hygiène publique et de médicine légale, 4 (1880), 498–519. (Extract from a communication to the Académie de Médecine, October 26, 1880.)

as stated above, to reveal the odious intrigues of a certain kind of simulator, intrigues which are little known, even unknown (as I have concluded), to a number of our colleagues and which can lead to the most serious judicial errors. Imagine for a moment the terrible situation of an honest man when he is suddenly and undeservedly accused of a contemptible assault. Imagine this man, until then justly held in high regard, who descends abruptly to the lowest depth of dishonor and moral degradation because of a mendacious accusation. What a blow for him! And, if he has a family—a wife and children—what a blow for them, upon whom this filth will fall as well!

Well, such cases exist. They have been written about. I know of them firsthand. Several times I have been present at occurrences of this kind, and it is because I have witnessed them with my own eyes—the simulators' perfidious cunning and the heartrending despair of their victims—that I promised myself I would denounce such monstrosities and expose them to public indignation the day my voice carried some weight.

I will even add that the cases in question are not, as one would assume *a priori*, extraordinarily rare. For without looking for them, without having access to the same material an expert would have, I count four, perhaps five cases in my notes taken at the hospital and in my private practice. For a single observer this surely constitutes a considerable number.

2

It would be an imposition on your kind attention if I were to recount these four or five cases, which, except for some minor details, seem cast from more or less the same mold. I will request your indulgence for only one of them. I selected it because it is typical of its kind and because it unfolded very openly, in a hospital, before many people and in front of a medical expert who had been delegated by the court. Here, in a few words, is the case:

A young girl, about eight years old, was admitted to my ward. I was told that in the last few days she had been the victim of a criminal sexual assault. "The guilty party," they added, "is a man of a certain age, rich, of irreproachable reputation up to that point. He has been imprisoned in Mazas in spite of his vehement denial."

I examined the child and confirmed the existence of severe lesions on her body. The vulva showed all the symptoms of a violent and extremely acute inflammation. She was literally bathed in a creamy green pus which appeared to be blennorheal. Her labia majora, enormously swollen, looked like the segments of an orange and completely masked the vulvar orifice. After being washed and dried, they presented a deep-red coloration, covered with many small inflamed dots, running together, purple in color. The labia minora were equally red, voluminous and swollen, but to a lesser extent. The swelling and pain in her genitals did not permit me immediately to examine her hymen; it was only some days later that I was able to determine the integrity of this membrane. Finally, in each groin there were two or three lymph nodes the size of small hazelnuts, slightly painful when touched.

For the rest, her general condition was good; apyrexia; her major bodily functions normal.

In order to speedily complete the clinical part of this examination, I will say in a word that her acute vulvitis was quickly cured by the most simple treatment (rest, daily baths, emollient lotions, dressing with zinc oxide and cotton, etc.). Within twelve to fifteen days the little patient was completely healed.

But it remained to determine the *etiological* problem, that is, the source of these symptoms; from the legal point of view, this was the major question, and the one of special interest to us here.

Now, in this respect, I must first point out that at her first examination I was vividly impressed by the unusual and surprising intensity of the inflammation manifest in the child's vulva. True, before this time I had scrupulously studied a number of cases of rape and sexual abuse of young children; cases which are, as we all know, hardly rare in certain hospitals. But never, absolutely never, had I seen anything similar to what was confronting me here. Never had I encountered a vulva in such a state, in such a condition of inflammatory fury. Moreover, remember that we are dealing with a single attack, lasting (according to the child) not more than a few moments. I was struck, in short, by the disproportion between cause and effect, clinically speaking, and I could not find an explanation for the singular intensity of the inflammation.

My suspicions thus aroused, I questioned the child repeatedly in an effort to get her to divulge new information. And soon she made what was from my point of view an important remark: it suggested that she was reciting a lesson learned by heart rather than telling the truth, a truth which comes from direct experience, a truth dependent only on her own (albeit negligible) intelligence. In fact, she invariably retold this tale in the same words, with the same inflections in her voice, with the same mistakes in grammar, etc.; in short, in the manner of children who repeat flattering civilities or fairy tales.

This new and very striking consideration, added to the unusual nature of the clinical symptoms, only increased my suspicions, and I asked myself whether we were not the victims of a charade, of some lie regarding the cause of the symptoms.

The matter was a grave one, for the honor of a man, possibly of a whole family, was at stake. But how could the mystery be solved? How to untangle the true from the false, and accord each its proper role in this dark affair? The difficulties notwithstanding, I set myself to the task, telling myself that with skill, with patience, and with persistence I would most likely be able to get the better of a little brain only eight years old. It was merely a question of getting the child to speak and obtain the truth from her. I proceeded by battering her defenses [*siège en règle*] and invading her will [*captation*], if you will excuse the conceit. I attacked her position by means of friendship, kindness, compliments, etc. A few sweets and a few coins succeeded in winning the little patient's confidence and friendship. I will be brief: a doll with moving eyes was a crucial factor in my triumph. Conquered by this irresistible munificence, the child, after much difficulty and after a long time, finally told me that it was not a *man* who had touched her but her mother, who on three different occasions had rubbed her genitals with a *waxing brush*, forbidding her to tell anyone and threatening her with more of the same if she said anything.

What followed then was very simple. Now that I was master of the truth, I demanded that the mother of the child come to the hospital; I told her of my discovery, adding that if she did not withdraw her charge without delay I would have the strict obligation to tell the examining magistrate the story of the waxing brush. The woman turned pale as she listened to me but did not offer a single word in response and left immediately. A few days later I learned that the investigation was suspended (probably because the charge was withdrawn) and that the affair, at least medically, would not have any consequences.

Thus my suspicions were absolutely justified. It was not a

rape that we were dealing with but rather a *simulation of rape.* *
The lesions I had observed on the child, which had struck me
as so strange, so unusual from a clinical point of view, were
not the result of sexual assault but rather the result of an
irritation which developed from manipulations of a different
kind. And I feel (though I obtained no confession to this effect)
that the intent of the simulation in this case almost certainly
was fraud, a form of "blackmail" (to use the technical expression) of the man accused of the crime.

A case of this nature, and others similar to it that I could
furnish, is no doubt open to widely varying interpretations. I
will suggest only two, which from a medical point of view
seem worthy of consideration because of their everyday interest.

3

First point: What was, in the case just cited, the *clinical symptom* which saved me from an error and set me on the path of
truth? The unusual intensity and extraordinary number of
inflammatory lesions and the disproportion between them and
their purported cause. Unable to account for such symptoms
with an ordinary rape, I searched for another cause, and I
have just explained how I found it.

But please note that in this case the profusion of local lesions
was but the result of a lack of cunning on the part of the
dissembler. She had wanted to prove too much; she was afraid
of not going far enough and instead she went too far. By an

* It is almost useless, I think, to note that the word "rape" is used here in its most
general sense (a violent sexual assault or an assault on a child) and not in its specific
sense, quite open to criticism incidentally, bestowed on it by judicial terminology,
namely that of an assault with complete penetration or, in the case of virgins, tearing
of the hymen.

excess of zeal she wound up giving herself away. But this obviously is only an incident specific to this particular case. If it had been more moderate and more skillful, the deception would have achieved its goal. For I cannot affirm too emphatically: *There is no visual distinction between a vulvar inflammation caused by a criminal assault and a vulvar inflammation caused by an assault of a different kind—at least none which would permit a solid differential diagnosis.* Sexual assaults, attempted rape, and even consummated rape do not have—in fact, they could not have—any local symptoms so unique that they would justify an absolute and decisive statement in court identifying the etiology of such cases. *

Well, public opinion—indeed, medical opinion—is such that a diagnosis of acute vulvar inflammation which arises or appears to arise suddenly is always deemed to be proof of criminal assault. Of course criminal assault does manifest itself in this manner. But it is not just a criminal assault which is capable of producing symptoms of this kind. Any violence whatever can produce lesions of the same kind, sometimes even more serious ones, without intending to do so. The preceding observation will bear me out. Further proof is furnished by an analogous case of a six-year-old girl whose vulvitis (of average intensity) had been caused by her mother rubbing "a rough and dirty rag" across her genitals a number of times. Proof, too, are the numerous cases where masturbation alone suffices to create vulvar inflammations in young children which are certainly equivalent in intensity and clinical details to those resulting from criminal manipulation.

Given the general attitude prevailing in society, a medical

---

* L. Penard, in *De l'intervention du médecin légiste dans les questions d'attentats aux moeurs* (Paris: J. B. Baillière, 1860), writes: "It is a very rare occasion in forensic medicine when a physician can positively affirm, using absolute and decisive arguments, that a given effect is necessarily produced by a given cause. Particularly in cases of sexual assault the physician must maintain a wise and prudent reserve."

certificate attesting to a vulvar inflammation in a young child becomes a powerful weapon in the hands of the simulator, a weapon he will use, no doubt, to terrify his victim and bring his ingenious exploitation to an auspicious end. This certificate is the trump card in his hand, if you will. Therefore we must be on our guard!

Hence there are two safeguards that must be applied to protect both our practice and the dignity of our calling:

1. Do not furnish such certificates except at the express request of a competent authority charged with the duty and obligation to do so.

2. If a certificate of this kind is *requested*, specify only the lesions you observe, *without making any statement about their etiology.* * This is because clinical evidence is unable on its own to differentiate in an absolute and categorical fashion between local lesions stemming from criminal abuse and lesions of a different sort.

4

Second point: In the case that I had the honor of submitting to you, my suspicions were first aroused by a purely clinical consideration (namely, the unusual intensity of local inflammatory symptoms); but the truth, you will remember, was revealed only through the confession of the child, and was realized only through procedures having nothing to do with medicine. There is no doubt that in this matter I went beyond

---

* The same applies to rape. Cf. Toulmouche, "Des attentats à la pudeur et du viol," *Annales d'hygiène publique et de médecine légale*, 6 (1856): "The forensic physician should not conclude solely on the basis of a torn or destroyed hymen *that a man has committed rape*. He should limit himself to declaring that *defloration has taken place*, leaving it to the district attorney to discover the true nature of the physical cause that produced it." An identical opinion is given by Professor Tardieu in his remarkable *Etude médico-légale sur les attentats aux moeurs*, 7th ed. (Paris, 1878), p. 77.

my obligations as a physician.* As a physician, it was my duty merely to treat and cure the child; nothing more was asked of me. But to serve my religion [?], to instruct myself and my students, I went further. I wanted—and this only on the condition that it would not violate the respect owed to childhood innocence—I wanted, as I say, to learn the exact etiology of the symptoms before my eyes. And I succeeded, by taking on the additional role of inquisitor for the investigating magistrate. I am far from repentant for having done this, because everybody (except the simulator) benefited from it, and above all, because an innocent man benefited from it. If it had to be done again I would do so. Should this opportunity arise, my only desire would be to be a recidivist!

The truth is—and this is precisely the second point I wish to stress here this evening—that in these sad cases it is the physician who in all respects is in the best position to track down and discover the truth. First, he is fully respected as a medical authority; thus, on occasion he is in a position to see the light. Then, as he is called upon to treat the young patient, to see her and her family frequently, to question her, to understand her background, her environment, he will be in a better position than anybody else to interpret events and people. He will be able to see the situation more clearly, because he will see it more intimately and from a closer range; in short, he will be able to sniff out a ruse, to suspect simulation, and even to uncover it on the spot, on the basis of some clue that might have escaped anybody else's notice. This is what hap-

---

* I went beyond my role of expert for a very good reason. A judicial expert who in a case of this kind would use methods of persuasion to reach the truth, such as I did, would certainly incur the reproach of having exceeded his mandate. But I was not an expert in the case in question; I was only a physician, a physician curious to learn the truth. I was only following my conscience, without any obligation to the court. It is thanks to this freedom that I was able to act as I did, and to discover what under any other circumstances would have been difficult, if not altogether impossible.

pened to me, twice, and twice I was lucky enough to have saved from infamy people who were nothing but victims of an odious plot.

It would certainly be far from my intention to raise to a universal truth the idea that the physician must always exchange his role for that of investigating magistrate; that is, to proceed by means of interrogation and investigation rather than bandaging and healing. What I claim is purely and simply that if during the exercise of his profession the physician, merely by chance, is put on the trail of one of these criminal simulations that I have just spoken of, he has the moral obligation both to society and to himself to free an innocent man from the heavy accusation that unjustly weighs on him.

I know and respect the Hippocratic oath. I know that the physician is obliged not to sit in judgment, and that when leaving the patient he is obliged to reveal nothing of what he may have learned during the examination. I know that when he is with his patients his eyes are not for seeing and his ears are not for hearing. But the situation is entirely different in the cases in question. Here, criminal fraud could cost a man something more than his life, namely, his honor and his liberty; on the other hand, an innocent man must be saved, whose criminal conviction the physician would risk by remaining blind and mute. Common sense and conscience tell me that, as a physician, I have not only a right but a duty to carry this out. Between my professional silence (from which a scoundrel could benefit) and the protection I owe an upright man, my choice is easy; in my opinion, no hesitation is possible in such a case. To stop a criminal intrigue and, when necessary, to denounce it publicly so as to protect an innocent man seems to me to constitute a *duty*—I am repeating the word deliberately—a veritable duty to society, which I, a physician, do not have the right to shirk.

5

To investigate and determine the moral motivation which inspires simulators, in the cases we are discussing, would be more of a philosophical analysis than a medical one. However, the physician, and even more so the expert, does not have the right to be indifferent to such an investigation, because the more he understands the reasons behind simulation, the more easily will he be able to uncover it.

I will, therefore, attempt to investigate and to show in a few words what could be called the *moral etiology* in such cases.

It is certainly difficult to reckon with a crime so rich in surprises. The inventive imagination of the offender defies any attempt at classification.* It is necessary in such cases to confine oneself to enumeration rather than classification, and to do so in a provisional fashion, always open to revision. I will therefore limit myself and merely state that, on the basis of my own observations or those collated from other sources, the simulation of sexual abuse on young children falls into two major categories, depending on the motivation. These categories are: (1) simulations inspired by expectations of monetary gain, that is, those that aim to extort money from the victim

---

* There are cases, moreover, where the motive, the objective of the simulation, escapes analysis. See, for example, the strange case related by Dr. H. Bayard: "Mémoire sur les maladies simulées," *Annales d'hygiène publique et de médecine légale*, vol. 38, p. 218. If I may be excused for straying a moment from my subject, I would like to remind you of a shocking case of simulation observed and recounted *in extenso* by Dr. Merland (of Napoléon-Vendée). The case is about a wretched hysteric, a hallucinator, a delinquent who accused two brothers of raping and torturing her. Now, in order to make her accusation seem plausible, this girl introduced into her vagina "thirteen pieces of old rusty metal, nails, a screw, half a horseshoe, a knife blade eight or nine centimeters long, and even a roll of wire"! "Nobody will be surprised," adds our colleague in ending his incredible account, "that the accused were acquitted by the jury, by the lower court, and by the appeals court. What is harder to understand is that in this case the simulation could have been believed by some people." *Annales d'hygiène*, vol. 22 (1864), p. 141.

who falls into the trap; (2) simulations inspired by a desire for vengeance.

The first category seems more common by far. Indeed, it is well known, thanks especially to the work of the late Professor Tardieu, an eminent forensic physician.* It has a specific technical name, *blackmail-rape*.

Blackmail-rape (please excuse me, gentlemen, for introducing this police jargon into our discussion) consists, in brief, of the following: extortion of the largest possible sum of money from a man by threatening to charge him with the sexual abuse of a young girl.

This is carried out according to a more or less unvarying formula, which is as follows: (a) choose a rich man, or at least a man of means (this is a major point, essential to the scheme); (b) arrange things so that this man, in circumstances that can be remembered and recounted, spends some time alone with a young girl, even if it is only for a few minutes; (c) then, by any means whatever (friction, rubbing, assaults, etc.), produce on the vulva of the child an inflammation similar to one that would result from rape; (d) then, when things have been arranged in this way, accuse this man of criminally abusing the child; accuse him loudly, with outbursts of anger, indignation, etc.; threaten him with public denunciation, with legal action, but (and this needs to be hinted at adroitly) indicate that he might be permitted to make up for his heinous crime with a large monetary compensation.

If it is well orchestrated and skillfully conducted, this play-

---

* "Nothing is more common than to see, especially in large cities, charges of sexual abuse dictated solely by selfish and sinful design. Parents do not hesitate involving young children; some even go so far as to inflict abrasions and bruises on their sexual organs in order to simulate the evidence of violence upon which their mendacious accusations are based . . . I have seen presented in court—shirts and sheets purposely stained with blood, sperm, and matter flowing from discharge." (*Etude médico-légale sur les attentats aux moeurs*, 7th ed., p. 131.)

acting has a chance of succeeding. It may indeed happen—
and this is precisely the hope of the simulator—that a man
suddenly faced with such a formidable accusation loses his
head, as we say, and then, bewildered, terrified, already seeing
himself dragged before the courts, seeing himself surely dishonored and possibly convicted, he will agree, in spite of his
innocence, to pay the money demanded of him in order to
avoid publicity. Within the last few years, I observed an example of this kind of case, which I will describe in a few words:

An outstanding and upright man, head of a family, highly
esteemed and absolutely incapable of any dishonorable act (I
will gladly vouch for this), allowed himself to get caught in a
trap of this kind. All the evidence, both material and moral,
spoke in his favor. The child he was supposed to have abused
(and whom I was called upon to examine) presented only
insignificant lesions of vulvar erythema, most probably scrofulous in origin. Moreover, the child's family was publicly
disdained for its deplorable lineage, etc. Well, in spite of all
that, and in spite of anything I could do, the man preferred
to pay the ransom that these vile exploiters demanded of him
rather than face a battle from which his innocence would most
certainly have emerged unharmed. "Yes, surely," he told me,
"I would win the case, and I would confound these impostors;
but I would lose more by insisting on a trial than I would gain.
Something of the calumny always remains, as Bazile showed.
An acquittal is not a badge of innocence; an acquittal leaves
behind a suspicion of guilt that could not be proven, and I
owe it to my family, to my children, to the honor of my name,
that such a suspicion not even be allowed to touch me . . .
Besides, who knows? Human justice has its shortcomings, and
the most worthy causes have sometimes been wronged before
the courts." These words, which I remember distinctly, and
these arguments, which are not totally faulty, compel us to
recognize, gentlemen, that the odious blackmail of which I

have just spoken exists for a reason, and comes along with conditions conducive to its own success. To unmask this blackmail, to divulge its motives and methods as I have here, is, I hope, to contribute to its prevention and discourage imitation.

I have said that there can be a second motive for simulation. It is vengeance pure and simple, without monetary demands.

In the two cases of this kind that make up my small sample, it was the vengeance of a woman who devised the plot and carried it out. Both cases involved retaliation on an unfaithful lover.

A third case was assigned to me by a worthy and very distinguished judge. The affair is completely factual. I will summarize it in brief, on the basis of a voluminous dossier that I have in my possession:

A young girl is brought by her boss to the commissioner of police. She makes a deposition to the effect that she has been the victim of sexual abuse, on three separate occasions, by a certain X, a workman in the store. "I didn't dare say anything until now," she added, "because X threatened me, saying that if I did, he would kill me by hitting me with an iron bar he always keeps in his pocket." She gives the exact dates, the places, the circumstances of the crime, even the posture, etc.; and all this in great detail and in language in which her explicit terminology rivals the ignoble subject matter. The *mise-en-scène* is as complete and revolting as only the imagination of a novelist in the realistic tradition could make it. X is arrested. Nevertheless, the skilled magistrate smells a ruse and intensifies his interrogations. The girl becomes upset, she contradicts herself, she retracts, she accuses first one person, then another, then herself, and finally she ends with the following declaration: The workman X did nothing to her; it is her boss who ordered her, with threats, to say everything she said and to accuse X; moreover, the same boss stuffed rags into her vagina to the point where they caused severe pain and made her bleed, etc.

I will be brief. The truth was established as a result of the impact of contradictory depositions, and it was confirmed (if not by definitive confessions, at least by factual evidence) that the whole affair was pure invention; that the girl was never a victim of the least sexual abuse (which is also confirmed by the report of the expert); that the girl's boss had had the workman X, younger than she was, as her lover; finally, after he left her for a younger woman, she could find no better vengeance than to accuse X of sexually abusing one of her apprentices.*

6

Finally, as a not unexpected appendix to the preceding discourse, I will mention a group of cases in a different category. These, as you will see, are no less insidious or dangerous to medical practice. Allow me, then, to withhold a complete narrative—which would carry me away from my subject—and to describe them as an aside, as a complement to this study.

Here it is no longer a matter of lesions produced for the express purpose of simulation, but of lesions which originate from some other source yet serve as the basis for the imputation of criminal abuse.

The accusation typically derives almost invariably either from the unconscious of the child, who is not aware of the meaning

---

* To the two motives that I have just described (monetary speculation and vengeance), I should add a third. Professor Brouardel, my dear and learned colleague, recently told me about a whole series of cases he had observed with respect to simulations, or at least imputations of sexual abuse, that were inspired by the desire to shake off an annoying guardianship—to get rid of a husband, a father, a guardian, etc. Women do not recoil, with this aim in mind, from accusing their husbands of abusing their children; girls accuse their fathers of fantasized sexual abuse, either of them or of other children, in order to achieve their liberty, so that they can give themselves over to debauchery, etc. Since I have not personally observed cases of this kind, I have refrained from discussing them here.

of her words, or who is answering questions without understanding them,* or from the evil-minded perversity of certain children in whom this vice is more advanced than their years.

For this third category of cases, I am happy to be able to enlist the aid of two considerable authorities, whose credentials cannot help but impress us.

Astley Cooper, the eminent surgeon who identified the vulvar discharges which occur frequently and absolutely spontaneously in young girls, t contributes the following:

---

* It is certain—and here I speak from experience—that if one persists in interrogating a child, one almost always obtains something, some answer, from the child. But what value should we assign to this answer? None, in my opinion, none at all, unless her words are confirmed by very precise and conclusive evidence. Who has not seen a child respond first positively and then negatively to the same question asked in different ways? Who has not caught a child red-handed giving an unknowing response, even though she seems to have understood the simple question that had been addressed to her? And so on.

An example of this, from Professor Brouardel: A very small girl claims to have been "touched" by a man, but she cannot give the name of this man, because she can "no longer remember." Several names are suggested to her. The child seems to reflect but does not answer. As a test, she is given the name of a great man, the political head of a foreign power. "Oh, yes," she says, "he's the one, definitely. I remember now." All commentary seems superfluous.

t Tardieu (loc. cit., p. 39) seems to question the frequency of these spontaneous vulvar discharges: "Physicians who have practiced or made observations in hospitals for sick children are very prone, as I know, to consider vulvar inflammations in little girls very ordinary and very natural. But I am convinced, from my experience as a court-appointed medical examiner of hospital cases, that these so-called spontaneous vulvar inflammations are often, in reality, the result of criminal violence." In spite of the respect I have for the great authority of Tardieu, I cannot disagree strongly enough with his opinion on this subject. I have in my own practice found a large number of vulvar inflammations that came upon young girls absolutely spontaneously, totally unrelated to any criminal violence, beyond the possibility of sexual abuse— for example, in cases of little girls who had not left for one instant the vigilant eyes of their mothers. Not only do I believe, like everybody else, in the existence of spontaneous vulvitis in childhood, I consider such cases *common, very common*, especially in little girls who are lymphatic, scrofulous, sickly, emaciated by poverty, etc.

An excellent chapter has been devoted to spontaneous vulvitis by Professor Brouardel in his *Commentaires de médecine légale*. I cannot commend it enough to the attention of my colleagues. (See *Nouveaux éléments de médecine légale*, by E. Hoffmann, translated by Lévy, commentaries by Brouardel [Paris, 1880].)

"From time to time it happens that a nervous woman becomes alarmed upon discovering a discharge of this kind and suspects that her child misbehaved . . . She seeks out a physician who unfortunately may not know this condition and may tell her that her child has venereal disease . . . What happens in such circumstances? The mother asks the child: 'Who played with you? Who took you on his knees recently?' The child in all innocence answers: 'Nobody, Mother, nobody, I swear.' The mother responds: 'Oh, don't tell me such lies. I'll whip you if you continue.' So the child is made to confess what never happened in order to escape punishment. Finally she says: 'So-and-so took me on his knees.' The man is questioned and energetically denies it. But the child, believing her mother's threats, persists in her accusation. The man is taken to court; a physician who is not familiar with the kind of discharge I am speaking of testifies, and the man is punished for a crime he did not commit."

Cooper continues: "I have seen such cases more than thirty times in my life and I can assure you that a number of men *have been hanged* as a result of this type of error."*

Now let us listen to Ricord:

It is not rare [this eminent professor told me in a recent conversation] for little girls, even very little girls, to be affected with vulvar discharges that are absolutely spontaneous; and I don't mean simple catarrhal discharges, but rather yellow discharges, definitely purulent, appearing to be blennorrheal, as blennorrheal as the vulvo-vaginitis that comes from venereal disease.

To pretend to be able to distinguish these discharges from other

---

* Surgical Lectures, *The Lancet*, vol. 3/4 (1824). p. 275; see, too, Capuron, *La médecine légale relative à l'art des accouchements* (Paris, 1821), p. 41; Toulmouche, loc. cit., p. 143, etc., etc.

kinds provoked by causes such as touching, criminal abuse, masturbation, etc., is to attempt the impossible, speaking from a clinical point of view. For clinically there is no single factor that allows us to make this differential diagnosis with any certainty.

Thus it has more than once happened that these spontaneous cases of childhood vulvitis have awakened suspicions of sexual abuse, and that these suspicions were investigated and even confirmed by physicians inexperienced in this matter. I have seen and could cite a number of examples.

In this connection, Ricord told me about the following case in the presence of several of our colleagues. Permit me to repeat it here.

A man of irreproachable background was accused of criminal abuse of a young child and was brought to trial. His situation was all the more critical in that the report of the expert, a highly esteemed forensic physician, concluded that he had probably committed the abuse. Ricord was asked by the president of the tribunal to examine the child. He was unable to find anything on her but a pure and simple vulvitis, one of those cases of vulvitis, discussed above, which can occur in a completely spontaneous fashion. He therefore energetically argued against the medical opinion supporting the plaintiff, and it will certainly surprise nobody here if I say that thanks to the clarity of his reasoning, his eloquence, and the respect he commands, he had the satisfaction of bringing everybody around to his opinion—everybody, even the expert, who, with a most honorable modesty, did not hesitate to make a public disavowal of his original conclusions.

For my part, I could also cite a number of cases in which vulvar inflammations of various origins, though they were all more or less acute, were at first falsely interpreted and imputed—even in good faith—to fantasized sexual abuse, until a more experienced medical expert was able to redress the error.*

But here I want to speak only about cases in which the matter was carried further; that is, in which the error served as the basis for judicial action. Well, examples of this kind are not lacking. Allow me to tell you about the following case, knowledge of which I owe to the wise investigating magistrate who was in charge of it.

A little girl, nine years old, suddenly presents symptoms of a vulvar inflammation with a purulent yellow discharge. Her mother becomes worried and anxiously questions her. The child at first does not answer, then after several days declares that she was "touched" by a man in the neighborhood who had been invited to pay frequent visits to the house. A complaint is immediately made to the police and the man is ar-

---

* Several observers have already related a large number of these cases. As an example I cite the following. The error came from a *high* source, as we shall see.

"Sometime in 1817, a little girl of less than six years of age was brought to my office. She was suffering from a considerable vaginal discharge, which had come about naturally. Her mother was armed with a certificate bearing the signature *of one of the most important surgeons in Lyon*. It attested that this discharge was syphilitic and that the child *had been sexually abused*. Since I had not been requested to examine this child, I confined myself to examining her genitals. There was no tear. The discharge was white, thick, and had formed, on the upper region of the inside of her thighs, layers of mucus that nonetheless did not give rise to any pimples or any discoloration of the skin. Moreover, the child seemed completely healthy and did not complain of any pain. I reassured the parents, prescribed a few baths with emollient lotions, syrup of quinine to be taken internally, etc., and I kept the certificate that had been so casually furnished, but which in their eyes seemed sure proof.

"The same day, on another matter, I went to the office of the police commissioner and there I found the same people whom I had seen that morning in my office. They were armed with a second accusatory certificate, far stronger than the first, made out by the same surgeon . . . When I was asked for my opinion, I based it on observations diametrically opposed to what was stated on the certificate . . . Justly surprised by such a contradiction, the Count of Fargues, at that time mayor of Lyon, secretly selected five physicians to examine the child again . . . these physicians did so without knowing the findings of the other reports. They established, as I did, that the child *had not been the victim of sexual abuse*, but was merely suffering from a *simple mucous discharge*." (Blessy, *Manuel pratique de la médecine légale*, Ch. 5 [Lyon, 1821], p. 149.)

rested in spite of his indignant protests: an investigation is begun. Pressed with questions, frightened by the judicial apparatus, the child finally confesses that she was touched not by a man but rather by one of her little girl friends, who almost daily engages in certain manipulations on the child's body and demands that she do the same to her. "She is the one who hurt me," she added (I am quoting her verbatim here), "but she urged me not to say it was she, but rather Monsieur X, because if the truth were known she would be punished and we would not be allowed to play together anymore," etc.

What would have happened if, in this case and in others similar to it, the truth had not come out, either through medical or judicial means? These accusations are so dangerous precisely because of their apparently innocent and disinterested motives. One shudders to think that in this manner the honor of a man is at the mercy of the unconscious mind of a child, or at the mercy of that child's precocious perversions.

Therefore, the characteristics of this third group, perhaps even more than the first two groups, deserve to be brought to the attention of physicians.

7

At the end of this study, I will not formulate any conclusions, for conclusions presuppose a clear grasp and a precision to which the simple outline I have just given cannot aspire, based as it is on only on a small number of personal observations.

Instead of a conclusion, therefore, I will confine myself to a summary of the principal points which may be derived from this study.

1. A certain number of cases exist to which we can assign the collective name "simulated sexual abuse on small children of feminine gender." In brief, these cases consist of artificially produced vulvar lesions on a young child which are meant to

resemble the lesions of sexual abuse, and the imputation of this abuse to a carefully selected perpetrator, to serve the simulator's self-interest.

2. Clinically, it is not impossible that these artificial lesions may betray themselves by some idiosyncrasy, some local peculiarity. But this is only a possibility. And in theory as well as in practice, we do not know of any clinical symptom which would permit us to conclusively differentiate an artificially produced vulvar inflammation from a vulvar inflammation caused by criminal abuse.

3. In cases of this kind, the discovery of the simulation will come about less as a result of clinical phenomena than from phenomena outside the purview of medical practice: attitude, answers, hesitations, contradictions of the child, past history of the simulator, varying circumstances, etc.

4. If the physician, in the exercise of his profession, happens to uncover a ruse and find the truth, he has more than the right, he has the duty to derail the criminal accusation and to protect the honor, the liberty, and the reputation of an innocent man.

5. It is in the interest of everyone's security and particularly in the interest of medical honor that in such cases the physician not issue a certificate attesting to the lesions he observed unless he has been expressly invited to do so by a competent authority whose duty it is to order such a certificate; and it is equally important that, in certificates of this kind, the physician confine himself to describing only the lesions he observed, without speculating about the origin of these lesions. The facts necessary to make such interpretations are almost always unattainable through clinical examinations.

6. Motives of every conceivable kind can inspire these deceptions. One of the most common is monetary gain, to which one can apply the clumsy but expressive term of blackmail-rape.

7. Finally, vulvar inflammations of various origins, which indeed are most often spontaneous, have often been used as proof of abuse; at times these unwarranted imputations appear plausible, either because of the unwitting replies of the alleged victims or even because of the mendacious depositions of prematurely perverted children.

Biographical Note

For a biography of Alfred Fournier (1832–1914), the distinguished and influential physician from Paris, see H. Bianchon's *Nos grands médecins* (Paris: 1891, pp. 163–70). See also Robert A. Nye's *Crime, Madness and Politics in Modern France: The Medical Concept of National Decline* (Princeton: Princeton University Press, 1984). My book *The Assault on Truth* (p. 50) contains a brief discussion of Fournier's influence on Freud.

Gustav Braun

The Amputation of the Clitoris

and Labia Minora: A Contribution

to the Treatment of Vaginismus*

The illness known as vaginismus—sometimes called vaginal spasm, irritable vagina (Hodge), "Vaginodynie" (Simpson), or vaginal neuralgia—refers to a peculiar set of symptoms which differ slightly from case to case but which have certain principal attributes in common. As a rule, vaginismus is characterized by a feeling of spasmodic constriction of the vagina and its surrounding areas, marked disturbances in physical sensibility, a distinct feeling of warmth, and intense pain.

The painful sensation of spasmodic constriction is described by some patients as a feeling of narrowing in the vagina, which is sometimes limited to the vagina itself but more generally is felt in the neck of the bladder, the urethra, the sphincters of the vagina, and the rectum. These spasmodic constrictions do not always appear in the sequence just mentioned, but from time to time during the functioning of the organs of secretion

* "Die Amputation der Clitoris und Nymphen, ein Beitrag zur Behandlung des Vaginismus." *Wiener medizinische Wochenschrift*, 15 (1865), 1325–28; 1341–44. For a biography of Gustav August Braun (b. 1829), see A. Kallay's *Curorte* (Vienna: 1889, pp. 1–4). Braun's *Compendium der Frauenkrankheiten* (Vienna: W. Braunmüller, 1863) also appeared in Dutch and Italian.

and excretion which have their orifices near the vagina, or during mechanical stimulation; for example, during coitus or a manual examination.

Its effect on urination is notable, because that function is hampered by pain and a constant need to urinate. These patients often must attend to their needs every ten to twenty minutes. This situation is particularly unpleasant in that the patients not only avoid all human society and therefore are excluded from going on walks, visiting the theater, etc., but they also forgo the rest that is so necessary to them at night. The sphincters of the neck of the bladder are set in motion by the constriction of the urinary bladder, and these in turn give rise to spasmodic constrictions of the urethra, the *constrictor cunni*, the entire musculature of the bowels, and the anal sphincters.

Just as it does during urination, the collection of fluids in the uterus during and after menstruation (especially when changes in the position of the uterus provide a physical obstacle) causes spasmodic contractions of the vagina, which spread to the bladder as well as to the rectum. Bowel movements are generally accompanied by pain, but one observes that it is either very hard or very loose evacuations that most often lead to cramping of the adjacent organs.

This sensitivity is generally limited to the vagina, and usually it is only in this organ that mechanical intervention elicits a strong sensation of pain. During a vaginal examination, considerable pressure is necessary to overcome the resistance of the vaginal sphincters. But even when the lubricated fingertip has reached the entrance of the vagina, the farther one penetrates, the more tightly the finger is gripped: that is, the lower portion of the vagina is somewhat less constricted than the upper portion. If the vagina is examined with a speculum, it is almost impossible to penetrate into the vagina, and even with the help of a mechanical occluding apparatus, it is difficult. The convulsive constrictions are often so strong that the speculum itself is expelled with unusual vehemence and to a considerable distance. Nor does this sensitivity confine itself to the vagina alone; it extends to the vulva as well. The slightest touch on the clitoris or the labia minora is sufficient to elicit spasmodic constriction in the entire peripheral area, so that coitus cannot, as a rule, be carried out. If attempted, it gives rise to strong convulsive spasms and agonizing pain.

In addition, there is a further problem, which with some women frequently entails unpleasant consequences. The rubbing of clothing against the clitoris and the labia first produces mild, then unbearable itching, followed by an overwhelming feeling of sensuality, forcing patients to rub their clitorises and the surrounding area with their fingers or any other object at hand. If just the finger is used for this activity, it is less common to discover evidence of mechanical activity on the external genitalia, unless long nails, now fashionable, have caused an abrasion. But if other objects are used, for example, a shirt or a rough towel, then one often finds the labia to be devoid of epidermis and even, in some cases, to be covered with swollen and edematous ulcers. In these cases, the labia minora are generally somewhat darker in pigmentation. Strong sexual excitement occasionally gives rise to the most absurd behavior, and leads to pitiful moral and physical disorders. Nymphomania, with its repulsive and intractable peculiarities, is not an uncommon result.

These initially erotic states of arousal, which can be caused by normal walking and sitting, provoke stronger stimulations with a finger or other objects. These stimulations continue until, with a severe shock to the nervous system, there is a sudden discharge of liquid from the vagina, which briefly frees the exhausted patient from her itching. But soon the itching returns, and where there are no environmental obstacles, these patients start the game again, so that sometimes, as has been confessed to me, there are eight to ten discharges during the day or, more commonly, at night.

In some cases, normal satisfaction of the sexual urge is not sufficient, and if coitus, though painful, is regarded merely as an unpleasant means of excitement, other methods are brought into play that can last much longer and are more responsive to individual needs. We must count, as examples of this, tin pepper boxes, drinking glasses, and other similar objects found in the vagina. It is certainly disturbing to discover that we must sometimes remove objects from the vagina which are out of proportion to its size. This may be explained by the fact that during an examination smaller objects such as the finger often cannot be tolerated in the vagina, whereas the more voluminous vaginal speculum seems to cause less discomfort.

Vaginismus is most often observed in young women. It can be caused by the following: metritis and chronic infarct, even after childbirth (either because of lack of proper care or prolonged lactation), excesses in venery; encolpitis, displacement or tilting of the uterus; irritating uterine secretions; and finally, the presence of ascarides or other foreign objects in the vagina. Closely connected to these factors is genital excitement caused by mental and moral impressions. Under the influence of a salacious imagination, which is stimulated by obscene conversations or by reading poorly selected novels, the uterus develops a hyperexcitability which leads to masturbation and its dire consequences. All of these conditions, combined with a neglected physical education, expose the female organism to the illness described above, even in early life.

It is not only young girls and newlyweds who remain abstinent for some time who are susceptible to this illness. Widows are also in danger, for similar reasons. In Simpson's opinion, one of the major causes of vaginismus is permanent cramping of specific muscle fibers around the vagina. He considers the contraction of some parts of the pelvic fascia a further

contribution. The condition probably originates with a sub-
acute inflammation. The anatomical center of these painful
vaginal contractions, he believes, is located in that part of the
levator ani which is close to the vagina. In some cases, according to Simpson, one can feel a bandlike strip on one or
both sides of the vaginal wall, approximately an inch below
the upper vaginal section. It is usually painful to the touch
and is characteristic of the disease.

Aside from these factors, it appears that anomalies of the
clitoris—particularly hypertrophy—play a role in causing and
exacerbating vaginismus. I would like to corroborate this statement by recounting a case I observed in my gynecological
clinic.

The case concerns J.P., twenty-five years old, single, heretofore in good general health. At thirteen she had her first
menstrual period, which normally lasted for eight days and
was regular and painless. She claims that her attention was
drawn to her clitoris by a friend, after which she would often
touch it with her finger and continue to do so to the point
where her whole body would vibrate and a sticky, peculiar-
smelling fluid would be discharged from her genitals. Because
of these manipulations, she would become very excited, particularly when she came in contact with men; and although
she supposedly gave herself with great abandon to sexual intercourse, she was never satisfied and always returned to these
manipulations of her clitoris. She did not become pregnant
until she was twenty-two, but aborted in her third month
allegedly due to a fall. As a consequence of the ensuing hemorrhage, she was sick for two months and her menses did not
occur as they had before. The flow, which was now pale red
and lasted for only one or two days, was accompanied by pain
and congestion. In February 1864, the patient again was ill
because of another fall, which left her unconscious, and as a
result of which she suffered vomiting and headaches for almost

two months. In April of the same year, she had a convulsive seizure, which is said to have affected her eyes, mouth, and neck muscles, especially. Since similar seizures recurred and became even worse, the patient was hospitalized. She stayed in the hospital until the end of October. The convulsions were experienced every eight days to four weeks, and took on such intensity that she supposedly fainted. Even her extremities were involved. Since the time of her abortion, and especially after she had started her convulsions, her irritability and unprecedented sexual excitability had only increased.

A physical examination revealed the patient to be medium-sized and well proportioned; musculature moderately well developed; eyes shine in a strange way; breasts well developed; much hair in her abdominal region, with the inner thighs especially thickly covered.

Auscultation and percussion of the thorax normal. The abdomen was slightly distended, but not sensitive to the touch. Only in the left inguinal region, where by pressing firmly one could feel a hard tumor about the size of a dove's egg, did the patient experience any discomfort. In the right groin, one could feel a slightly smaller tumor.

Inspections of the vulva revealed that the labia minora were extended somewhat more than an inch beyond the labia majora, hanging down, and were of a dark brown pigmentation. Their mucous membrane was hardened, almost like skin. The foreskin of the clitoris was highly developed and could easily be retracted. When touched lightly, the clitoris readily became erect. It was over one inch long, firm, and of the thickness of a raven's feather, protruding like a small male penis, palpable and visible. The vaginal opening was somewhat tight, and when I touched it, she experienced spasms of the *constrictor cunni* and surrounding sphincters. Her eyes began to roll and her breathing became rapid. The abdominal muscular pressure was so intense and opposed the slowly advancing finger so strongly that it seemed almost impossible to proceed into the upper vagina.

The uterus rejected the finger with such force that one distinctly felt a spasmodic constriction of the round and broad ligaments. The abdominal pressure and constriction in the vagina were so strong that the fingertip was violently clasped by the vagina and expelled. During the entire procedure, her pelvis moved convulsively in such a manner that the audience of physicians present during the examination found themselves involuntarily seized by a desire to laugh. These movements were repeated regularly during every subsequent examination.

The *portio vaginalis* is one inch long, shaped like a bowling pin, tough, tilted slightly forward. The external cervical os opens into a fissure and shows on its lower lip two erosions the size of lentils, very close together. Through the vaginal wall, in back, toward the left and somewhat in back of the cervix a tumor almost the size of a walnut could be felt. It was firm and mobile. With the use of the speculum one could see, in addition to the erosions noted above, catarrhal secretions in the cervical canal.

The uterine sound could not be inserted with its concave part turned upward; if turned downward, it could be inserted as far as 1¼ inches into the cervical canal, where one met with an obstacle, beyond which one could penetrate only by turning the concave part of the sound upward. Then one could insert it 3¹⁄₁₆ inches farther into the uterine cavity.

The entire examination caused great sexual arousal in the patient.

There is no doubt that the previously diagnosed anteflexion of the uterus was bound to be a major cause of the spasms. Frequently, hysterical convulsions can be traced exclusively to accumulated secretions in a flexed cervix, which in turn cause painful contractions in the uterus. The direction in which the uterus is flexed is not without significance; the strongly curved posterior wall of the cervix continued in the uterus in a steady, convex direction, whereas the uterus proper was situated below the upper vaginal section but positioned in such a way that the angular bend occurred on the anterior uterine surface.

This is not a common form of anteflexion, but one that I have observed several times.

In order to return the uterus to its proper position, a #2 closed lever pessary with double curves was inserted through the vagina. One could immediately see that, with the pessary in place, the uterine sound could be easily inserted in a normal manner through the cervix.

My most urgent concern was to prevent the patient from touching her outer genitalia, as had been her custom. Thus, on November 11, 1864, a good part of the labia minora and the foreskin of the clitoris were cauterized with a cauterizing instrument. To limit the copious discharge from the uterus, the uterine cavity was cauterized with Chiari's caustic solution. At the same time, the patient was given Lupulin, in dosages of three grains to combat her sexual excitement, and lactic iron.

During the afternoon of the same day, there was a brownish-red, light discharge with grayish-black particles—from the vagina. The patient complained of a steady pain in the vagina which seemed to be caused by the somewhat large pessary. The pessary was removed for that reason. Since urination was also painful, and in particular caused burning in the labia minora, urine was removed via catheterization.

The next day, November 12, a somewhat smaller lever pessary was inserted into the vagina, and vaginal pain did not recur. On November 16 the patient complained that the pessary seemed to increase her excitement, especially at night, and it was therefore removed.

During the night of the seventeenth, the patient claimed to

have had spasms lasting approximately five minutes in all. They were said to have particularly affected the muscles on the left side of the neck, the pronators on the upper extremities, and the back. Only toward the end of the attack did convulsive movements of the extremities occur.

On November 20 the pessary was reinserted, and then removed after two days because of increased irritation.

On November 22 the uterine cavity and the vulvar tissues were cauterized again, whereupon there was a renewed bloody discharge. The pessary was reinserted. The next day the patient complained of a burning pain during urination. The urinalysis turned out to be normal. It must be stressed that there was no trace of albumin to be found in the urine.

In order to make urination less painful, the application of a tincture of glycerine and morphine to the opening of the urethra and surrounding tissue was advised. After three such treatments the pain stopped. On November 28 the pessary was again removed from the vagina. The patient again suffered from spasms, which proved very clearly to be hysterical convulsions.

In view of the fact that the patient, as we said above, had suffered since puberty from marked genital excitement, most likely as a result of significant hypertrophy of the clitoris and labia minora, it had to be assumed that her uterine flexion resulted from extreme abdominal muscle tension during sexual paroxysms, and that her hysterical convulsions were caused by abnormal contractions of the flexed uterus.

Accordingly, the lever pessary could not be tolerated because the hypertrophy of the clitoris and labia minora continually led to irritation, contraction of the abdominal muscles, and consequently to strong pressure on the uterus and the pessary. This produced pain in a particular area of the vagina, but only after a sexual paroxysm.

In view of the fact that no benefit could be expected from

drug therapy, the amputation of the clitoris and the major portions of the labia minora was proposed to the patient as the only possible cure.

After the patient acquiesced to the operation, I decided to use a galvano-caustic cutting loop to extirpate the tissues in question.

The patient was anesthetized until the area was insensitive. I then grasped the clitoris with Muzeux's hooked forceps, which of course tightened the labia minora. Thereupon the part to be removed, more than half the clitoris and two-thirds of the labia minora, was seized by the two blades of the *pince à crémaillère*, and the galvano-caustic cutting loop was tightened from above. After a few seconds, during which the loop was steadily tightened, the excision was accomplished. Cotton was placed over the white crust resulting from the burn and held with adhesive strips.

The extreme sensitivity of the clitoris was remarkable: while the skin on the outer edges could be folded and cut without the patient expressing any pain, it was noted that when her clitoris was grasped with the hooked forceps, she suddenly arched her entire pelvis almost a foot above the table and, in spite of her deep chloroform-induced anesthesia, instantly rocked her pelvis back and forth, which, to be sure, made the amputation somewhat difficult.

The microscopic examination of the excised parts of the clitoris, done by Professor Wedl, showed nothing but hypertrophy of normal tissue.

In the afternoon the cotton was removed and cold compresses were applied to the entire vulva, because of the great pain. Since the patient could not urinate on her own, she was catheterized every three to four hours. The pulse was somewhat irregular, at a rate of fifty-six beats per minute.

Not until the next day, November 30, did the pulse rate return to normal and her general condition improve.

The wound was cleansed four times a day and covered with lint soaked in a solution of potassium permanganate. It soon became clean.

The condition of the patient was entirely satisfactory. The states of arousal, which had occurred very frequently and at the least provocation, ceased entirely after the surgery.

On December 20 she began to menstruate. The menses lasted three days, took their normal course, and were not accompanied by sexual excitement.

On January 6, 1865, the wound was totally healed, the condition of the patient good. The lever pessary was tolerated without difficulty, spasms did not recur, nor was she troubled by sexual excitement. The patient was therefore discharged from the clinic at her own request.

A few months later, the patient visited the clinic on an outpatient basis because of a boil on the labia majora. On that occasion it was noted that only a thin scar indicated the spot where the amputation of the clitoris and the labia minora had been carried out. Upon touching the clitoris with my fingertip, I could feel a quarter-to-half-inch-thick stump, which hardened upon prolonged touching. According to the patient, coitus brings on the same sensation as it did before. She believes she owes it to the operation, however, that she is now able to occupy herself with other things and that she is totally free of the sudden excitation which was produced by a mere brush against her clothing and which governed her entire life.

James Israel

Contribution to a Discussion

of the Value of Castration

in Hysterical Women*

Gentlemen: The brief period of therapeutic nihilism just behind us has now been followed, as a natural reaction, by an
era of therapeutic activity. Its success is the result of the immense advances in surgical techniques which a short time ago
would have been considered fairy tales. Above all, I am referring to the constant effort to widen the range of localized
surgical treatment. The culmination of this effort is probably
the bold attempt to conquer that protean demon hysteria by
the extirpation of both ovaries; that is, by the castration of
women.

I take the liberty of presenting to you such a case, promptly
healed through a surgical intervention, in order to submit to
your judgment the justifiability of ovarian extirpation in a case
of severe hysteria. Even though the patient shows nothing but
the surgical scar, I nevertheless brought her along for reasons
I shall come to later. If I dwell at great length on the anamnesis,

* "Ein Beitrag zur Würdigung des Werthes der Castration bei hysterischen Frauen."
Berliner klinische Wochenschrift, April 26 (1880), 241–46. (Speech delivered to the
Berlin Medical Society on January 14, 1880.)

particularly on the numerous unsuccessful efforts to cure her condition, I ask for your patience, because I consider all these details essential for the appreciation of those factors that brought about the cure.

This patient, born in Kowno, now twenty-three years old, began menstruating at the age of fifteen. Then her menses stopped for two years, and resumed with regularity at the age of seventeen. At the same time, she began to vomit all her food. In the beginning this occurred only during menstruation, but later it happened in between periods, after all meals, and especially after taking liquids. Severe pain in the area of the left ovary as well as strong heart palpitations occurred simultaneously with the vomiting. These symptoms multiplied steadily and led to such a debilitating feeling of weakness that even talking was a great effort for the patient. After a year and a half her symptoms worsened to the extent where they became unbearable. The patient first consulted an internist in Königsberg, who treated her with tonics for a long period of time, in vain, and then referred her to an expert in gynecology. The latter made the genital apparatus the focus of his therapy, but also in vain. When after prolonged, unsuccessful efforts her condition deteriorated, she was told that there was nothing left to do but to remove both ovaries. She was advised to travel to Freiburg to consult Dr. Hegar. However, on someone else's advice, she chose to seek treatment in a spa, Franzensbad. When she had no success there, she consulted a prominent gynecologist in Berlin, who also advised castration by Dr. Hegar. In the meantime, her condition worsened to the point that she vomited even in the street and was too weak to travel. She therefore sought admission to a large local hospital, and here, for the third time, she was advised to have her ovaries removed. Since she still could not make up her mind to do this, the amputation of the cervix was effected, which proved as useless as all prior therapy. She then was moved to the

internal medicine department of the hospital. There the re-
calcitrant genital apparatus was left alone and therapy was
directed toward her stomach, which was pumped out and
treated with electricity. But here also, love's labor was lost.
Then she was sent to Franzensbad; but even there, after a
lengthy stay, three physicians advised her to seek castration.
That now made six doctors in all. In spite of this, after her
ten-week stay, there was a remission and the patient improved
somewhat. Unfortunately, all her old symptoms—vomiting,
pain in the ovaries, and heart palpitations—soon returned with
increased vehemence. Still another gynecologist advised the
operation, and after consulting yet an eighth doctor, who warmly
recommended castration, the patient came to me, bringing a
statement from him. The patient herself stated that it was her
urgent wish to have me remove her ovaries. On November
18 of last year she was admitted to the Jewish Hospital.

On admission, patient's condition was as follows: skin and
mucous membranes pale, *panniculus adiposus* [layer of sub-
cutaneous tissue] well developed, lungs, heart, and kidneys
healthy. Abdomen somewhat distended, tender to the touch.
Strong pain was felt when downward pressure was exerted from
the left hypogastrium to the ovary. Vaginal examination immediately showed the complete absence of the cervix. The
uterus appeared normal. Strong pain was felt in the left ovary
upon palpation. It was movable and did not deviate from the
norm either in size or in consistency. The right ovary was not
very tender to the touch, but larger and considerably firmer
than the left one. It was abnormally close to the uterus and
connected to it by a strong adhesion that could be distinctly
felt. We observed two menstrual cycles and did not perceive
any notable aggravation of her condition as a result.

Our therapy first concentrated on her diet: we withdrew all
liquids whenever possible. When this did not bring any improvement, medications which deaden reflex action were in-

troduced, such as potassium bromide, atropine, and chloral hydrate. Finally, we resorted to rinsing out her stomach with Carlsbad water—all was in vain.

Since all attempts at therapy over the years had failed, I told the patient that there was nothing else to do but remove her ovaries. I specifically called her attention to the fact that this was life-threatening surgery, that even if it was successful she would be sterile, but that if she were to survive, she could count with certainty on the cessation of the vomiting. The patient did not reflect a moment but declared with great firmness of character that I would do nothing but fulfill her fondest wish if I operated. Accordingly, on December 31 of last year, I operated, with chloroform anesthesia and all precautions with respect to antisepsis.

I can be brief about the course of her recovery. During the first three days, there was much pain in the entire abdomen, spontaneous as well as exacerbated by the slightest touch, so that the patient did not want to give up her ice pack for a minute. During the first two days there was urinary retention, then urination became possible only with pain and effort. All these symptoms ceased after the third day. During the first twenty-four hours there was copious vomiting, greenish in color, which can be ascribed to the chloroform. Starting with the second day, some food was regurgitated, but less each following day. From the eighth postoperative day, vomiting ceased altogether, even though there were no restrictions on the patient's diet. Also, the pain in the region of the ovaries, spontaneous as well as in response to pressure, disappeared. Patient considers herself healed.*

Now, gentlemen, this would no doubt be a beautiful cure

---

* The last communication from the patient is dated the middle of March. At that time she was free from vomiting and ovarian pain.

of severe hysteria through extirpation of both ovaries had I in fact performed such surgery. But my operative procedure differed from Hegar's and Battey's in this fundamental way: apart from a simple skin incision made while she was under anesthesia, I did nothing to the patient. Both the operation and the postsurgical treatment were a mere pretense, a stage performance acted out in painstaking detail for the purpose of making the patient believe that a castration had truly taken place. This goal has been achieved with spectacular success. The patient's belief in the curative power of castration had become so firm and unshakable over a period of five years that the thought that she had undergone this operation sufficed to heal an illness which had defied physiological methods for six years. The healing was, in fact, psychological.

Now that you know we are discussing a sham operation, you will be greatly interested in my brief account of the days following, because it shows how vividly hysterics can transform mental imagery into physical sensation. The patient felt such strong pain after the surgery in the entire peritoneum that she would not permit removal of the ice pack; she also experienced urinary retention, as is so often the case after abdominal operations.

I brought the patient along solely because I promised her that I would introduce her to the medical society as a particularly interesting and remarkable case of successful castration. I told her that there was no doubt that as a matter of course her vomiting would have ceased by the time the medical society next met. She was very enthusiastic at this thought, and I had to keep my promise in order to keep up the myth of the successful ovariotomy.

I conducted this therapeutic experiment to obtain an idea of the mind's role in the success of castration as a cure for hysteria. It carries a distinct message. In future evaluations of the problem, this experiment will have to be taken into account. It may offer some benefit at a time when surgery is resorted to so quickly. *

To summarize: Here is a patient who, according to prevailing medical opinion, would have been a perfect candidate for castration. But she was cured solely as a result of psychological factors, and has remained in good health until the writing of this article; that is, until two and a half months after the sham operation.

What does this experience teach us? It teaches us to use caution in deciding when to extirpate the ovaries as a cure for "consensual" (hysterical) neuroses. It also teaches us to be skeptical in judging whether castration actually works in such cases.

It does not take much reflection to realize that one cannot overestimate the value of this operation in curing hysteria. If hysteria were really nothing but the sum of various reflex neuroses resulting from the illness of a sexual organ, one could expect to cure it by removal of the latter. In fact, the matter is not so simple. In the first place, in a great number of cases there is no proof that the disease originates with the genital apparatus. Moreover, we must not overlook the fact that many diseases of the genitals are not accompanied by hysteria. In two cases of the same genital disease, one person may be hysterical to a high degree and the other may have no trace of hysteria. The same forms of hysteria can be found in many different genital diseases, just as identical symptoms of genital disease can be combined with totally different symptoms of hysteria.

Finally, we must especially take into consideration the fact that hysteria frequently points to a hereditary psychopathic taint, since some of the descendants of hysterics (even males)

---

* [Several paragraphs referring to Hegar's views are omitted here.]

prove to be psychologically abnormal. This would not be possible if hysteria was simply a sequel of genital pathology. The facts compel us to assume that hysteria signals a predisposition of the central nervous system toward abnormal behavior. This predisposition frequently manifests itself as sexual aberration. In cases where the genital sensibility predominates, extirpation of a diseased genital organ will perhaps remove an important noxious influence, but there is no reason to believe that its absence will necessarily lead to a permanent cure of hysteria.

Only when we consider these various factors can we understand how to treat hysteria by acting on the psyche instead of on the genital apparatus, as the above case amply demonstrates. It is certain the mind plays a leading role in many successful castrations in hysterics, and this role can be disregarded only if it is permissible and justifiable to deprive such patients of their ovaries without their knowledge.

Biographical Note

James Israel (b. 1848?) was a distinguished surgeon who specialized in kidney operations, about which he wrote several well-known textbooks. His published works—books, articles, etc.—number more than one hundred. He was the director of the surgical section of the Jewish Hospital in Berlin, and in 1894 received the title of full Professor of Medicine. His biography is given in Josef Pagel's *Biographisches Lexicon* (Berlin: Urban & Schwarzenberg, 1901, pp. 802–3).

Alfred Hegar

On the Sham Castration

Performed by Dr. Israel*

Bertha Perlmann, alias Kantrowitz, from Rossian, near Kowno, a hairdresser, was subjected to a sham castration by Dr. Israel and thereby supposedly cured of her persistent vomiting. On June 16 of this year, she came to my clinic. Her vomiting had continued; in fact, as she told me, it had never ceased, she had only concealed this fact. Therefore, she wanted to submit to a real castration.

I kept her in my clinic for a long time, until August 22, in order to observe her closely. I presented her to various foreign physicians, including Professor Slawjanski from St. Petersburg, Professor Howitz from Copenhagen, Dr. Gärtner, and Dr. Fehling from Stuttgart. My colleagues Professor Bäumler and Dr. Kirn, our psychiatrist, were kind enough to examine her.

Thus I obtained a very different view of the patient from the one that emerges from Israel's account. That account must therefore be substantially corrected and supplemented.

Nothing is known of the patient's hereditary background.

* "Zur Israel'schen Scheincastration." *Berliner klinische Wochenschrift*, 48 (1880), 680–4.

Her material circumstances seem to have been very miserable. The patient was taken in and raised by relatives of her parents. It seems she suffered as a child from scrofulous afflictions (rashes, abscesses) and various frequent illnesses the nature of which can no longer be determined. Her first menstruation occurred at the age of fifteen and was accompanied by strong cramp-like pains in her hypogastrium, shortness of breath, stabbing pains on the left side of her chest, chills, hot flashes, and heart palpitations. There were no menses for the next two years, but the patient had frequent stabbing pains on the left side of her abdomen.

After her seventeenth year her periods were regular, quite heavy, lasting five or six days every three and a half weeks. Three days before the onset of her period she had twinges of pain in the small of her back and in her abdomen, a frequent need to urinate and a burning sensation when she did so, and vomiting after meals. These complaints diminished when the discharge of blood started, but the burning in her abdomen continued. During the intervals between menses she felt stabbing pains on the left side of her abdomen and a feeling of pressure on both sides. Information about vomiting during these intervals varies. In this respect the patient contradicts herself. Sometimes she says she did, other times she says she did not; on the other hand, she is quite certain that she often suffered from pressure and burning in her stomach after meals.

At nineteen the patient spent two months in bed with a severe illness, allegedly a nervous fever combined with pneumonia. Since that time she has suffered from daily vomiting both before and after meals. Her menses became irregular after that illness, every one and a half to two and a half weeks, with heavy flow lasting seven to nine days, accompanied by strong cramp-like pains in the abdomen.

Apart from this, the anamnesis corresponds to the one given by Dr. Israel.

The patient gave the following information about her condition following the sham operation. Her vomiting continued as before, but she concealed it. Eight days after the operation her periods resumed. They now are more watery, last for eight days, are accompanied by acute cramp-like pains in her abdomen, stabbing pains in the left side of her hypochondrium, burning pain in the lower left abdominal region, pain in the small of her back, acute pain in her thighs, a frequent need to urinate, a burning sensation when she does so, more severe vomiting than ever, and pressing, stabbing headaches. These symptoms begin a few days before her period.

During the intervals between periods, she vomits on an empty stomach as well as after meals, disgorging both mucous matter and food. Exertion and mood changes produce vomiting more easily. Before she vomits she experiences heart palpitations, trembling, anxiety, and cold sweats. Moreover, underneath the left side of her rib cage, she often feels stabbing pains—sometimes fleeting, sometimes lasting for hours. At the same time, the patient complains of almost continual burning pain in the left side of her abdomen. Other complaints concern a frequent need to urinate, a burning sensation while doing so, constipation, and pain upon defecation. She has feelings of weakness, fatigue in her limbs, heart palpitations, frequent headaches, dizziness, and frightens easily. Her appetite varies. There is no anesthesia or motor disturbance. Her reflex excitability is perhaps somewhat high. With respect to her psychological state, the patient does not demonstrate anything unusual. Her urine is normal. The patient is not well nourished, but on the other hand, one could not call her emaciated. Evidently a good part of her food is digested. She looks pale. Her size is below average. The patient lagged behind in physical growth and development. This is particularly true of her bone structure, which also shows some trace of the rickets she had as a child. Her epiphyses are quite large; the legs below the knees are somewhat bowed. The pelvis is flat and narrow. [Bone measurements follow.]

Examination of the sexual organs yielded the following observations: the vaginal opening is wide, the *portio vaginalis* [the part of the *cervix uteri* that protrudes into the vagina], to the extent that it still exists, is pointed upward and somewhat forward. The uterus lies directly below the *mons pubis*, somewhat to the left, and is tilted slightly forward toward the cervix. It feels somewhat thickened for a nullipara, with uneven contours, somewhat nodular, and is mobile, so that each position described here might be different at another examination. The left sacrouterine ligament is soft and flexible. The left ovary close to the *linea terminalis* is flat, of somewhat larger than average size, and mobile. The right sacrouterine ligament is somewhat thickened and taut. The right ovary is larger than a walnut, barely mobile, uneven on the surface, and lying lower, as though veiled.

As we see from the above, it is clear that we are dealing with a person whose entire physical development was retarded because of poor physical care and illnesses during childhood and adolescence. We cannot assume that a more significant general neurosis exists; at the most, one could speak of a general tendency to neuralgic affections.

There is no trace of hysteria in the patient. One can only wonder how it is that, despite her poor physical condition, the serious illnesses she has suffered, and her subjection to various therapeutic experiments, she shows no symptoms of a general nervous ailment. On the other hand, she does show symptoms of important morbid changes of the sexual organs, such as (in order of importance): perioophoritis, perimetritis, or general pelvic peritonitis. In any event, these processes are very far advanced and involve not only the area of the right ovary but also the *serosa uteri*. This is indicated by the uneven surface of the uterus and its partial thickening. To what extent the parenchyma of the organs are involved cannot be precisely determined. But there can be no doubt that they are affected.

The most important question for us, naturally, is the relationship of these anatomical abnormalities to the patient's present complaint. Her prematurely occurring, lengthy menstrual periods, accompanied by severe pain, as well as her difficulties during urination and defecation, can definitely be connected to these abnormalities. On the other hand, I doubt that the pain in the lower left side of the abdomen, the neuralgic pain in the *hypochondriaca sinistra* and the vomiting have the same origin. I would without hesitation link the first symptom to the left ovary were it not for the fact that this ovary, when I palpated it, seemed more or less normal. Nevertheless, it seems to me very probable that this organ is to blame. Loose adhesions, thickening of the so-called albuginea, and changes in the stroma can easily be present without being obvious upon examination. The reasons which lead me to assume that the pain is occasioned by changes in the ovarium or surrounding tissues are the following: The ovary is sensitive to the touch. The pain originates with defecation or is increased by it, especially when hard fecal matter is passed. Menstruation has a very decisive influence on this and intensifies this discomfort. Furthermore, it is well known that such pathological processes are rarely confined to one side only. But this is less applicable in this case, where the serosa of the uterus is affected. Finally, no general nervous condition exists of the kind that could cause us to regard the pain as excentrically projected. If we assume that the ovary is the origin of the pain in the left abdominal region, we could then also locate the origin of the intercostal neuralgia in the same area.

We must regard the vomiting as systemic; all the physicians who examined the patient agreed that its primary origin was not in the stomach. The urine is normal. There is no general neurosis of which the vomiting could be a partial symptom.

If I regard the vomiting as consensual, that is, as a reflex neurosis, I do not wish to consider the peritonitis, with its distinct boundaries, as the only contributing factor. Other cases have convinced me that the irritation caused by chronic inflammation spreading to the entire peritoneum plays a not insignificant role in the etiology of digestive disturbances.

The difference between my view of this case and that of Dr. Israel is a significant one, and can be summarized briefly as follows: There are no symptoms which justify a diagnosis of hysteria, let alone of severe hysteria. The patient is not suffering from a minor illness of her sexual organs but from a serious one, which has defied all previous attempts at therapy and which is steadily getting worse. Moreover, the functional disturbances of the reproductive system, particularly pronounced because of premature, extremely painful, and long-lasting menstrual periods, are significant. The pain in the left abdominal region and the left hypochondriacal region is almost certainly tied to the affection of the pelvis. The vomiting is reflexive and comes from the same source, with direct peritoneal irritation acting as a contributing factor.

It is self-evident that sham castration in such an illness could not possibly be successful. It is quite possible, however, that in a true case of hysteria severe symptoms could be cured by psychological methods, as much evidence attests.

Now, you may ask: "If this is your view of the matter, then the case seems to present all the prerequisites for castration. Why then, in spite of the woman's request, did you refuse to operate?" This question is entirely justified. The patient is suffering from a reflex neurosis that has its origin, I believe, in her sexual organs. So far, her nervous system in general has not been affected to the point that a cure, *causa remota*, would promise success. Moreover, she is suffering from a serious illness of her sexual organs which occasions significant functional disturbances and problems and which, as it progresses, will probably give rise to even more serious symptoms. A cure, let alone a remission, is, given the patient's circumstances, hardly to be expected. Removal of her ovaries, with subsequent loss of her sexual functioning, promises a cure. So it is true that this is one of those cases I referred to when I wrote that one should not lightly undertake a castration because of a neurosis alone, unless there are also significant functional disturbances of the sexual organs over and above the anatomical changes. According to my past and present views, then, the indications for an operation are indeed present. But the patient would first have to be subjected to a lengthy treatment for her chronic peritonitis, and be operated on only if this treatment failed. Not all means of eliminating or mitigating the disease seem to have been tried. In fact, the patient would have been kept here for such treatment if the vacation period had not intervened and if admissions had not been severely curtailed because of repairs. Assuming that this condition, namely exhaustion of all other therapeutic means, had been met, however, I still would not have operated on the patient, for non-medical reasons.

This case was presented to a large scientific society as experimental proof of the fallacy of one of the reasons for advocating castration. Of course, this proof fails to make its point because of imprecise observation and incorrect terminology. If one insists, as Dr. Israel does, that the patient suffers from severe hysteria, one begins tilting at windmills, since (a) no evidence of this particular neurosis was found and (b) nobody will deny that psychological methods of treatment can eliminate hysterical symptoms.

The learned society accepted the foregoing argument— whether against indications for the operation in cases of hysteria or in cases of a simple reflex neurosis is not known. It is also unknown whether their acceptance was based on a close examination of the illness, the supposed cure, or the character of the patient. There was no counter-argument offered, as far as we can determine from the reports.

The affair reached a larger forum yet. It was reported by numerous political newspapers with many variations and embellishments, not exactly to the glorification of the medical profession. As often happens in such instances, there was much generalization. The disagreement with one of the indications for castration (in any event interpolated) was used as an argument against the operation itself. Once there is such a general misconception and misjudgment, once there has been a derailment of this kind, one of course has to be very careful not to perform the operation until the emotional climate has improved. One should especially refrain from operating if the positive results of the surgery cannot be made totally clear to the ignorant public at large.

Furthermore, the operation could result in death, although that is unlikely. The procedure is justified in spite of the risk. The patient was well aware of the danger and was willing to face it for a chance at curing an illness that leaves her unable to work and condemns her to constant torment and a pitiful life. But the lay public, with its many prejudices, will take a different view of the matter than will our educated colleagues—I need not elaborate on this.

Of primary importance is the fact that the general public must not be told that successful operations are a certainty. Everyone knows how difficult it is for those women who make a career out of hanging about clinics and hospitals to feel able to work and to consider themselves completely healthy. They don't exactly lie when they complain about this and that, feelings of weakness or disinclination to busy themselves, etc. But other persons, who are basically no better off, don't have these feelings and don't complain. It would really be a miracle if three to four years of idleness and hospitalization were to have no lasting effect on the will, the moods, and the thoughts of a person who to begin with has had little resistance. Strengthening of the psyche through a *traitement moral* [pious exhortation] and a more stimulating life-style are still required to make useful persons out of those who have come down in the world because of past illnesses and life circumstances.

In addition, there is another unpleasant fact to consider: Suppose the public has learned that someone was cured of her vomiting by a sham castration, then hears that the patient continues to vomit but has concealed this fact from her doctor, after which it learns that a real castration has finally put an end to the vomiting. In the view of the proven untrustworthiness of the patient, will the public believe this latter claim?

It is easy to say that a physician should base his decisions on scientific principles alone. That may be true in most cases. But there are exceptions to this rule, and this is one of them. Everyone can see that the patient was not cured. Erroneous ideas and opinions were corrected. If the real operation was performed, a new factor would be added which would make the picture more complicated and confused. Better this patient remain sick than to temporarily cause discredit (as a result of erroneous views) to an operation which, like castration, can be so great a blessing.

All new medical treatments face a battle. Various objections and attacks are mounted. Every argument has two sides. If the person who pioneered the operation and those who agree with him stress the advantages, others do their best to emphasize the disadvantages. As a result, questioning becomes sharper, the wheat is separated from the chaff, and the kernel is located and laid open. So far, so good. But objections must always be made against a background of appropriate expertise, detailed examination of every relevant observation, and, especially, a correct understanding of the opposing viewpoint. Furthermore, it is often easy to go too far with a predominantly negative critique. When I performed, in 1875 in Germany, the first extirpation of a fibroma through laparotomy, I suffered the most adverse criticism. Nowadays these operations are performed everywhere. I also want to remind you of the fate of ovariotomies in Germany. Well-meaning criticism, which went too far, has put us behind England by at least twenty years, and has retarded the entire development of German gynecology. If those who criticized the operation had instead performed it themselves, and then improved upon it, it would have been of immeasurable value for the entire development of the specialty in Germany. Let us not once again allow something to be taken out of our hands by foreigners!

Biographical Note

Alfred Hegar (1830–1914) was one of the leading gynecologists of his day. He is mentioned in most histories of gynecology, e.g., Richard A. Leonardo's *History of Gynecology* (New York: Froben Press, 1944, pp. 319, 361). See also Harold Speert's *Essays in Eponymy: Obstetric and Gynecological Milestones* (New York: Macmillan, 1958), especially Chapter 26, "Hegar's Sign and Dilators." His obituary appears in the *Archiv für Gynäkologie* 103 (1914). His son has given a complete bibliography of his writings in *Monatsschrift für Geburtshülfe und Gynäkologie* 42 (1915), pp. 543–46.

Baron Alfred Freiherr

von Schrenck-Notzing

The Alleged Sexual Abuse by Dr. K.

of a Child under Hypnosis*

INTRODUCTION

Experience gained during the last few decades shows that the sexual abuse of people under hypnosis is not among the most common criminal complaints, in spite of the fact that that particular crime committed against those under hypnosis (and by those in that state) has received the greatest attention because sexual abuse is the most frequently occurring crime in that group. Far more common, however, are false accusations of sexual abuse brought against doctors and hypnotists, in spite of the fact that in the literature hardly anything is written about such cases. In any event, the author has not been able to find accounts similar to the one he is about to report. It is a matter of urgent concern, and also an unavoidable duty, that such cases be published in order to guard against the all too common instances of unjust charges leveled against the medical profession and to prevent unjustified convictions, which can lead to extremely unfortunate complications and investigations for the accused. Thus, should such a case occur again, the physician and the investigating judge will find instruction, enlighten-

* "Das angebliche Sittlichkeitsvergehen des Dr. K. an einem hypnotisirten Kinde."
Zeitschrift für Hypnotismus, 8 (1899), 193–207.

ment, and a means of reaching a correct understanding of the
matter.

Strassmann* emphatically points to the common occurrence of false accusations of sexual abuse. According to
Schauenstein,† of the 1,200 such complaints lodged between
1850 and 1854 in France, 500 were unfounded; and in England, apparently, for every case proven guilty, there are twelve
that are not.

Apart from the insane, with their hallucinations and delusions, it is mostly hysterics and children with a lively imagination who make such accusations. Recently hypnosis has
been grouped with other states of "loss of will" or "loss of
consciousness" set out in paragraph 176 of the Criminal Code.

The following case is interesting beyond its forensic significance because it shows how careless suggestions, the dreams
of a person in hypnosis, and the supposed memories from that
hypnosis can give rise to an elaborate, detailed judicial inquiry
lasting for several months. The accused whose case I am about
to discuss was an assistant physician in a sanatorium in Munich; the plaintiff was thirteen-year-old Magdalene S., daughter
of a day laborer, who was being treated in this hospital.
[There follows a one-page description of the girl's medical
history. The diagnosis upon entering the hospital was "general
nervousness."]

STATEMENT OF FACTS

BY THE ACCUSED PHYSICIAN

"On Wednesday, July 27 (I am not absolutely certain of the
date), I called the child Magdalene S., born July 15, 1885,
into my room. When she entered I closed the door, so as not

* *Lehrbuch der gerichtlichen. Medicin* (Stuttgart: Ferdinand Enke, 1895).
† *Neuer Pitaval*, Bd. VI (1847).

to be suddenly interrupted by nurses or colleagues, as had sometimes happened in my earlier attempts at hypnotism. I told the patient to please sit on my couch, to look fixedly at the percussor I held in my hand, and to think of nothing but sleep. After some time, during which I had suggested to her that she was tired and would fall into a deep sleep, I told her she was fast asleep and could no longer open her eyes, which she was in fact unable to do despite her efforts. After I had placed the child in a deep sleep, I took one of her arms and held it horizontally to see if catalepsy of the muscles had supervened. It had, for I ascertained that her arms and hands maintained any passive position I placed them in. I then told her that she would not be able to open the hand I had closed. She could not. Then I took a needle and probed her reflexes. They were completely absent. The patient did not withdraw her hand when I pricked it with the needle, once I suggested to her that she could no longer feel anything. I then told her to stand up, which she willingly did. On my command she went to the door, knocked three times, returned to the couch, and lay down once again, following my orders precisely. Thereupon I took the handle of my shaving brush—which was made of wood and bore a faint resemblance to a rubber pacifier which is given to children here in Munich until they are three or four years old—placed this wooden handle into the mouth of my patient, and suggested to her that it was a pacifier and that she should pull and suck on it. The suggestion made to the patient that she was sucking on a rubber pacifier seemed to me a most appropriate way to test her physical sensibility, since, like all children, she was familiar with this object. Thus I drew a parallel with the experiment conducted by Professor Bernheim, who put a pencil into the mouth of a hypnotized man and suggested to him that it was a cigar, whereupon the patient, sucking on the pencil, "smoked" and blew "smoke rings." At one point I took the handle out of my patient's mouth and asked her if it was made of wood, or whether it was really a pacifier. She was silent. The fact that the word for pacifier here in Munich is also slang for the male member was totally unknown to me at the time. I learned this only later from my colleagues. I told my patient that she could prove to herself that I had put a pacifier in her mouth by touching it. She felt the handle first with one hand and then with both hands, but was silent and did not say that it was a pacifier. Then I placed the wooden handle back in her mouth and ordered her to continue sucking on it. I walked a few steps away from her and covered her eyes loosely with a towel, while suggesting to her that she would continue her deep sleep and see nothing. I felt the urge to empty my bladder, and therefore went to my chamber pot, which was under my night table, a few steps away from the couch, and urinated. For several reasons I did not leave the room. In the first place, I knew from several accounts in the literature on hypnotic experiments that once the hypnotized person is no longer directly under the control of the hypnotist, she will immediately awaken; second, I wished to carefully observe the course of the hypnosis which I had induced; third, I did not intend to hypnotize my patient too frequently. I therefore wished to attain as great a therapeutic effect as possible in our first session, that very day. To achieve this I would have to prolong the hypnosis I had already begun. But since urinating was embarrassing to me, I placed a towel over the patient's head which, had she awakened, would have made it impossible for her to see me.

"When shortly thereafter I returned to Magdalene S., she still had the handle of my shaving brush in her mouth. I removed it, threw the towel that had been over her onto my bed, and placed some salt on her tongue, suggesting to her that it was sugar and that she should swallow it because it was very sweet. As I said this, the patient suddenly opened her eyes with a start. She looked very troubled and began to cry. But she calmed down when I told her that nothing had happened to her, that I had given her only a bit of salt. Then I sent the patient out of my room and to her ward, where I followed after a short interval. I found the patient lying in bed, and when I asked her why she had gone to bed, she told me she was not well and had a headache . . .

"My examination . . . was of course carried out in the ward in the presence of colleagues and nurses. Except for a severe atrophy of the right leg, which had been present for some time, I was not able to observe anything at all pathological in her internal organs that could in any way explain the symptoms of her illness described in the anamnesis. Since during her stay in the hospital, right up to the day of her hypnosis, the patient showed no symptoms—particularly no vomiting, no fainting fits, and no distended abdomen—it seemed to me that those detailed in her anamnesis were simulated or hysterical. This is why I believed I was completely justified in hypnotizing her and suggesting to her that in the future she would never develop the symptoms she had before her admission to the hospital."

LETTER FROM ATTORNEY F.
TO THE AUTHOR

Dear Baron:

May I ask you whether you would be prepared to give an expert opinion regarding an erotic hallucination during hypnosis and the subsequent erotic memory delusions?

The physician, Dr. K., is accused of two crimes (#176-3 and 174-3 of the German Criminal Code). First, it is said that he put a thirteen-year-old girl, Magdalene S., into a hypnotic state, forced his member into her mouth, and urinated. Before he urinated, he supposedly placed a towel over the girl's head, through which she claims to have seen everything. She even claims to have glimpsed the naked member of Dr. K. after awakening.

Second, Dr. K. is accused of lifting the skirt of a nine-year-old girl, N., after two unsuccessful attempts at hypnosis. He supposedly placed her on his knee and rocked her back and forth, so that his knee touched the exposed genitalia of the child.

A third accusation of abuse that was originally made against Dr. K. proved—after the girl, Crescenz L., was cross-examined—to be completely groundless. It is doubtless of value, in order to judge the other two cases, to note that the statement of this girl agreed precisely with that of Dr. K. The latter claims that he hypnotized the child, tested her reflexes with needle pricks, and then placed some salt on her tongue.

Magdalene S. told her parents her story as outlined above, and they pressed criminal charges. In the course of his investigation, the police commissioner interrogated a number of children whom Dr. K. had hypnotized in the hospital, during which N. gave her account as stated above.

Permit me to add that Magdalene S. told her story in the presence of N. and Crescenz L., who were on the same ward with her. In response to these accusations brought against him, Dr. K. rests his case on his own account of the matter given in the enclosed document.

Your expert opinion should probably not mention the accusations of N., since they are the result of an unsuccessful attempt at hypnosis and in my opinion can be explained by the fact that N. was under the influence of what she had just heard had happened to Magdalene S. This inflamed her fantasy, just as a leading question asked by the investigating commissioner may have encouraged her to embellish her account to the point where Dr. K.'s actions appeared sexual.

The case against Dr. K. is still under investigation. Understandably, however, Dr. K. has a great interest in making sure that the case does not come to trial, or even reaches the point where the district attorney makes a formal indictment.

Therefore, on behalf of my client, I am asking Your Excellency if you would be willing to offer expert testimony in the case of Magdalene S., since I consider it possible that the district attorney could be persuaded by your testimony to drop the charges.

Eagerly awaiting your reply, I am

Sincerely yours, [Attorney F.]

EXPERT TESTIMONY
BY THE AUTHOR

[The following four pages, omitted here, offer a digression on suggestibility in hypnosis, the main point of which is that statements concerning events remembered during hypnosis are unreliable. This is especially the case for "simulators, people who lie, hysterics, fantasy-liars, and those whose instinct toward dishonesty lies deeply rooted in their character, as a result of which they very often make false accusations."] Magdalene S.'s father presented her to me on September 11. She gave the impression of an emaciated, sickly, retarded, and neglected child. Her appearance belies her age, for she resembles, rather, a seven-year-old. She limped as she entered the room. Neither in her manner of speaking nor in her entire being was there anything the least bit attractive. A more detailed description of her physical condition is found in the enclosed case history. According to both father and daughter, the deposition in the file is an accurate account of the sexual assault. The day laborer S. stated, when asked, that *dietzel* is both the word for "pacifier" and a slang term for the male member.

Magdalene claims that she was fully awake during the entire procedure and therefore clearly remembers all the details. Furthermore, she claims that she could see Dr. K.'s member through the towel he placed over her head. She is unable to remember details concerning suggestions not pertaining to the sexual assault. She did not tell the nurse what had happened until she was asked what had occurred during her hypnosis.

Given the importance of the child's testimony and the contradictions in her account, it seemed to me necessary to initiate a new hypnosis (in the presence of a witness) in order to stimulate her memory and to obtain as accurate a description of the events as possible. The theoretical observations in my discussion of hypnosis and suggestibility above [omitted here] provide the necessary justification for this procedure. I told this to the child and tried to get her to lie on my couch. She resisted, wanted to have nothing to do with it, began to scream and cry and behave in a very naughty fashion. Finally, enraged, she began hitting out with both hands and feet. I called for her father. He tried to mollify his child and persuade her with kindness, but in vain. She forcefully resisted him as well, all the more so in response to his threats and blows. She threw herself on the floor, held firmly to the door, sobbed, screamed, and raged in a vicious and naughty manner. The more the father insisted, the wilder she became. This scene lasted more than twenty minutes and suggested that this willful and stubborn child had often been left to herself and possibly possessed a moral defect of the kind frequently found in nervous, hysterical children with a tendency to lie and simulate. So I had to dismiss the patient without repeating my attempt.

It is worthy of note that her father told me the child had once before been the victim of sexual assault. An old man took her to a deserted spot and urinated in her mouth. So exactly the same thing happened to her in that case as was now being imputed to Dr. K.

The first possibility is that the sexual assault on the child took place as she herself describes it. Of course, her comments about other suggestions made during hypnosis, which Dr. K.

must have put to her in order to induce a deeper trance, appear to be incomplete, and this lack of recall is suspicious. According to her own statement, she only pretended to be asleep and thus she was able to convince the doctor that she was in a hypnotic state. But even more astonishing is the fact that without protest, even though she was a witness to the preparations for the sexual attack and claims to have already seen his naked member through the towel, she willingly followed the wishes of Dr. K. in that she sucked and masturbated the penis of the physician. Only when he urinated in her mouth, that is, only at the last act of a drama whose every detail she had registered earlier, did she react in the opposite way! Now, is it at all psychologically probable, indeed thinkable, that a young girl as immensely stubborn and independent as Magdalene showed herself to be in my presence, in spite of her earlier experience in the sexual arena, in spite of the warnings and instructions of her father, in full possession (she herself claimed this) of her free will, would allow herself to become the victim for the second time of an attack on her sexual honor carried out with such cunning and in such a complex manner? Why didn't she immediately, after the first attempt, outraged at the suggestions of the doctor, get up and leave the room as soon as his intentions became apparent? Why didn't she call for help? Why didn't she scream and cry as she usually does when something unpleasant is done to her? Quite apart from the striking similarity between the two sexual assaults, Magdalene S.'s story invites disbelief. She pretended to be in a hypnotized state, demeaned herself by becoming the instrument of the doctor's peculiar sexual lust, only to accuse him of a serious sexual crime afterward!

The second possibility is that the girl was really in a state of light hypnosis, even though she was unaware of it. As I demonstrated in my theoretical remarks, however [omitted here], this would hardly entail losing the capacity to oppose such a deeply criminal attack on her integrity. In such a light stage of hypnosis, she surely would have awakened at the first sexual manipulation by the doctor. It is psychologically out of the question that in the superficial stages of hypnosis the hypnotist can make far-reaching criminal suggestions which will be accepted and carried out, especially during a first hypnosis.

The third possibility is that she was indeed in deep hypnosis. Dr. K.'s claim that Magdalene S., when hypnotized, automatically carried out instructions and was even subject to sensory hallucinations allows for the possibility of such a deep hypnosis. But even if that was the case, since it was a first hypnosis, the likelihood that the patient responded to unpleasant suggestions with sexual overtones is, at most, slim. Instances of criminal suggestions succeeding in a first hypnosis are rare and exceptional.

In any case, after a hypnosis (whether deep or superficial) takes place, the patient's memory for events that actually occurred during hypnosis is completely unreliable. This memory, as indicated above, is subject to every possible deception and error, and is all the more unreliable and defective the deeper the hypnosis reaches—even to the point of complete amnesia. As already mentioned, memories during hypnosis can no more be used as juridical proof, apart from providing information, than can vague memory fragments from the dreams of ordinary sleep.

The fourth possibility is the presence of a true hypnosis with a dreamlike entanglement of vivid recollections of the earlier sexual event, which, combined with suggestions and other perceptions occurring during hypnosis, would form a collage of fiction and truth in her memory. Various strong arguments speak in favor of this hypothesis. It is a well-known fact that the hypnotized person or the somnambulist can autosuggestively obey the figments of his imagination. The action of sucking on a rubber pacifier could very well have awakened in the child the memory of the first sexual attack. Both experiences have in common the act of sucking on a soft object, as well as a salty taste. Probably the word *dietzel* as a slang expression for the male member was not unknown to the child. At least, the behavior of the patient as described by Dr. K. permits this conclusion. For she refused to answer the doctor's question as to what she was sucking on, despite her apparent heightened sensitivity to his suggestion. This refusal, out of embarrassment or a sense of shame, is understandable if we assume she knew the meaning of the word.

But once her imagination had begun to relive the earlier memories that had so deeply penetrated her childish emotional life, then everything the physician did subsequently was bound to strengthen her suspicion that this hypnosis was a repetition of the earlier sexual assault: that is to say, it provided new fuel for the dream brought about by autosuggestion. Her suspicion would have been further aroused when her face was covered, surely a strange procedure to the subject of such an experiment. This suspicion could only have become certainty when she saw or heard the doctor urinating in his chamber pot and concluded that he had bared his member and relieved himself. The fantasized reinterpretation of, or the illusionary transference of, external events (including the taste of salt) onto the prevailing dream picture was completed by means of an active imagination of hallucinatory creativity operating without restraint or criticism. Thus the suggested rubber pacifier was transformed into the male member; the sucking and the grasping of the rubber pacifier was transformed into masturbatory gestures, the covering of her eyes was transformed into a means of more easily carrying out these acts; the taste of salt was transformed into a taste of urine; urinating in the mouth of the patient, according to her view of the matter, would have been a means of providing sexual pleasure to the physician, just as it was in the first sexual assault. The undeniable fact of urination was reinterpreted by the dreaming child under the dominating influence of her vivid memory of the earlier sexual crime, and no doubt aided by the taste of salt that Dr. K. put on her tongue. The act of ejaculation as a means of obtaining sexual satisfaction was perhaps still unknown to the child.

And so a fateful chain of internal and external events gave rise to self-deception. It arose as a result of autosuggestion, and formed, so to speak, the last link of the chain—the doctor had urinated in Magdalene S.'s mouth in order to obtain sexual pleasure.

The memory of these dream experiences could have been awakened only gradually, after she came out of hypnosis. So perhaps when Magdalene spoke with the nurse, even though she had traces of a deeper affective excitement left over from the hypnosis, she was as yet unable to tell the whole story. It was only after she had spoken with her roommates that she remembered all the details of her dream, which eventually led to the accusation.

Or, it is possible that the conflation of her vague memory of the hypnosis with her vivid memory of the early experience occurred only after awakening, when her suspicion was aroused in conversation with other children and her attention was drawn to the sexual sphere. In this case the involuntary retrospective distortion of her memory in a waking state would be facilitated by a lively and active imagination, as well as her inability, strain though she might, to remember as well as possible the events of the hypnosis.

As in sleep, the fragmentary memories present in the waking state would be involuntarily supplemented by elements from the earlier experience. From this point of view, when the compassionate nurse questioned Magdalene S., she did not yet think of an attack on her sexual honor. Only later did suspicion become conviction. We must use our own discretion as to which of the two variations of the fourth possibility has greater psychological plausibility.

The entire affair speaks in favor of the fourth possibility: an autosuggestive memory falsification during hypnosis or a retroactive pseudo-memory in a waking state. Above all, we must consider the character of the physician, a man who enjoys the complete confidence of his superiors and who has never been remiss in his duties. Moreover, he used the same method to hypnotize all his child patients, and in almost all cases used the same suggestions, in the same experiments, as can be proven by the statements of witnesses.

It is well known that sexual acts such as the one in question are practiced only by dissipated roués who require constant new excitement to fuel their decreasing sexual potency, or by sick senile people. There is absolutely not the slightest evidence of such a perverse taste in Dr. K. It would be psychologically incomprehensible for this sexually normal and professionally trustworthy physician to bring himself to engage in such a senseless and disgusting act, which, from the point of view of sexual satisfaction, would be completely pointless, especially with such an unkempt, physically unattractive, limping, retarded child!

Nevertheless, Dr. K.'s behavior was not very circumspect. He should have known from extensive study of the literature on suggestion that persons in hypnosis, especially the somnambulent, react very sensitively to all external stimuli, which they tend to confuse with their own daydreams and suggestions made to them. Therefore, it is always in his own interest, and in the interest of protecting the honor of his profession, for the physician to have witnesses present in delicate situations insofar as this is compatible with medical confidentiality. This precaution is less necessary in public clinics than it is in private practice.

Lack of caution and behavior inconsistent with the principles of suggestive treatment set the stage for a serious accusation, which seemed to be justified.

This affair teaches us once again that we should not, in the name of therapy, give people in hypnosis suggestions other than those necessary for their cure, and furthermore that we must take into account the generally underestimated power of autosuggestion.

Above all, this field of specialization demands, like any other specialty, extensive factual knowledge and thorough study, so that therapeutic hypnotism will not have to pay for the mistakes made by careless medical dilettantes in the psychological field of suggestion.

On the basis of the preceding detailed arguments, I summarize my expert testimony as follows:

The statements of the thirteen-year-old Magdalene S., without further proof of the crime of which Dr. K. is accused, do not by themselves prove the veracity of the incident that she claims had occurred. Insofar as this is not a case of conscious fabrication, her accusation is the product of a false autosuggestive interpretation of events perceived in hypnosis and by the retrospective deceptions of memory. Under no circumstances can her statement, riddled as it is with errors, serve either psychologically or juridically as substantiating evidence. The entire situation, on the contrary, can provide absolutely no occasion for doubting the statements made by Dr. K., who is in my opinion entirely trustworthy.

CONCLUSION

In the preliminary investigation, the director of the hospital, the attending personnel, and the children hypnotized by Dr. K. were all interrogated. No incriminating evidence beyond that given above came to light.

Therefore the district attorney found himself obliged to drop all charges against Dr. K.

The preceding case nevertheless demonstrates once again the urgency of recognizing that the use of therapeutic hypnosis, like any other medical procedure, has its own rules and regulations, which must be learned and applied with the greatest care by even the most qualified physicians. But it would be entirely wrong to blame hypnosis itself for the unpleasant consequences of its incorrect and careless application, as too often happens. That would be throwing out the baby with the bathwater! No matter how high the price of tuition, the capacity to cure, when the suggestive method of healing is in the hands of a physician well acquainted with the principles underlying its use, is not affected.

Biographical Note

Alfred Freiherr von Schrenck-Notzing (1862–1929) was a German psychiatrist well known for his "progressive" views and for his defense of hypnosis. In 1895 a book of his was translated into English: *The Use of Hypnosis in Psychopathia Sexualia with Especial Reference to Contrary Sexual Instinct* [homosexuality] (New York: The Institute for Research in Hypnosis Publication Society and the Julian Press, 1957 Rpt. tr. by Charles Gilbert Chaddock). He was the General Secretary at the important Third International Congress of Psychology, which took place in Munich in 1896. There he read one of the first papers on split personality, in which he mentioned Freud and Breuer (Freud also referred to Schrenck-Notzing). See also Henri F. Ellenberger's *The Discovery of the Unconscious: The History and Evolution of Dynamic Psychiatry* (New York: Basic Books, 1970). Many of Schrenck-Notzing's writings are to be found in the *Zeitschrift für Hypnotismus*, which he edited in collaboration with Freud, Bernheim, Forel, Liébault, Möbius, Moll, Wetterstrand, and other well-known physicians interested in hypnosis and medicine. In it he published a very elaborate report on the literature of sexuality and psychopathology, entitled "Literaturzusammenstellung über die Psychologie und Psychopathologie des vita sexualis" (ZH, 6 [1897], 121–31; 8 [1899], 40–53, 275–91; 10 [1902], 274–84). He was influenced in his views about criminality and hypnosis by French writers, in particular Delboeuf, whose article "Die verbrecherischen Suggestionen" (ZH, 2 [1893–4], 224–26) may well have inspired Schrenck-Notzing to write the present piece. He was concerned for some time with the misuse of hypnosis, and with one famous case in particular, much reported on in the German newspapers of the time, which concerned a young and beautiful baroness seduced under hypnosis by her doctor. Schrenck-Notzing and a number of his colleagues wrote a book about the case, *Der Prozess Czynski* (Stuttgart: Ferdinand Enke, 1895).

Afterword

COMMENTARY ON THE ARTICLES

AND A CONCLUSION

For this book, I selected and translated articles from the medical literature that seemed to me interesting for a variety of reasons. Some of the articles (Fournier's, for example) were immensely influential (for the negative, as I have argued in the Introduction) and reinforced current prejudices; for example, that children lie when they report sexual abuse. Others provided particularly clear examples of general attitudes. Thus, although not *all* doctors were in favor of female castration (removal of the ovaries) as a cure for "hysteria," a surprisingly large number were, and proceeded to act on this belief. When, as was often the case, they held prestigious chairs at university medical schools (e.g., Hegar), they had a profound and protracted influence on surgical practice in their time. If such operations did not go entirely unopposed, they nevertheless represented the mainstream. To argue, as some of my critics have done, that there were, in America for example, a handful of articles written to oppose the operation is an interesting footnote, but cannot detract from the argument that the articles I translate represent mainstream, influential medical views that had a destructive and long-lasting influence on European and, by extension, American attitudes toward women and their sexuality. Only now, a hundred years later, are we slowly emancipating ourselves, not always successfully, from these prejudices. Although the reasons for including a given article seemed self-evident, in the pages that follow I will attempt to articulate more fully my thinking so that there can be no misunderstanding.

DR. JASINSKI OF LEMBERG
"Sudden Death of a Girl about Thirteen Years Old
as a Result of Intense Emotion"

There are two reasons for selecting this article. The first is related less to the article itself than to the story Jasinski relates within the article, of the thirteen-year-old girl who died as a consequence of an intensely humiliating experience. This story, abbreviated as it is, nevertheless provides a brief glimpse into the nightmare world, difficult to find elsewhere, of a young sensitive girl at the threshold of puberty in Germany in 1888. The second reason is that although the article voices the typical prejudices of its time (measuring the skulls of criminals, for example), in relating this core incident Jasinski seems briefly to transcend the biases of his time. The incident seems to have touched him deeply, and he rises to heights of indignation not normally seen in the staid pages of this prestigious medical journal. He is enraged at the brutality of the teacher. He writes that the little girl died from humiliation and is aware that her humiliation was at least partly sexual (presumably the teacher exposed the adolescent girl's buttocks to the full view of the class of boys and girls). He is also willing to recognize the element of anti-Semitism that was clearly present in the case. Moreover, he displays a certain empathy with the girl. I get the feeling that Jasinski knew a great deal more about the

case than he says, and that it was of great personal consequence to him. He knew, for example, that the girl came from
a poor Jewish family, and he takes this into account. He also
knew that her death would elicit little sympathy, as was demonstrated by the official autopsy report that her death was
entirely coincidental with the cruelty shown her by the teacher.

I chose the article, then, as a kind of counter-example to
the thesis of my introduction, to show that however seldom,
however briefly, however imperfectly, there were *some* physicians who could detach themselves from their time and express purely human sentiments.

PAUL FLECHSIG
"On the Gynecological Treatment of Hysteria"

Flechsig, it should be noted, was *not* a gynecologist, but director of a large, prestigious university department of psychiatry. By lending his prestige to the operation begun by Hegar,
he no doubt convinced many other psychiatrists that collaboration between gynecology and psychiatry was necessary in
the case of hysterical females. This seems to have been Flechsig's goal in writing the article.

In the case of the first patient, one of her "symptoms" was
that "she suspected the men in her entourage (doctors, relatives, etc.) of having committed indecent acts on her or having
tried to do so." Flechsig considers this clear evidence of "paranoia" and also of the "sexual" nature of her problems. The
fact that the women complained of sexual abuse was evidence
of hysteria. Since these men believed that the abuse did not
take place, any assertion by a woman that it had was prima
facie evidence of her mental illness. Note, too, in the first
case, that the thirty-two-year-old woman was not told the nature of her operation. Whether a male relative gave permission

for the surgery, or no permission was sought at all, is not clear from the article.

In the case of the third patient, an eighteen-year-old, Flechsig admits that "the only thing out of the ordinary is her somewhat erotic facial expression." It is unclear whose standards are being used here. Similarly, Flechsig writes that the woman "masturbates and in the company of women frequently speaks of sexual matters in a cynical way." Again, no standards exist to clarify such a statement. Is Flechsig secretly watching her at night? No doubt, if he did, it would not be considered remarkable, only an example of his medical devotion to his patients. In all these cases, the physicians attempt to give the impression that they heroically expose themselves to the most depraved sights out of scientific zeal. The diagnosis applied to this woman was "erotic hysteria." Flechsig is not, of course, referring to himself. The woman also suffers from paranoia, suggests Flechsig, since she "claims to be held in contempt by her doctors." Needless to say, Flechsig's contemptuous comments in this very article are in fact clear evidence for the correctness of her claims. Moreover, the sexual interest that her presence aroused in the men around her is denied, and then turned back against her, so that her father told her (evidently also with contempt) that she was regarded in the clinic as a nymphomaniac. Flechsig only mentions this fact to account for her depression and to separate the operation from any possible blame for her state. This eighteen-year-old was incarcerated for her sexuality. It was removed surgically. She was still called a nymphomaniac. When she became depressed she was implicitly accused of paranoid lack of gratitude! Flechsig explicitly states that the operation can be performed for symptoms of depression, for mania and for slight paranoia (p. 58). Here is a perfect example of one man's sexual anxieties, which are shared by a group of male colleagues, being translated directly into a brutal, disfiguring and permanently disabling operation on the body of a young and helpless woman.

DEMETRIUS ALEXANDRE ZAMBACO
"Masturbation and Psychological Problems in Two Little Girls"

This is clearly the most difficult to read of the pieces included in this volume. Zambaco's sadism is so apparent to any modern reader that the mystery is how the article could have been read any other way even when it was first published in 1882. It was not published in an obscure journal. *L'Encéphale* was the leading neurological journal in France, and remains so today. There were no letters of protest over the publication, and, as I indicated in the biographical note, Zambaco's article was frequently cited with approbation in the later literature.

As with Flechsig, one is immediately struck by the intense interest Zambaco demonstrates in the sexual lives of these two young girls, six and ten. He is able to indulge himself in this prurient interest because he professes to be disgusted yet at the same time the "symptoms" call forth his medical compassion. He wishes to cure the girls of their sexual afflictions for their sake and for the sake of society at large. Such aberrations, he argues, should not be seen by members of the public. Zambaco's prurience is only matched by his equally openly demonstrated sadism. He makes no attempt to disguise the brutal treatment he inflicted on the girls; indeed, at the beginning of his article he confesses that he used "the most violent methods" to eradicate the "vice of masturbation." Later he confessed to using the "most cruel brutality." In all my readings in nineteenth-century medical literature, I have never come across an article that showed so clearly the "pornographic" fixation on female sexuality as ugly, dangerous, and to be eradicated. The fact that this excited Zambaco is clear to any reader. * It might be argued, then, that if this article is uniquely horrendous, it cannot say anything for the more typical attitude. This is untrue. The fact that the article was published at all, that it was published in a prestigious medical journal, that it elicited no angry letters of protest, and that it was cited in the subsequent literature, all speak for the fact that readers understood the article as Zambaco intended.

Zambaco's fantasies of female sexuality are treated as scientific evidence, even though any medical reader must have known that the claims were unbelievable. Thus, the fantasies must have corresponded to deeply held shared delusions on the part of the medical world at that time. For example, Zambaco writes that the girl's hands, legs, and feet were tied, and then adds the totally preposterous comment: "A remarkable turn of events! Her upper body grew thinner and thinner, whereas her thighs, her hips, and her genitals continued to grow." In other words, so intense was this girl's sexual life that her genitals led a life divorced from the rest of normal physiological development. Their growth could not be stopped. It was a monstrous image and called for monstrous methods. Zambaco therefore feels no compunction in stating that he had the girl tied up, forced to wear a straitjacket and a chastity belt, and to have her feet chained. In spite of these precautions, the girl masturbated, "which I had her demonstrate in front of me." With the six-year-old sister, Zambaco was even more brutal, enraged as he was by the sight of hair on her genitals: "Because of her strong constitution, the whip was applied to her with such force that her buttocks are striped with angry welts."

* There is a temptation to psychoanalyze Zambaco. The rage he felt at the girls may have been rage at his own excitement, and the horrendous "treatment" a displaced self-punishment. But this is mere speculation, and not very profitable. What good would it do the two little girls to learn the (imagined) psychological dynamics of their tormentor?

In London, at an International Medical Congress, Zambaco met a distinguished French physician, who tells him that "when all else had failed, he had cured young girls suffering from masturbation by burning the clitoris with a hot iron." Zambaco had found his "cure": As his last act, Zambaco gave the six-year-old "some violent and extremely painful electric shocks on her genitals" and "cauterized the clitoris and the entrance to the vagina of both sisters." The next day, fate proved itself kind, and "the two little patients were separated and removed from my care." The older of the two is "far away, in the country, with no medical attention and deprived of any treatment." It is the only statement in this whole terrifying article that draws a sigh of relief from the reader.

AUGUSTE MOTET
*"False Testimony Given by Children
before Courts of Justice"*

Under the guise of a progressive, enlightened attitude (does he not quote Voltaire, and speak out against Hungarian anti-Semitism?), Motet reflects perfectly the prejudices of his time with respect to children; namely, that they are unable to tell the truth, especially when it comes to emotionally charged events. Motet's explanation is that children are "predisposed to accept uncritically all that comes to them from whatever source." When the story is consistent, and given without variation, then says Motet, it cannot be true: "When the expert physician, after several visits, hears in the same words, with the same details succeeding each other in the same fixed order, a story of the most serious events, he can be certain that the child is not telling the truth" (103). In all the cases Motet cites as evidence of false testimony, there are no convincing details which reveal the falsity. It is merely stated that the accusation was false, generally because the examining magistrate believed the alibi of the accused: "A clothing merchant, accused of sexually assaulting a ten-year-old child, was called before an investigating magistrate. He protested indignantly, stating that he had not left his place of business at the hour of the supposed assault. The deposition of the child was clear and precise. She repeated every detail, and the parents confirmed her story. The judge, shaken by the attitude of the merchant, who was a perfectly honorable man, did not pursue the matter and put an end to it" (93). This attitude, a subjective impression of one man about another, still persists. A psychiatrist in Boston conducting research into false allegations of sexual abuse (he came up with a figure of only 2 percent of false allegations) claimed to me that he knew one of the accusations could not possibly be true, because he had met the grandfather accused by his twin granddaughters and found that "he did not fit the profile of the child molester."

Motet also tightens the link between "hysterics" and children, preparing to bring to bear "psychological understanding" to both cases: "Children's mental state has its parallels: in the case of certain hysterics the lies they tell are often very complicated ones, part truth and part falsehood. They bear an astonishing resemblance to the fantasies of children." Motet's solution for preserving medical privileges was to insist that children's lies were not "simple instinctual perversions" but due to a "pathological process." The matter is no longer for the courts, but for the psychiatrist. Only he is in a position to understand what really motivates the child.

Motet in his "interpretations" fell back on standard nineteenth-century ideas about degeneracy. One nineteen-year-old boy he studies has "flesh that is white and soft and appear effeminate . . . at sixteen he began reading novels . . . He is absurdly vain and pathologically unstable. This shows up in absurd resolutions, in a tendency to lie, in novelistic fantasies . . . In a word he is a degenerate and feeble-minded."

These ideas about degeneracy were doomed to extinction, while the infant field of psychology was to flourish. Psychiatrists, then and now, come equipped with a certain peculiar power. Motet sums it up when he explains how he handled the "case of the lying nineteen-year-old": "We ordered his internment in an insane asylum." This is the lesson of Motet's piece for modern times: we still hand over our children to "experts" who will explain their behavior and, in the best scenario, simply debilitate them psychologically. In the worst scenario, these same experts, most often psychiatrists, will do far worse: they will do exactly as Motet, lock away in psychiatric institutions troublesome people whose ideas are not similar enough to their own.

ALFRED FOURNIER
"Simulation of Sexual Attacks on Young Children"

Fournier's paper attracted a great deal of attention, being printed twice in the same year. Fournier was considered a formidable medical authority. His citations are evidence of the fact that the attitudes he expressed did not originate with him; they are part of the climate of the time. As he notes, Brouardel, the prestigious professor at the University of Paris Medical School (to whom Freud was deeply indebted), shared them entirely. In his eloquent style Fournier put forth what must have appeared to many people as a reasonable point of view.

Nevertheless, his presentation masks the conservative nature of his ideas. Fournier reverses our ordinary vocabulary; he uses the word "victim" exclusively to refer to the man accused of rape, reserving the word "simulator" for the person bringing the charge. He uses the word "truth" only to refer to his unmasking of the child (an activity eagerly engaged in by most of the authors cited in this anthology). He confesses that as a physician his only duty is to treat the child brought to his attention, but as a citizen he has a greater duty to expose the truth and save the innocence of the man accused. This is Fournier's concern throughout the article. Just as Fournier automatically assumes a girl who makes such an accusation is guilty, so does he believe that a man who is so accused is innocent. Several times Fournier notes that when a man is so accused, the man "energetically denies it," as if the denial itself were proof of innocence. Fournier implies that a man justly accused would acknowledge his guilt. In fact, to this day, it is extremely rare for a man to admit his guilt in such cases, even when the proof is overwhelming. What leads Fournier to this remarkable and consistent inversion of the truth? His faith that an "impeccable background" would make such an act impossible. Fournier gives the case of "an excellent and perfectly honest man, head of a family, justly honored and absolutely incapable (I will gladly vouch for it) of any dishonorable act," for whom "all the evidence, both material and moral, spoke in his favor." In short, the man was rich and well connected. As for the little girl whom he is accused of raping, Fournier tells us: "The family of the child was publicly disdained for its deplorable lineage." In short, the girl was poor. For Fournier, these facts are sufficient to decide the "truth," in this case that the girl was inventing the story. What leads children to make these false allegations? Fournier says that they do it for money and for vengeance (in all of Fournier's examples, the adult who profits is a woman). But in a footnote his explanation goes much further. He cites his friend Brouardel, who told him that "girls accuse their own fathers of fantasied sexual abuse . . . in order to achieve their liberty so that they can give themselves over to debauchery." The implication of this is that if children accuse an adult of sexual abuse, it is really only because they themselves yearn for it. No proof is given, not even so-called clinical evidence. In fact, if we look at the cases cited by Fournier from his own medical practice, there is not a single one which supports, even in his own telling, the claims he makes. Fournier bemoans the fact that "the honor of a man could be at the mercy of a child's precocious perversions." The evidence of these "precocious perversions" is masturbation, which Fournier believes to be responsible for most of the genital inflammatory symptoms not caused by an avaricious mother.

Fournier's prejudices are not museum pieces. The debate is very much alive today. Fournier speaks of "hysterical" women, and with a slight shift, from adjective to noun, the debate is entirely current: a great deal has been appearing in the press in the last months about the public (read "female") "hysteria" over child abuse. The word has become a common insult. Recently, male society seems to have found a new method of punishing women who tell the truth about sexual abuse: judges are awarding custody to men accused of the sexual abuse of their children, on the grounds that a woman who could make such an accusation (even when there is medical evidence) is engaged in a Salem-like witch hunt, and does not deserve her children. *

In Fournier's article, proof is nowhere advanced that cases of false allegation are common. The prejudice underlying the assumption is therefore patently obvious. The modern literature has not supplied that proof either. The importance of Fournier's article, quite apart from the influence it undoubtedly had on medical opinion in the nineteenth century (sending shock waves down to our time through the mediation of Sigmund Freud), is that it enables us to see clearly the reality underlying these attitudes: prejudice against women and hatred

---

* See the excellent impassioned article by Louise Armstrong and the cases she cites in her article "Challenging the Courts: Mothers and Children Seek Sanctuary," in *Sojourner: The Women's Forum*, Vol. 13, Number 7 (March 1988), pp. 10–11.

of their sexuality. It demonstrates the elevation of a prejudice into a scientific method of evaluation, a theme that runs through almost all the articles in this collection.

GUSTAV BRAUN
"The Amputation of the Clitoris and the Labia Minora: A Contribution to the Treatment of Vaginismus"

We have seen, from the preceding articles, that what men thought about women was hardly ever confined to the realm of pure thought: it spilled over, very quickly, into action. Fournier acted indirectly on the girls who accused men, by having their "stories" invalidated and dismissed in court; Motet acted more directly by confining those whose imaginations he did not approve of to insane asylums; Zambaco acted directly upon the sexual organs of the children whose imagination she found too lurid. But Gustav Braun, following in the tradition of the English surgeon, I. Baker Brown,* went further still, and acted not only directly but also irreversibly on the sexual organs of his patients. It was the beginning of a long tradition of male doctors operating on organs exclusive to women, their genitals, their breasts, and their reproductive organs.

For Braun, physical pathology in the female genitalia is caused by an overactive sexual sensibility. As he put it: "Under the influence of a salacious imagination, which is excited by obscene conversations or by reading poorly selected novels,

---

* See his *On the Curability of Certain Forms of Insanity, Epilepsy, Catalepsy and Hysteria in Females* (London: Robert Hardwicke, 1866), which was the first textbook to describe clitoridectomies as a means of curing "hysteria" in women. See, too, G. J. Barker-Benfield, *The Horrors of the Half-Known Life: Male Attitudes Toward Women and Sexuality in Nineteenth Century America* (New York: Harper and Row, 1976). Finally, the article on Brown by Elaine Showalter, "Victorian Women and Insanity," in Andrew Scull, ed., *Madhouses, Mad-Doctors, and Madmen: The Social History of Psychiatry in the Victorian Era* (Philadelphia: University of Pennsylvania Press, 1981), pp. 313–39, is well worth reading.

the uterus develops a hyperexcitability leading to masturbation and its dire consequences."

The term "vaginismus" has by no means disappeared from medicine. The latest edition of *Dorland's Medical Dictionary* defines it thus: "painful spasm of the vagina due to local hyperesthesia"; and even speaks of "mental vaginismus," which is defined as "extreme aversion to coitus on the part of a woman attended with contractions of the muscles when the act is attempted." For Braun the "hyperesthesia" was concrete, for he speaks of the "hypertrophy of the clitoris." What he means by this becomes clear when he presents his patient. In his account of her we note something that seems to occur frequently in these case histories: whatever strikes Braun as unusual or unattractive or threatening is taken as a sign of degeneracy. Often it is the eyes (or "the look in the eyes") but usually it is the appearance of the entire genital region. Nature is considered to have run rampant there. So Braun writes that his patient's "eyes shine in a strange way; breasts well developed; much hair in her abdominal region with the inner thighs especially thickly covered." We remember that Zambaco, too, was impressed with "the unnatural development of the thighs" in little X. This morbid curiosity about secondary sexual characteristics had disastrous results.

Braun continues his investigations: "The clitoris itself could easily be seen beneath the clitoral hood. When lightly touched it became erect and took on the appearance of a member over one inch long, firm and of the thickness of a raven's feather, protruding like a small male penis, palpable and visible." There is no doubt that Braun first masturbated the patient and then used her normal physiological response as proof of her degeneracy and the need for surgery: "The vaginal opening was somewhat tight, and as soon as I touched it, she experienced constrictive spasms of the constricter cunni and surrounding sphincters, her eyes began to roll and her breathing became rapid." We learn from an astonishing remark that the examination was carried out in front of an audience of physicians, who all observed the rape of this woman and found it amusing: "During the entire procedure her pelvis moved convulsively in such a manner that the audience of physicians present during the examination found themselves involuntarily seized by a desire to laugh." What made them laugh? Embarrassment at their participation in such an abuse?

Once Braun had established that the woman had sexual sensations and masturbated, his energy was devoted to stopping both: "My most urgent concern was to prevent the patient from touching her outer genitalia as had been her custom. In order to achieve this end, on November 16, 1864, a good part of the labia minora and the foreskin of the clitoris was cauterized with a cauterizing instrument." But this did not suffice, for her clitoris and labia minora were too far "hypertrophied"; that is, they were too big for Braun's liking: "The patient from puberty on steadily suffered from significant genital excitement, most likely as a result of significant hypertrophy of the clitoris and the labia minora." The only solution was surgery: "In view of the fact that no benefit could be expected from drug therapy, the amputation of the clitoris and the major portions of the labia minora was proposed to the patient as the only possible cure." Braun goes so far as to claim that the surgery was made difficult because of the "extreme sensibility of the clitoris," such that "the patient suddenly arched her entire pelvis almost a foot above the surface and in spite of the deep chloroform-induced anesthesia instantly rocked her pelvis with forward and backward motions." Her supposed sexual arousal during the operation only confirmed for Braun the necessity of the operation.

Many readers will wonder, after reading this article, to what extent fantasy played a role in the minds of the physicians. No doubt, it was considerable. But the important point is to realize that these physicians were mandated by society to carry their fantasies into direct action. Braun and his colleagues were not merely speculating, they were operating. Once again, I must stress that this article was no aberration. It was cited by Hermann Rohleder in his influential book *Die Masturbation* (Berlin: Fischer, 1899), p. 300, and by Ludwig Fleischmann in the first article ever written about masturbation in infants, "Ueber Onanie und Masturbation bei Säuglingen" (*Wiener medizinische Presse*, 19, 1898), p. 50. Fleischmann writes there: "But for infants still at the breasts, one will hardly ever find it necessary to use these surgical methods. Rather one can try cauterizing the labia or the entrance to the vagina."

JAMES ISRAEL
"Contribution to a Discussion of the Value of Castration in Hysterical Women"
ALFRED HEGAR
"On the Sham Castration Performed by Dr. Israel"

These articles must be read in the context of ovariotomy. For, after the medical profession (temporarily) gave up the direct assault on the clitoris that we saw illustrated in Braun's article, they discovered another "cure" for hysteria, one that was more radical and far more dangerous: castration; that is, the removal of healthy ovaries. Bringing about an artificial menopause was thought to have enormous benefits for female sexuality: it caused it to disappear.

The man who performed the first ovariotomy was Alfred Hegar, professor of gynecology at the University of Freiburg. An enormous literature grew up around this operation, which was beset with controversy from the beginning. James Israel was one doctor who dared to suggest that castration might not be a good idea, although he is as guilty as Hegar and others of violating medical ethics and of a misogynistic approach to sexuality. The twenty-three-year-old woman who came to see Israel had been told by one gynecologist after another (eight in all) that she should have herself castrated at Hegar's clinic. Her symptoms included vomiting, abdominal pains, and heart palpitations. She finally consulted Israel, who agreed to remove her ovaries: "On December 31, 1879, I operated, with chloroform anesthesia and every antiseptic precaution." The woman seemed to be cured. However, the operation was a charade: "Now, gentlemen, this would no doubt be a beautiful cure of severe hysteria through extirpation of both ovaries, indeed, had I only performed such surgery. But my operative procedure differed from Hegar's and Battey's in this fundamental way: besides a simple skin incision under anesthesia, I did nothing further to the patient." It was a "sham castration—theater—performed to prove a point. It remains one of the most elaborate "placebo" experiments in medical history.

The woman, of course, was not informed at any time of what had been done to her. She was presented to a gathering of physicians in order to keep up the pretense: "I brought the patient along solely because I promised her that I would introduce her to the medical society as a particularly interesting and remarkable case of successful castration . . . She was very enthusiastic at this thought, and I had to keep my promise in order to keep up the myth of the successful ovariotomy." (Presumably she was out of the room when Israel made this comment.) Clearly, Israel had little concern for the interests of the patient: he was conducting a personal vendetta against Hegar, and perhaps genuinely felt that castration was a medically dangerous operation. After all, many patients had died from it. The case immediately became something of a *cause célèbre* in Berlin, and was written about in several newspapers.

Evidently the woman eventually discovered that she had not truly been castrated, no doubt as a result of reading the newspapers, and she soon presented herself at Hegar's clinic for castration. Hegar claimed that the patient was not cured of her main symptom, vomiting. Moreover, he disagreed with Israel that she was a hysteric; i.e., that her illness was psychosomatic. According to Hegar, she was "suffering from a reflex neurosis that has its source, I believe, in her sexual organs . . . she is suffering from a serious illness of her sexual organs." We recall that Wilhelm Fliess, Freud's friend and collaborator, claimed that Emma Eckstein was suffering from a nasal reflex neurosis, which caused dysmenorrhea. Hegar believed that, given the serious nature of the illness (nowhere clearly defined), only a genuine castration would help: "The indications for an operation are doubtlessly present." But Hegar refused to operate even though he agreed on medical grounds that she required surgery, because the case had been too widely publicized and the climate was therefore not right for success: "Furthermore the patient could die from the operation . . . the operation is justified in spite of this risk."* Hegar was convinced that he was depriving the patient of her only hope of living a normal life, but he insisted that he would not operate. He even managed to blame the victim: "In addition there is another unpleasant fact to consider. The public has learned that someone was cured by a sham castration, and then hears that this was a deception and that the patient continues to vomit. Now they are told that a real castration put an end to the vomiting. In view of the proven untrustworthiness of the patient, will the public now assume that this is true?" In other words, Hegar is damned if he does and damned if he doesn't: if he operates, either she dies, for which he will be blamed, or she is cured, in which case no one will believe

---

* Several of Hegar's first patients died undergoing the operation. For further bibliographical information, see Dr. Medicinalrath Kroemer, "Beitrag zur Castrationsfrage," in *Allgemeine Zeitschrift für Psychiatrie*, 52 (1896), pp. 1–74, which surveys over 220 articles dealing with the castration of women by gynecologists and psychiatrists.

her. Hegar will not compromise his medical integrity merely to save this one poor soul. Let her suffer, he seems to be saying. If only all the other women had managed to incite Hegar's wrath before he operated! Obviously, Hegar and his colleagues were far less happy to operate in the clear light of day than they were under the protection of obscurity.

BARON ALFRED FREIHERR
VON SCHRENCK-NOTZING
"The Alleged Sexual Abuse by Dr. K.
of a Child under Hypnosis"

Schrenck-Notzing was one of the nineteenth century's best-known medical authorities on the use of hypnosis.* His article is an example of the damaging uses to which the theories about childhood mendacity that we read about in the articles by Motet and Fournier were put. The article consists primarily of his "expert opinion" on whether a thirteen-year-old girl was fabricating her accusation of sexual abuse. The accused physician sent a letter to Schrenck-Notzing with his version of the story. Here is a summary of that version in his own words:

I took the handle of my shaving brush, which was made of wood and bore a faint resemblance to a rubber *dietzel* [pacifier] . . . and I stuck this wooden handle into the mouth of my patient and suggested to her that it was a *dietzel* and that she should pull [*ziehen*] on it and suck [*saugen*] on it . . . The fact that the term *dietzel* here in Munich is slang for the male member was totally unknown to me at the time I hypnotized my patient . . . I felt the urge to empty my bladder, and therefore went to my chamber pot, which was in

---

* See Frank Sulloway, *Freud, Biologist of the Mind* (New York: Basic Books, 1979), pp. 286–87. Freud had a reprint of Schrenck-Notzing's paper in his private library (see the *Hinterberger Catalogue*, 4, No. 696).

my night table a few steps away from the couch, and urinated . . .
When shortly thereafter I returned to Magdalene S., she still had
the handle of my shaving brush in her mouth. I took it into my
hand, threw the towel that had been over her onto my bed and
placed some salt on her tongue, suggesting to her that it was sugar,
and that she should swallow it since it was very sweet.

This is an extraordinary account, by any standards. It is entirely
implausible and sounds like what it is: a description of fellatio.
(*Ziehen*, by the way, in German slang, means to masturbate,
and *saugen* is the common word for fellatio.) What the doctor
called urinating in his chamber pot was probably actually ejaculation in the child's mouth, and the salty taste of ejaculate
was explained as the taste of salt on her tongue (though perhaps
he actually urinated in her mouth). Surely Dr. K. could have
come up with a better lie than this! It is a situation typical of
male pornography: the man is able to do what he wants under
the guise of a medical procedure.

When Dr. K's attorney sought an expert opinion from
Schrenck-Notzing, he admitted that Dr. K. had been accused
of sexually assaulting patients three times previously. Of one
case, he writes: "Dr. K. is accused of lifting the little girl's
skirt, and of then placing her on his knee and rocking her back
and forth in such a fashion that his knee touched the exposed
genitalia of the child." But this case can be dismissed: "Your
expert opinion should probably not consider the accusations
of N., since they are the result of an unsuccessful attempt at
hypnotism and in my opinion they can be explained by the
fact that N. was under the influence of what she had just heard
had happened to S. This influenced her inflamed fantasy."
We can assume that this reasoning appealed to Schrenck-
Notzing because he used it himself. (It is interesting to note
how many shared prejudices are repeated in these articles under the guise of independent observations.)

When he saw Magdalene S., however, Schrenck-Notzing was immediately suspicious: "Neither in her manner of speaking nor in her entire being was there anything the least bit attractive." Of course, Dr. K. was not accused of having been attracted to her, only of having abused her. Had she been attractive in Schrenck-Notzing's eyes, she would have been blamed for being seductive.

Schrenck-Notzing decided to rehypnotize the girl, though if she was telling the truth (which is something he was there to determine, not to have decided in advance), this repetition of a traumatic event would prove unbearable to her. It did. The girl was "enraged and began hitting out with both her hands and feet." Schrenck-Notzing calls in the father, who threatens and beats her, but to no avail:

This scene lasted more than twenty minutes and gave me the impression that this willful and stubborn child had obviously often had her own way and possibly possessed a certain moral defect of the kind that is so often found in hysterical, neurotic children with a tendency to lie and to simulate.

The case has already been decided against the child, as it is against any other child, well in advance of anyone's hearing the evidence. Nothing the child does or says makes the slightest difference. Just as Magdalene S. was judged guilty long before she came into the room, so was Dr. K. judged innocent before Schrenck-Notzing heard his account. He was, after all, a medical doctor, a colleague. Schrenck-Notzing notes quite openly that, for the case to be judged, "the personality of the physician is particularly important in this respect." This is followed by the usual cliché: "Dr. K. is a man who enjoys the complete confidence of his superiors and has never been remiss in his duties." He then proceeds with his judgment: "It would be psychologically totally incomprehensible for this sexually nor-

mal and professionally trustworthy physician to bring himself
to engage in such a disgusting act which from the point of
view of sexual satisfaction would be completely pointless, especially with an unkempt, retarded, physically unattractive,
limping child!" "Psychologically incomprehensible," perhaps,
but true. According to Schrenck-Notzing, the child halluci-
nated and "transformed" harmless everyday events into sexual
acts. But the real act of transformation was performed by
Schrenck-Notzing, when he transformed a callous sexual assault into the fantasy of the child. Everything that Schrenck-
Notzing claims the child transformed was simply part of the
attempt by Dr. K. to hide and rationalize what he was doing.
The child perceived it correctly. For this correct perception
she was attacked and punished. We can only imagine what
would happen to such a child in later life. It would not be
surprising that, if she insisted on her perceptions, she would
be diagnosed as paranoid schizophrenic and locked away
indefinitely.

CONCLUSION

A few years ago, the majority of the population would have
dismissed the possibility of child abuse. When Florence Rush
and Louise Armstrong first spoke of it in the seventies, their
works were largely ignored (except by the feminist press), certainly by professional journals. Today a book like John Crewd-
son's *By Silence Betrayed: Sexual Abuse of Children in America*
(Boston: Little, Brown & Co., 1988) is prominently and positively reviewed on the front page of *The New York Times Book
Review*.

I have been startled to see how much sympathy I receive
from audiences when I talk about abuse of power in psychotherapy, the theme of my latest book, *Against Therapy: Emotional Tyranny and the Myth of Psychological Healing* (New

York: Atheneum, 1988), whereas just a few years ago when I tentatively broached this topic in lectures I was practically stoned. We are, I believe, as a society, gradually becoming more sophisticated in our willingness to recognize and acknowledge the reality and the extent of atrocities in our world.

At the same time, such progressive steps seem almost inevitably accompanied by a (temporary?) backlash. I can think of no better example than the recent article in *New York* by Ellen Hopkins, "Fathers on Trial" (January 11, 1988), pp. 42–49, the theme of which is best captured by the subtitle: "Trumped-up Charges of Child Abuse is Divorce's Ugly New Weapon."

We should, I think, be wary of attempts to substitute interpretations for historical facts. The nine articles that Marianne Loring and I translated for this volume *exist*. They were accepted for publication by standard, indeed, prestigious medical journals. These facts are indisputable. What has been disputed, by a number of critics of my book, is that these articles represent anything other than a fringe, minority view. Without actually saying so, these critics have implied that the articles in my book were part of a nineteenth-century debate, and represent but one side. In fact, these articles were *not* part of a debate. There *were* no published articles giving voice to the other side. The other side, women's suffering, went unrecognized by these official professional journals. This is not my interpretation. I say this because I spent a good deal of time reading through the primary literature; namely, the medical journals in French and German. The opposing literature was conspicuous by its absence. It was simply not there (with very few exceptions, which can be found in my annotated bibliography).

As for the selection of the articles themselves, I chose what I regarded to be the most interesting, even if their interest derives from the clarity of their negative views about women and children. But I cannot stress often enough that these articles and the views they express are *typical* and were acceptable to the vast majority of the medical authorities in the nineteenth century. This is what gives them their value today, and that is why I have gone to the trouble of translating them. Reading these primary texts tells us more than any amount of interpretation about what professional men in France and Germany thought of the sexuality of their female patients. We might not all draw the same conclusions, but we ignore the historical precedents to current-day practices in psychiatry at our peril.

I sent a copy of *A Dark Science* to Tim Beneke, a friend who has written extensively about men and sexism, and received this thoughtful reply.

Dear Jeff,

Thanks for a terrifying but valuable book. What I find perhaps most terrifying about these men (Jasinski excluded) is their prodigious, fastidious powers of observation, their scrutiny in the service of rationalization, their evident intelligence, all coupled with a pervasive blindness to the reality of women's experience. How is it possible for these men to look so closely and see so little?

It seems to me that in these articles science has gone mad. These doctors observe, annotate, quantify, and inspect; they constitute women and children as objects to be understood objectively; they take pride in their scientific coldbloodedness; but they almost never offer the patients they "treat" (or the children they interrogate) something they desperately need: simple human understanding. It is a little like trying to understand grief by examining tears under a microscope. Their misplaced need to be scientific causes (enables?) them to distance themselves so that they miss everything. Or is that precisely the point? Perhaps these men are so full of anxieties about women that they use science as a means of dominating women without having to empathize with them.

Science in the late nineteenth century, and especially medicine, which had to sell itself to a skeptical public, faced a crisis of legitimation. Doctors were in a bind: they felt a pressure to be scientific and authoritative about things of which they knew very little and which, in the case of women, children, and the "mad," caused them immense anxiety. So they masked their ignorance behind a defensive scientific façade that no doubt inhibited their empathy. For these men to have been "enlightened scientists" instead of "dark scientists" would have required them to acknowledge how little they understood about the suffering they ostensibly treated. But that would have undermined their power and hurt them economically.

As you know, I spent a great deal of time interviewing men on the subject of rape for my book *Men on Rape*, and found many men willing to justify rape as a kind of revenge against women's sexual capacity to arouse. In *A Dark Science* we see some doctors attack women's genitals and reproductive organs under the guise of medical treatment; others use their analytical powers to find ways to disbelieve children who have been sexually assaulted. I sense in these men the same resentment against women's capacity to arouse that I found in the men I interviewed.

Another point. There are many kinds of sexism, but it seems useful here to distinguish two: the sexism that views women as mere bodies to be used for pleasure and disregards or narrowly stereotypes women's experience; and the sexism that claims a superior knowledge of women's psyches and insidiously seeks to dominate women through defining and interpreting their subjectivity. The first kind of sexism, which pervades pornography, views women as objects to be degraded; the second views women as subjects, usually children, whose subjectivity is to be understood and articulated by male authority. In *A Dark Science* we see psychiatry claiming a superior knowledge of women's psyches and using that "knowledge" to justify medical abuse. It is the kind of superficially benign, sometimes avuncular sexism that has come to pervade psychiatry in the twentieth century. *A Dark Science* shows psychiatry just beginning to oppress women by telling them who they are.

How much have things really changed? Some, but not nearly

enough. In 1981, with my tape recorder running, a nationally prominent psychiatrist thought nothing of telling me an egregiously sexist
rape joke that I included in my book. A few years later I saw him
offering his psychiatric expertise on national television.

Well, as you can see, I have more questions than answers, which
I suppose points to the immense amount of work to be done.

Sincerely,

Tim Beneke

I maintain that we cannot understand modern psychiatric
attitudes toward female patients unless we know the literature
translated in these pages. Until psychiatry has firmly and
openly and publicly renounced the reprehensible, indeed mur-
derous, past of its own science, psychiatrists cannot be surprised
that many women will continue to view them, quite rightly
in my opinion, as the unrepentant heirs to a very dark science
indeed.

Notes

1. Below is a complete list of the journals I read through (an asterisk indicates that material from it was used in this book):

FRENCH JOURNALS
Bulletin de l'académie de médecine
Annales de gynécologie
Annales médico-psychologiques
L'Encéphale: journal des maladies mentales
Nouvelle iconographique de la salpêtrière
Le progrés médical
Revue neurologique
Revue médico-chirurgicale des maladies des femmes
L'Union médicale
**Annales d'hygiène publique et de médecine légale*
GERMAN JOURNALS
Allgemeine Zeitschrift für Psychiatrie
Archiv für Kinderheilkunde
Archiv für Psychiatrie und Nervenkrankheiten
**Berliner klinische Wochenschrift*
Correspondenzblatt für schweizer Ärzte
Deutsche medicinische Wochenschrift
**Neurologisches Centralblatt*
Deutsche Zeitschrift für Nervenheilkunde
Jahrbuch für Kinderheilkunde
Jahrbücher für Psychiatrie

> Monatsschrift für Psychiatrie und Neurologie
> Münchener medizinische Wochenschrift
> Archiv für Psychologie
> Prager medizinische Wochenschrift
> Sammlung klinischer Vorträge (Gynäkologie)
> Schmidts Jahrbücher der gesammten Medicin
> Vierteljahrschrift für gerichtliche Medicin
> Wiener klinische Rundschau
> Wiener medicinische Presse
> *Wiener medicinische Wochenschrift
> Zeitschrift für Geburtshülfe und Gynäkologie
> Centralblatt für Gynäkologie
> *Zeitschrift für Hypnotismus
> Internationale klinische Rundschau

2. See the chapter "Feminism and Hysteria: The Daughter's Disease" in Elaine Showalter's *The Female Malady: Women, Madness and English Culture, 1830–1980* (New York: Pantheon Books, 1985).

3. I believe the first published feminist interpretation of the sexual abuse of children came from Florence Rush's "The Sexual Abuse of Children: A Feminist Point of View," which was presented at the New York Radical Feminist Conference on Rape in April 1971, and subsequently published in Noreen Connell and Cassandra Wilson's *Rape: The First Source-book for Women* (New York: New American Library, 1974). See Rush's article "The Freudian Cover-up" in *Chrysalis* (1977), 1, 31–45, and her important book *The Best Kept Secret: Sexual Abuse of Children* (New York: McGraw-Hill, 1980). Significant, too, in changing people's attitudes were the article by J. Herman and L. Hirschman, "Father-Daughter Incest," in *Signs* (1977), 2: 1–22, and the valuable book by Judith Herman, *Father-Daughter Incest* (Cambridge: Harvard University Press, 1981). Valuable, too, is the research by David Finkelhor in *Sexually Victimized Children* (New York: The Free Press, 1979) and, more recently, in *Child Sexual Abuse: New Theory and Research* (New York: The Free Press, 1984). The work of Diana E. H. Russell has also been very influential. See her collection of essays, *Sexual Exploitation: Rape, Child Sexual Abuse, and Workplace Harassment* (Beverly Hills: Sage Publications, 1984). The most complete and authoritative work on incest is her book *The Secret Trauma: Incest in the Lives of Girls and Women* (New York: Basic Books, 1986).

4. I believe the term and the concept were given their first wide publicity in a brilliant book called *Blaming the Victim* by William Ryan (New York: Vintage Books, 1972, rev. 1976).

5. Hannah Arendt, *Eichmann in Jerusalem: A Report on the Banality of Evil* (New York: Viking Press, 1965), p. 125.

6. Revised and Definitive Edition (New York: Holmes & Meier, 1985), vol. 2, p. 216.

7. *Krakauer Zeitung*, December 4, 1940, "Generalgouvernement" page. I was fortunate to find a complete set of this newspaper in the Hoover Institution in Stanford, where I was able to see the "article" that Hilberg used. Here is a literal translation of the passage: "Warsaw's Jews are no longer permitted to buy up scarce goods with an oily smile and then drive the prices to dizzying heights, or to find their crooked way to the black market and swindle the 'goyim'—in particular the good-natured and trusting poor Polish farmers. Now they are trying their luck with their own race, only to quickly discover that there is not much to be had there. The best business, though, seems to be in armbands, a trade taken up some time ago by street merchants grasping at the opportunity. Of course the armbands are available in two varieties: a simple cloth one with the star of David sewn on, or the more durable ones made of celluloid for the upper classes, washable like a rubber collar . . . That life for the Jews is still 'sweet' [*süss*] is shown by the greasy [*schmierig*], unshaven, grinning peddler who sells candied fruit with unwashed fingers." I am completely at a loss to explain how Hilberg could bring himself to cite, presumably as an "objective" observation, this ugly anti-Semitic cartoon. For a further discussion on this issue, see my "Hilberg's Holocaust," *Midstream*, 32 (1986), 51–55.

8. Recent examples of this trend, even among liberal and left-leaning people, are to be found in the September 1985 issue of *The Progressive*, where the cover story is entitled "Invasion of the Child Savers," and the spring 1985 issue of *Women and Revolution*, with a cover article entitled "Children, Sex, State Witchhunters: The Uses of Abuse." In *The New York Times* of Sunday, January 26, 1984, Robert Lindsey, in an article entitled "Boy's Responses at Sex Abuse Trial Underscore Legal Conflict," quotes the defense in the McMartin case as asserting that "every psychological expert will tell you that children fantasize about sex."

9. Highly respected research on sexual abuse of girls has been published by Diana E. H. Russell in "The Incidence and Prevalence of Intrafamilial and Extrafamilial Sexual Abuse of Female Children," in *Child Abuse and Neglect* (1983), 7: 133–46. Her conclusion (p. 145) is that "over one-quarter of the population of female children have experienced sexual abuse before the age of 14, and well over one-third have had such an experience by the age of 18 years." The *Los Angeles Times* of August 26, 1985, on the front page, reported the results of a survey of 2,627 adults, "which is thought to be the first comprehensive study of the extent of child sexual abuse in the United States. The survey, supervised by *Times* poll director I. A. Lewis, found that at least 22 percent of Americans had been molested as children." It is clear that the most recent trend is to find a greater amount of abuse than was imagined earlier. Thus Gail Elizabeth Wyatt at the Neuropsychiatric Institute in Los Angeles, in her article "The Sexual Abuse of Afro-American and White-American Women in Childhood," published in *Child Abuse and Neglect* (1985), 9: 507–19, found that 62 percent of 248 women reported at least one incident of sexual abuse prior to age eighteen. This is the highest percentage yet, as revealed in one of the most rigorous studies undertaken.

10. Third edition (Washington, D.C.: American Psychiatric Association, 1980), No. 301.50, p. 313.

11. See Judith Lewis Herman, "Masochism Unmasked," in *The Women's Review of Books* (February 1986).

12. See John Putnam Demos, *Entertaining Satan: Witchcraft and the Culture of Early New England* (New York: Oxford University Press, 1982). From his appendix, which lists known witchcraft cases in seventeenth-century New England (pp. 401–9), we can ascertain that only two men were executed for witchcraft during that entire century. This list excludes Salem. For a list of all the known witchcraft cases in the Salem trials, see Paul Boyer and Stephen Nissenbaum, eds., *Salem Village Witchcraft: A Documentary Record of Local Conflict in Colonial New England* (Belmont, California: Wadsworth Publishing Co., 1972). See, too, Paul Boyer and Stephen Nissenbaum, *Salem Possessed: The Social Origins of Witchcraft* (Cambridge: Harvard University Press, 1974), and Chadwick Hansen, *Witchcraft at Salem* (New York: George Braziller, 1969).

13. One of the best books on witchcraft was first published in 1843 by Wilhelm Gottlieb Soldan: *Geschichte der Hexenprozesse aus den Quellen dargestellt*, 2nd ed., by Heinrich Heppe (Stuttgart, 1880); 3rd ed., by Max Bauer (Munich: G. Mueller, 1912). Also see Joseph Hansen, *Zauberwahn, Inquisition, und Hexenprozess im Mittelalter und die Enstehung der grossen Hexenverfolgung* (Munich: R. Oldenbourg Verlag, 1900; rpt., 1964). See especially his sensible comments on women (pp. 481 ff.). See, too, his *Quellen und Untersuchungen zur Geschichte des Hexenwahns und der Hexenverfolgung im Mittelalter* (Bonn: C. Georgi, 1901; rpt., Hildesheim, 1963). The prejudice against women can be seen in such modern works as the very influential book by H. R. Trevor-Roper, *The European Witch-Craze of the Sixteenth and Seventeenth Centuries* (New York: Harper, 1956), where he writes: "So the Hammerers of Witches built up their systematic mythology of Satan's kingdom and Satan's accomplices out of the mental rubbish of peasant credulity and feminine hysteria" (p. 116).

14. The point of view that the women were socially marginal is expressed in H. Erik Midelfort's *Witch Hunting in Southwestern Germany, 1562–1684: The Social and Intellectual Foundations* (Palo Alto: Stanford University Press, 1972). Such views strike me as continuing in the tradition of Nicola Rémy, Attorney General of Lorraine, who, boasting on the title page of his influential book *The Demonolatreiae* (1595) that he had condemned 900 witches in ten years, wrote: "It is one of the clearest and surest proofs against those who have been accused of witchcraft, if it is found that they come of parents who have previously been convicted of that crime." The view that children inherited the degenerative disease of witchcraft from their mothers was not uncommon (cf. the nineteenth- and twentieth-century view that "mental illness" is inherited). Soldan (vol. 2, p. 26) noted that Rémy, after many years as the highest judge of the land, and after having sentenced countless witches to their death, had one regret, the case of a seven-year-old. He had allowed himself to be misled by the compassion of his colleagues, and instead of sentencing the child to death by burning

(as he had in so many other cases), he had her stripped of all her clothes and dragged to the same plaza where both her parents had been burned to death, there to be forced to run around it three times as she was whipped. He wrote: "I never thought that the law was fully satisfied by such methods." Eleven-year-old Sybille Lutz of Würzburg was accused in 1628 of *coitus cum demone* and was subsequently put to death. The real "devil" was the man who sexually abused her, for which she had to pay with her life.

15. New York: The Free Press, 1965, p. 164.

16. 28 (1983), 34–39.

17. Vol. 13 (1887), pp. 119–20.

18. Reported in *The Boston Globe*, February 11, 1982, under the headline FOR THREE GIRLS, JUSTICE TAKES A HOLIDAY.

19. "Confusion of Tongues Between Adults and the Child: The Language of Tenderness and the Language of Sexual Passion." Translated by J. Masson and Marianne Loring. Appears as Appendix C of *The Assault on Truth* (New York: Farrar, Straus and Giroux, 1984), pp. 283–95.

20. It should be mentioned that there is also, thanks to feminists and the women's movement, a growing body of writings about the truthfulness and trustworthiness of children as witnesses. Thus, an entire issue of the *Journal of Social Issues* (40, 1984) devoted to that subject discussed recent experiments demonstrating just how reliable children can be. See, for example, the work of Gail S. Goodman at the University of Denver, particularly her paper "Child Sexual Assault: Children's Memory and the Law" (written with Vicki S. Helgeson), to appear in J. Bulkley, ed., *Papers from a National Policy Conference on Child Sexual Abuse* (Washington, D.C.: American Bar Association).

21. San Francisco: Glide Publications, 1976.

22. New York: Springer Verlag, 1983.

23. New York: Springer Verlag, 1979.

24. "The Return of Lobotomy and Psychosurgery" (*Congressional Record*, February 24, 1972, E1602–12); reprinted in *Quality of Health Care: Human Experimentation*, Hearings before Senator Edward Kennedy's Subcommittee on Health, U.S. Senate (Washington, D.C.: U.S. Govt. Printing Office, 1973); also in B. Edwards, ed., *Psychiatry and Ethics* (Buffalo, N.Y.: Prometheus Books, 1982, pp. 350–88).

25. March 30, 1972, E3380, "New Information in the Debate over Psychosurgery."

26. "The Return of Lobotomy and Psychosurgery."

27. New York: Times Books, 1975.

28. Vol. 133:4 (April 1976), p. 459.

29. New York: McGraw-Hill, 1978.

30. See *Madness Network News Reader*, eds. Sherry Hirsch et al. (San Francisco: Glide Publications, 1974). An outstanding account of the history of the Psychiatric Inmates Liberation Movement is to be found in a fine book by Lenny Lapon, published in 1986: *Mass Murderers in White Coats: Psychiatric Genocide in Nazi Germany and*

the United States. (It can be obtained from the Psychiatric Genocide Research Institute, P.O. Box 80071, Springfield, MA 01138–0071.)

31. This is reprinted on pages 26 and 27 of an excellent anthology, *The History of Shock Treatment,* edited by Leonard Roy Frank in 1978. (Available from L. Frank, 2300 Webster St., San Francisco, CA 94115.)

32. Pp. 76–77.

33. A. M. Freedman, H. I. Kaplan, and B. J. Sadock, eds., *Comprehensive Textbook of Psychiatry,* 2nd ed. (Baltimore: Williams & Wilkins, 1975), p. 1532.

34. See the sources given above, in note 9. See also the chapter "Sexual Abuse as a Social Problem" in David Finkelhor's *Child Sexual Abuse: New Theory and Research* (New York: The Free Press, 1984), where the statistics are soberly evaluated.

35. C. H. Kempe et al., "The Battered Child Syndrome," *Journal of the American Medical Association,* 181 (1962), 17–24.

36. In *Sexual Assault of Children and Adolescents,* edited by Ann Wolbert Burgess et al. (Lexington, Mass.: Lexington Books, 1978).

37. *American Journal of Orthopsychiatry,* 7 (1937), p. 514. One might suppose that the years have changed her views, but this is not the case. Writing about her career in the book *Explorations in Child Psychiatry,* edited by E. James Anthony (New York: Plenum Books, p. 443) in 1975, she says that "incest was a frequent pattern to which these children were exposed. Fantasized incestuous experiences also presented a challenging problem. It was not always possible to determine if in reality the child had had the sexual relations he claimed with parents or parent surrogates or had fantasized them. Our child patients were for the most part schizophrenics, to whom fantasy comes more readily and is often retold as reality or maybe, in puberty, acted out realistically." Even the syntax of this sentence is confusing.

38. *Comprehensive Textbook of Psychiatry,* edited by Alfred M. Freedman and Harold I. Kaplan (Baltimore: Williams & Wilkins, 1967), p. 986.

39. Op. cit., 1975, p. 1537.

40. This document was cited by Lloyd H. Martin, who had worked in the child sexual-abuse unit of the Los Angeles Police Department, in *Kiddie Cop Watch,* Vol. 1, No. 1 (March 1984), p. 3.

41. Andrea Dworkin and Catharine MacKinnon, the authors of the city of Minneapolis ordinance against pornography, define pornography "as the graphic sexually explicit subordination of women through pictures or words that also includes women dehumanized as sexual objects, things, or commodities, enjoying pain or humiliation or rape, being tied up, cut up, mutilated, bruised, or physically hurt, in postures of sexual submission or servility or display, reduced to body parts, penetrated by objects or animals, or presented in scenarios of degradation, injury, torture, shown as filthy or inferior, bleeding, bruised, or hurt in a context that makes these conditions sexual."

42. In her 1984 Francis Biddle Memorial Lecture, given at Harvard Law School, April 5, 1984, "Pornography, Civil Rights, and Speech," *Harvard Civil Rights Civil Liberties Law Review,* 29 (1985), 1–78.

43. From a speech to the Morality Colloquium, University of Minnesota, February

17, 1983, "Not a Moral Issue," *Yale Law and Policy Review*, 2 (1984), 321–45. Both speeches will appear in print in a collection of MacKinnon's essays to be published by Harvard University Press in 1986.

44. *The Mother Machine: Reproductive Technologies from Artificial Insemination to Artificial Wombs* (New York: Harper & Row, 1985), pp. 308, 317. See also Corea's *The Hidden Malpractice: How American Medicine Mistreats Women* (New York: Harper & Row, 1975; rev. 1985), p. 271: "The unnecessary removal of ovaries (castration) is another danger women face. In a study of gynecological surgery performed between 1947 and 1951 in five hospitals, the investigator found that only 21 percent of the unilateral oophorectomies (removal of one ovary) were justified." The source is an article in *Obstetrics and Gynecology* for February 1953 by A. W. Diddle et al. See also: Ellen Frankfort's *Vaginal Politics* (New York: Quadrangle, 1972).

45. In *The Hidden Face of Eve: Women in the Arab World*, tr. and ed. by Dr. Sherif Hetata (Boston: Beacon Press, 1982). See also: *The Hosken Report: Genital and Sexual Mutilation of Females* by Fran P. Hosken (3rd rev. ed., Lexington, Mass: Women's International Network News, 1982).

46. Vol. 2 (1977–78), 499–509.

47. New York: Random House, 1970, p. 70.

48. In *Sexual Exploitation* (Vol. 155 of the Sage Library of Social Research, Beverly Hills, 1984), p. 225.

49. Op. cit., p. 258.

50. Rev. by James A. Chadbourn (Boston: Little, Brown & Co., 1970), vol. 3a, pp. 735–46.

Bibliography

Adler, Laure. *Secrets d'alcôve: histoire du couple de 1830 à 1930*. Paris: Hachette, 1983.

Adler, Otto. *Die mangelhafte Geschlechtsempfindung des Weibes*, 3rd rev. ed. Berlin: H. Kornfeld, 1919.

Anthony, James E., ed. *Explorations in Child Psychiatry*. New York: Plenum, 1975.

Arendt, Hannah. *Eichmann in Jerusalem: A Report on the Banality of Evil*. New York: Viking, 1965.

Armstrong, Louise. *Kiss Daddy Goodnight*. New York: Hawthorn, 1978.

———. *The Home Front: Notes from the Family War Zone*. New York: McGraw-Hill, 1983. An impassioned statement about child abuse.

Aron, Jean-Paul, ed. *Misérable et glorieuse: la femme du XIXe siècle*. Paris: Fayard, 1980.

Barker-Benfield, G. J. "Sexual Surgery in Late-Nineteenth-Century America." *International Journal of Health Services*, 5 (1975): 280–98.

———. *The Horrors of the Half-Known Life: Male Attitudes Toward Women and Sexuality in Nineteenth Century America*. New York: Harper & Row, 1976. A pioneering work with valuable information on sexual surgery performed in America.

Barry, Kathleen. *Female Sexual Slavery*. Englewood Cliffs: Prentice-Hall, 1979. An early, groundbreaking account.

Bart, Pauline B. and Patricia H. O'Brien. *Stopping Rape: Successful Survival Strategies*. New York: Pergamon, 1986. An excellent, myth-shattering study.

Berze, Josef. "Ueber moralische Defectzustände." *Jahrbücher für Psychiatrie und Neurologie*, 15 (1897): 62–115.

Bleuler, Eugene, ed. *Dulden: Aus der Lebensbeschreibung einer Armen*. Munich:

Ernst Reinhardt, 1899. The life story of one of Bleuler's patients from his asylum, who wrote it down in 1882, when she was twenty-two. It contains one of the rare descriptions in the nineteenth century of a rape in childhood by a relative.

Boileau de Castelnau, P. "Des maladies du sens moral." *Annales médico-psychologiques*, 6 (1860): 348–76, 515–37. Sympathetic case histories of a criminal who helps his victims, and who is also a fascinating impostor.

————. "Misopédie ou lésion de l'amour de la progéniture." *Annales médico-psychologiques*, 7 (1861): 553–68. An early recognition of the often fatal abuse that children suffer at the hands of adults.

Bolande, Robert P. "Ritualistic Surgery—Circumcision and Tonsillectomy." *New England Journal of Medicine*, 280 (1969): 591–95.

Boyer, Paul and Stephen Nissenbaum, eds. *Salem Village Witchcraft: A Documentary Record of Local Conflict in Colonial New England*. Belmont, California: Wadsworth, 1972.

————. *Salem Possessed: The Social Origins of Witchcraft*. Cambridge: Harvard University Press, 1974.

Breggin, Peter Roger. *Electroshock: Its Brain-Disabling Effects*. New York: Springer Verlag, 1979. A brilliant criticism of the use of electroshock in psychiatry.

————. *Psychiatric Drugs: Hazards to the Brain*. New York: Springer Verlag, 1983. A sustained examination of the dangers of psychiatric drugs.

Brown, Isaac Baker. *On the Curability of Certain Forms of Insanity, Epilepsy, Catalepsy and Hysteria in Females*. London: Robert Hardwicke, 1866. The first textbook to describe clitoridectomies as a means of curing hysteria in women.

————. The Obstetrical Society: "Meeting to Consider the Proposition of the Council for the Removal of Mr. I. B. Brown." *British Medical Journal*, 1 (1867): 395–409. A fascinating discussion.

Brownmiller, Susan. *Against Our Will: Men, Women and Rape*. New York: Simon and Schuster, 1975. Landmark analysis of the history of rape as violence, not sex.

Bruns, L. *Die Hysterie im Kindesalter*. Halle am den Saale: Carl Marhold, 1897. An influential text on hysteria in childhood.

Bullough, Vern L. *Sexual Variancy in Society and History*. Chicago: University of Chicago Press, 1976.

———— and Bonnie Bullough. *Sin, Sickness and Sanity: A History of Sexual Attitudes*. New York: New American Library, 1977.

———— and Martha Vogt. "Homosexuality and Its Confusion with the 'Secret Sin' in Pre-Freudian America." *Journal of the History of Medicine and Allied Sciences*, 28 (1973): 143–55.

Burgess, Ann Wolbert et al. *Sexual Assault of Children and Adolescents*. Lexington, Mass.: Lexington Books, 1978.

Carlson, Eric T. and Norman Dain. "The Meaning of Moral Insanity," *Bulletin of the History of Medicine*, 36 (1962): 130–40.

Carmen, Elaine, Patricia Rieker and Trudy Mills. "Victims of Violence and Psychiatric Illness." *American Journal of Psychiatry*, 141 (1984): 378–83. Excellent account of the alarmingly high incidence of sexual and physical violence in the lives of psychiatric patients.

Castel, Robert. L'ordre psychiatrique: l'âge d'or de l'aliénisme. Paris: Minuit, 1976.

Chamberlin, Judi. On Our Own: Patient-Controlled Alternatives to the Mental Health System. New York: McGraw-Hill, 1978. One of the classics of the Psychiatric Inmates Liberation Movement.

Chesler, Phyllis. Women and Madness. New York: Doubleday, 1972. A fine work.

———. Mothers on Trial: The Battle for Children and Custody. New York: McGraw-Hill, 1986. An eye-opening, impassioned book.

Chombart de Lauwe, Marie-José. Un monde autre: l'enfance de ses représentations à son mythe. Paris: Payot, 1971.

Chorover, Stephan L. From Genesis to Genocide: The Meaning of Human Nature and the Power of Behavior Control. Cambridge, Mass.: M.I.T. Press, 1979.

Comfort, Alex. The Anxiety Makers: Some Curious Preoccupations of the Medical Profession. London: Thomas Nelson & Sons, 1967.

Connell, Noreen and Cassandra Wilson. Rape: The First Sourcebook for Women. New York: New American Library, 1974.

Corea, Gena. The Hidden Malpractice: How American Medicine Mistreats Women. New York: Harper & Row, 1975.

———. The Mother Machine: Reproductive Technologies from Artificial Insemination to Artificial Wombs. New York: Harper & Row, 1985.

Delbrück, Anton. Die pathologische Lüge und die psychisch abnormen Schwindler. Stuttgart: Ferdinand Enke, 1891. One of the first books about "pseudologia phantastica"; very influential in the nineteenth century.

Demos, John Putnam. Entertaining Satan: Witchcraft and the Culture of Early New England. New York: Oxford University Press, 1982.

Descuret, Jean Baptiste Félix. La médecine des passions. Liége: J. G. Lardinois, 1851.

Dictionnaire Encyclopédique des Sciences Médicales. A. Dechambre and L. S. Lereboullet, eds. Paris: Masson, 1889.

Dictionnaire des Sciences Médicales. C.L.P. Panckoucke, ed. Paris: Rue Serpente, 1812.

Dobash, R. Emerson and Russell Dobash. Violence Against Wives: A Case Against the Patriarchy. New York: The Free Press, 1979. Convincing, penetrating study.

Dreifus, Claudia, ed. Seizing Our Bodies: The Politics of Women's Health. New York: Random House, 1977.

Duffy, John. "Masturbation and Clitoridectomy: A Nineteenth-Century View." Journal of the American Medical Association, 186 (1963): 246–48.

Duvoisin, M. "Ueber infantile Hysterie." Jahrbuch für Kinderheilkunde, 29 (1889): 286–332.

Dworkin, Andrea. Woman Hating. New York: E. P. Dutton, 1974. A brilliant study.

———. Our Blood: Prophecies and Discourses on Sexual Politics. New York: G. P. Putnam's Sons, 1976. A brilliant analysis of the political meaning of pornography.

————. *Pornography: Men Possessing Women*. New York: G. P. Putnam's Sons, 1979.

Edel, Alexander. "Was kann die Schule gegen die Masturbation der Kinder thun?" *Berliner klinische Wochenschrift*, 32 (1895): 90–91, 628–31.

Ehrenreich, Barbara and Deirdre English. *For Her Own Good: 150 Years of the Experts' Advice to Women*. New York: Anchor Press/Doubleday, 1978.

Ellis, Havelock, "Auto-Erotism: A Psychological Study." *Alienist and Neurologist*, 19 (1898): 260–99. Considered to be one of the most liberal nineteenth-century views of masturbation.

Emminghaus, Hermann. *Die psychischen Störungen des Kindesalters*. Tübingen: H. Laupp, 1887. One of the most widely read books on childhood psychopathology.

Engelhardt, Tristam. "The Disease of Masturbation: Values in the Concept of Disease." *Bulletin of the History of Medicine*, 48 (1974): 234–48.

Erb, Wilhelm. *Akademische Rede zum Geburtsfeste des hochseligen Grossherzogs Karl Friedrich, am. 22. November 1893*. Heidelberg: J. Hürning, 1893.

Fehling, H. "Zehn Castrationen: Ein Beitrag zur Frage nach dem Werthe der Castration." *Archiv für Gynäkologie*, 21 (1883): 441–55.

Féré, Charles. "Notes pour servir a l'histoire de l'hystéro-épilepsie." *Archives de Neurologie*, 2 (1881): 281–309. Proposes the use of an ovarian belt in the prevention of hysterical attacks.

Feshback, Normal Deitch. "Corporal Punishment in the Schools." In George Gerbner, Catherine J. Ross and Edward Zigler, eds., *Child-Abuse: An Agenda for Action*, 204–24. New York: Oxford University Press, 1980.

Finkelhor, David. *Sexually Victimized Children*. New York: The Free Press, 1979.

————. *Child Sexual Abuse: New Theory and Research*. New York: The Free Press, 1984. A very useful series of essays.

————, Richard J. Gelles, Gerald T. Hotaling and Murray A. Straus, eds. *The Dark Side of Families*. Beverly Hills: Sage, 1983.

Fischer-Dückelmann, Anna. *Die Frau als Hausärztin*. Stuttgart: Süddeutsches Verlags-Institut, 1908. Describes, with pictures, the various devices and mechanical shields used to prevent children from touching their genitals.

Fischer-Homberger, Esther. "Hysterie und Misogynie—ein Aspekt der Hysteriegeschichte." *Gesnerus*, 26 (1969): 117–25.

————. *Die traumatische Neurose: vom somatischen zum sozialen Leiden*. Bern: Hans Huber, 1975.

————. *Krankheit Frau: und andere Arbeiten zur Medizingeschichte der Frau*. Bern: Hans Huber, 1979.

Flechsig, Paul. *Meine myelogenetische Hirnlehre*. Berlin: Julius Springer, 1929.

Fleischmann, Ludwig. "Ueber Onanie und Masturbation bei Säuglingen." *Wiener medizinische Presse*, 19 (1878): 8–10, 46–50. Possibly the first article written about masturbation in infants.

Fournier and Bégin. Entry on masturbation in *Dictionnaire des sciences médicales*. Paris: C.L.F. Panckoucke, 1819. Vol. 31: 100–33.

Frank, Leonard. *The History of Shock Treatment*. San Francisco: 2300 Webster St., 1978. An excellent anthology.

Frankfort, Ellen. *Vaginal Politics*. New York: Quadrangle, 1972.

Freedman, Alfred M. and Harold I. Kaplan., eds. *Comprehensive Textbook of Psychiatry*. Baltimore: Williams & Wilkins, 1967.

———, Harold I. Kaplan and B. J. Sadock, eds. *Comprehensive Textbook of Psychiatry*, 2nd ed. Baltimore: Williams & Wilkins, 1975.

Friedberg, John. *Shock Treatment Is Not Good for Your Brain*. San Francisco: Glide, 1976.

Friedman, M. "Ueber Nervosität und Psychosen im Kindesalter." *Münchener medizinische Wochenschrift*, 39 (1892): 359–61, 388–392.

Friedreich, N. "Zur Behandlung der Hysterie." *Archiv für Anatomie und Physiologie und für klinische Medicin*, 90 (1882): 22–242.

Friedrich, William M. and Jerry A. Boriskin. "The Role of the Child in Abuse: A Review of the Literature." *American Journal of Orthopsychiatry*, 46 (1976): 580–90.

Garnier, Paul. *Onanisme seul et à deux. Sous toutes ses formes et leurs conséquences*. Paris: Garnier Frères, 1883. Influential work with bizarre case histories.

Gornick, Vivian and Barbara K. Moran., eds. *Woman in Sexist Society: Studies in Power and Powerlessness*. New York: Basic Books, 1971.

Gotkin, Janet and Paul Gotkin. *Too Much Anger, Too Many Tears: A Personal Triumph over Psychiatry*. New York: Times Books, 1975. A beautiful, moving work.

Graham, Harvey. *Eternal Eve: The History of Gynaecology and Obstetrics*. New York: Doubleday, 1951.

Graux, P. J., H. Rossignol and J. Parigot. "Rapport médico-légal sur l'état mental d'Eugénie-Adélaide Hayez." *Annales médico-psychologiques*, 7 (1861): 569–87. An eighty-two-year-old independent woman philosopher and eccentric, living by herself. An important case.

Griffin, Susan. "The Politics of Rape" (1971). In *Made from This Earth: An Anthology of Writings by Susan Griffin*. New York: Harper & Row, 1982. The first study of rape as a political act.

Haller, John S. and Robin M. Haller. *The Physician and Sexuality in Victorian America*. New York: W. W. Norton, 1974.

Hansen, Chadwick. *Witchcraft at Salem*. New York: George Braziller, 1969.

Hansen, Joseph. *Zauberwahn, Inquisition, und Hexenprozess im Mittelalter und die Entstehung der grossen Hexenverfolgung*. Munich: R. Oldenbourg, 1900.

———. *Quellen und Untersuchungen zur Geschichte des Hexenwahns und der Hexenverfolgung im Mittelalter*. Bonn: C. Georgi, 1901.

Hare, E. H. "Masturbatory Insanity: The History of an Idea." *Journal of Mental Sciences*, 108 (1962): 2–3.

Harrison, Fraser. *The Dark Angel: Aspects of Victorian Sexuality*. New York: Universe Books, 1977. An interesting, Marxist account.

Hartman, Mary S. *Victorian Murderesses.* New York: Schocken, 1977.

Hegar, Alfred. *Die Castration der Frauen: Vom physiologischen und chirurgischen Standpunkte aus.* Leipzig; Breitkopf & Härtel, 1878.

————. *Der Geschlechtstrieb: Eine Social-medicinische Studie.* Stuttgart: Ferdinand Enke, 1894.

————. "Castration als Mittel gegen nervöse und psychische Leiden." *Archiv für Gynäkologie,* 23 (1884): 317–24.

————. *Der Zusammenhang der Geschlechtskrankheiten mit nervösen Leiden und die Castration bei Neurosen.* Stuttgart: Ferdinand Enke, 1885.

———— and R. Kaltenbach. *Die operative Gynäkologie.* Erlangen: Ferdinand Enke, 1874. One of the first German medical textbooks to discuss clitoridectomy.

Heine, Maurice. *Confessions et observations psycho-sexuelles tirées de la littérature médicale.* Paris: Jean Crés, 1936.

Hellerstein, Erna Olafson, Leslie Parker Hume and Karen M. Offen, eds. *Victorian Women: A Documentary Account of Women's Lives in Nineteenth-Century England, France, and the United States.* Palo Alto: Stanford University Press, 1981.

Henoch, D. "Die hysterischen Affektionen bei Kindern." *Wiener medizinische Presse,* 22 (1881): 916–1010. On how to catch children in the "crime of masturbation."

Herman, Judith. *Father-Daughter Incest.* Cambridge: Harvard University Press, 1981. An outstanding work.

————. "Masochism Unmasked." *The Women's Review of Books,* February 1986.

———— and L. Hirschman. "Father-Daughter Incest." *Signs,* 2 (1977) 1–22.

Herz, Maximilian. "Ueber Hysterie bei Kindern." *Wiener medizinische Wochenschrift,* 35 (1885): 1403–.

Hesse, Hermann. *Kindheit und Jugend vor Neunzehnhundert: Briefe und Lebenszeugnisse, 1877–1895.* Frankfurt: Suhrkamp, 1966. Contains an altogether remarkable letter written by Hesse when he was fifteen about being sent to an "Insane Asylum for Epileptics and the Mentally Retarded." This is, in my opinion, the one great thing Hesse wrote.

Hilberg, Raul. *The Destruction of the European Jews,* revised, definitive ed. 3 vols. New York: Holmes and Meier, 1985.

Hilberman, Elaine. "Overview: The 'Wife-Beater's Wife' Reconsidered." *American Journal of Psychiatry,* 137 (1980): 1336–47.

———— and Kit Munson. "Sixty Battered Women." *Victimology* 2 (1978): 460–70. An excellent, humane account.

Hirschprung. "Erfahrungen über Onanie bei kleinen Kindern." *Berliner klinische Wochenschrift,* 23 (1896): 628–31. Recommends hospitalization for the "disease" of masturbation, on the grounds that, if left to their parents, the children will be too severely or too leniently treated.

Houghton, Walter E. *The Victorian Frame of Mind, 1830–1870.* New Haven: Yale University Press, 1975.

Hudson, Robert P. "The Biography of Disease: Lessons from Chlorosis." *Bulletin of the History of Medicine,* 51 (1977): 448–63.

Huschka, Mabel. "The Incidence and Character of Masturbation Threats in a Group of Problem Children." *Psychoanalytic Quarterly*, 7 (1938): 338–56. A valuable study of how parents terrify children with threats about the dire consequences of masturbating.

Israel, J. *L'hystérique, le sexe et le médicin*. Paris: Masson, 1980.

Jeffreys, Sheila. *The Spinster and Her Enemies: Feminism and Sexuality 1880–1930*. London: Pandora, 1985. A brilliant study of the historical silencing of women's organized resistance to sexual exploitation.

Jolly, F. "Ueber Hysterie bei Kindern." *Wiener medizinische Presse*, 22 (1892): 841–45. On the "symptom" of fantasy as a pathogenic agent.

Kaplan, J. Martin. "The Misdiagnosis of Child Abuse." *American Family Practitioner*, 30 (1984): 197–200. An example of how physicians underestimate the seriousness of sexual abuse of children.

Keilson, Hans. *Sequentielle Traumatisierung bei Kindern*. Stuttgart: Ferdinand Enke, 1979. A remarkably complete study of Jewish orphans in Holland during the Second World War.

Kempe, C. H. et al. "The Battered Child Syndrome." *Journal of the American Medical Association*, 181 (1962): 17–24. The classic article, recognizing the prevalence of the physical abuse of children.

Kern, Stephen. *Anatomy and Destiny: A Cultural History of the Human Body*. Indianapolis: Bobbs-Merrill, 1975.

Kittrie, Nicholas N. *The Right to Be Different: Deviance and Enforced Therapy*. Baltimore: Johns Hopkins University Press, 1971.

Krafft-Ebing, Richard von. "Ueber pollutionsartige Vorgänge beim Weibe." *Wiener medizinische Presse*, 29 (1888): 466–69. A classic article which considers women's sexual desires as a sign of psychopathology.

———. "Bemerkungen über 'geschlechtliche Hörigkeit' und Masochismus." *Jahrbücher für Psychiatrie*, 9 (1890): 199–211.

———. *Psychopathia Sexualis*, 15th ed. Stuttgart: Ferdinand Enke, 1918 (first pub. 1880).

Kroemer, Dr. Medicinalrath. "Beitrag zur Castrationsfrage." *Allgemeine Zeitschrift für Psychiatrie*, 52 (1896): 1–74. Surveys over 220 articles dealing with the castration of women by gynecologists and psychiatrists.

Lancet, 1866. "The Operation of Excision of the Clitoris." Saturday, December 22, editorial.

———, June 12, 1866, to December 26, 1866. Letters to the Editor, concerning clitoridectomy and the Baker-Brown Case.

Lapon, Lenny. *Mass Murderers in White Coats: Psychiatric Genocide in Nazi Germany and the United States*. Springfield, Mass.: Psychiatric Genocide Research Institute (P.O. Box 80071), 1986. A commendable study.

Laquer, B. "Aphorismen über psychische Diät." *Deutsche Zeitschrift für Nervenheilkunde*, 23 (1902–3): 336–41. Prescriptions for keeping children from any kind of mental or intellectual stimulation.

La Roche, Julie. *Irrenanstalt und Millionenerbe: Streiflichter aus einer Basler Millionärsfamilie und einer thurgauischen Irrenanstalt.* Zurich: J. Enderli, 1897. An extraordinary autobiographical comment by a nineteen-year-old woman who was incarcerated in the Binswanger psychiatric clinic, Bellevue, for attempting to marry the man she loved.

Leavitt, Judith Walzer, ed. *Women and Health in America: Historical Readings.* Madison: University of Wisconsin Press, 1984. A useful anthology.

Lederer, Laura, ed. *Take Back the Night: Women on Pornography.* New York: Morrow, 1980. A groundbreaking collection.

Lerner, Melvin J. *The Belief in a Just World: A Fundamental Delusion.* New York: Plenum, 1980.

Levy, David M. "Critical Evaluation of the Present State of Child Psychiatry." *American Journal of Psychiatry,* 108 (1952): 481–94.

Lévy, Marie-Françoise. *De mères et filles: l'éducation des Françaises, 1850–1880.* Paris: Calmann-Lévy, 1984.

Linden, Robin Ruth, Darlene R. Pagano, Diana E. H. Russell and Susan Leigh Star. *Against Sadomasochism: A Radical Feminist Analysis.* Palo Alto: Frog in the Well, 1982. An excellent collection.

Loimann, Gustav. "Ueber Onanismus beim Weibe als eine besondere Form von verkehrter Richtung des Geschlechtstriebes." *Therapeutische Monatsschrift,* 4 (1890): 165–68. One of the first articles about "female" masturbation.

London Rape Crisis Centre. *Sexual Violence: The Reality for Women.* London: The Women's Press Handbook Series, 1984.

Longo, Lawrence D. "The Rise and Fall of Battey's Operation: A Fashion in Surgery." *Bulletin of the History of Medicine,* 53 (1979): 244–67.

Löwenfeld, Leopold. *Sexualleben und Nervenleiden: Die nervösen Störungen sexuellen Ursprungs.* Wiesbaden: J. F. Bergmann, 1891.

MacDonald, R. H. "The Frightful Consequences of Onanism." *Journal of the History of Ideas,* 28 (1967): 1–25.

Macfarlane, Kee, Barbara McComb Jones and Linda L. Jenstrom, eds. *Sexual Abuse of Children: Selected Readings.* Department of Health, Education and Welfare, Pub. No. (OHDS): 78-30161. Washington, D.C.: Government Printing Office, 1980.

MacKinnon, Catharine A. *Sexual Harassment of Working Women.* New Haven: Yale University Press, 1979. A landmark, brilliant study.

———. *Feminism Unmodified: Occasional Discourses on Life and Law.* Cambridge, Mass.: Harvard University Press, 1987. A collection of important and influential speeches.

Malamuth, Neil M. and Edward Donnerstein, eds. *Pornography and Sexual Aggression.* Orlando, Florida: Academic Press (Harcourt Brace Jovanovich), 1984.

———. "Rape Proclivity among Males." *Journal of Social Issues,* 37 (1981): 138–57.

———. "The Mass Media and Aggression Against Women: Research Findings and

Prevention. In A. Burgess, ed., *Handbook of Research on Pornography and Sexual Assault*. New York: Garland, 1984.

Martin, Del. *Battered Wives*. San Francisco: Volcano Press, 1981. One of the first important books on this subject.

Masson, Jeffrey Moussaieff. *The Assault on Truth: Freud's Suppression of the Seduction Theory*. New York: Farrar, Straus and Giroux, 1984.

————. *The Complete Letters of Sigmund Freud to Wilhelm Fliess, 1887–1904*. Cambridge: Belknap Press, Harvard University, 1985.

Melton, Gary B. "Children's Competency to Testify." *Law and Human Behavior*, 5 (1981): 73–84. A scholarly analysis that demonstrates children's reliability.

Merner. "Zur Frage der Züchtigungen durch die Lehrer: Zwei Fälle." *Vierteljahrsschrift für gerichtliche Medicin und öffentliches Sanitätswesen*, 50 (1889): 254–64. One of the rare accounts of the death of a child from the violence of a schoolteacher.

Metzger, Deena. "It Is Always the Woman Who Is Raped." *American Journal of Psychiatry*, 133 (1976): 405–8. Excellent, passionate statement about rape and other forms of violence.

Midelfort, H. Erik. *Witch Hunting in Southwestern Germany, 1562–1684*. Palo Alto: Stanford University Press, 1972.

Möbius, Paul. *Ueber den physiologischen Schwachsinn des Weibes*. Halle: C. Marhold, 1900. An often-cited book on the physiological feeblemindedness of women.

Moll, Albert. *Das nervöse Weib*. Berlin: F. Fontane, 1898.

Moreau de Tours, Paul. *La folie chez les enfants*. Paris: Baillière, 1888. Describes the dire consequences of masturbation for children.

Morris, Michelle. *If I Should Die Before I Wake*. Los Angeles: J. P. Tarcher, 1982. One of the most moving accounts of incest ever written.

Murray, Janet Horowitz. *Strong-Minded Women and Other Lost Voices from 19th-Century England*. New York: Pantheon, 1982. Excellent anthology of original sources.

Nelson, S. *Incest: Fact and Myth*. Edinburgh: Stramullion, 1982. A tiny but forceful book packed with excellent ideas.

Niederland, William. "Schreber and Flechsig: A Further Contribution to the 'Kernel of Truth' in Schreber's Delusional System." *Journal of the American Psychoanalytic Association*, 16 (1968): 740–48. A brilliant and orginal piece of research.

Oppenheim, Hermann. *Nervenkrankheit und Lektüre. Nervenleiden und Erziehung. Die ersten Zeichen der Nervosität des Kindesalters*, 2nd ed. Berlin: S. Karger, 1907. A classic statement by one of the leading psychiatrists of his day.

Pagelow, Mildred Daley. *Woman-Battering: Victims and Their Experiences*. Beverly Hills: Sage, 1981.

————. *Family Violence*. New York: Praeger, 1984.

Pearsall, Ronald. *The Worm in the Bud: The World of Victorian Sexuality*. New York: Macmillan, 1969.

Pelman, C. *Nervösität und Erziehung*, 3rd ed. Bonn: Emil Strauss, 1888.

Penfold, P. Susan and Gillian A. Walker. *Women and the Psychiatric Paradox.* Montreal: Eden Press, 1983.

Peretti, J. "Gynäkologische Behandlung und Geistesstörung." *Berliner klinische Wochenschrift,* 20 (1883): 140–45.

Perillon, Marie-Christine. *Vie de femmes.* Paris: Horvath, 1981.

Perrot, Philippe. *Le travail des apparences: ou les transformations du corps féminin XVIIIe–XIXe siècle.* Paris: Editions du Seuil, 1984.

Pfohl, Stephen J. "The 'Discovery' of Child Abuse." *Social Problems,* 24 (1977): 310–23. Excellent explanation for the "medicalization" of child abuse.

Pichevin, R. *Des abus de la castration chez la femme.* Paris: G. Steinheil, 1890. An excellent overview with a fine bibliography. This is the only nineteenth-century work I found that unqualifiedly opposes castration of women as barbarous, inhumane torture.

Pizzey, Erin. *Scream Quietly or the Neighbours Will Hear.* London: Penguin, 1974.

Platt, Anthony M. *The Child Savers: The Invention of Delinquency.* Chicago: University of Chicago Press, 1969.

Pouillet, Thésée. *Psychopathie sexuelle: De l'onanisme chez la femme.* Paris: Librairie Vigot Frères, 1897.

Quetel, Claude and Pierre Morel. *Les fous et leurs médecins de la Renaissance au XXe siècle.* Paris: Hachette, 1979.

Rafter, Nicole Hahn and Elizabeth A. Stanko. *Judge, Lawyer, Victim, Thief: Women, Gender Roles, and Criminal Justice.* Boston: Northeastern University Press, 1982.

Redlich, Johann. "Ein Beitrag zur Kenntniss der Pseudologia phantastica." *Allgemeine Zeitschrift für Psychiatrie,* 57 (1900): 63–86.

Reuter, Gabriele. *Aus guter Familie: Leidensgeschichte eines Mädchens.* Berlin: S. Fischer, 1895. The last chapter of this novel deals with the emotional breakdown of the heroine, who is slowly driven to madness by her oppressive environment. The description of the German mental asylum for women in which this takes place is unusually vivid.

Rhodes, Dusty and Sandra McNeill, eds. *Women Against Violence Against Women.* London: Onlywomen Press, 1985. Excellent collection of radical feminist pieces.

Rieger, Conrad. *Die Castration in rechtlicher, socialer und vitaler Hinsicht.* Jena: Gustav Fischer, 1900.

Riemer, Eleanor S. and John C. Fout. *European Women: A Documentary History, 1789–1945.* New York: Schocken, 1980.

Rohleder, Hermann. *Die Masturbation.* Berlin: H. Kornfeld, 1899. A major work, often cited by German authors.

Rosenberg, Rosalind. *Beyond Separate Spheres: Intellectual Roots of Modern Feminism.* New Haven: Yale University Press, 1982.

Rosenfeld, Alvin A. "Endogamic Incest and the Victim-Perpetrator Model." *American Journal of Diseases of Children,* 133 (1979): 406–10. An example of how psychiatrists can appear to be sympathetic but actually maintain the standard views of the profession.

Rouy, Hersilie. *Mémoires d'une aliénée* (Publiés par Le Normant des Varannes). Paris: Paul Ollendorff, 1883. The most remarkable autobiography I have ever seen of a person incarcerated in psychiatric institutes.

Rush, Florence. "The Sexual Abuse of Children: A Feminist Point of View." *The Radical Therapist*, 2 (1971): 4. Probably the first published recognition of the problem.

———. "The Freudian Cover-up." *Chrysalis*, 1 (1977): 31–45. The first feminist critique of Freud's abandonment of the seduction hypothesis.

———. *The Best Kept Secret: Sexual Abuse of Children*. New York: McGraw-Hill, 1980. An outstanding work that did much to awaken people's conscience and awareness.

Russell, Diana E. H. *The Politics of Rape: The Victim's Perspective*. New York: Stein and Day, 1975.

———. "The Incidence and Prevalence of Intrafamilial and Extrafamilial Sexual Abuse of Female Children." *Child Abuse and Neglect*, Vol. 7 (1983), 133–46. The classic, authoritative study.

———. *Sexual Exploitation: Rape, Child Sexual Abuse, and Workplace Harassment*. Beverly Hills: Sage, 1984. Outstanding collection of essays by one of the leading scholars in the field.

———. *The Secret Trauma: Incest in the Lives of Girls and Women*. New York: Basic Books, 1986. Perhaps the best book on incest.

Rutschky, Katharina, ed. *Schwarze Pädagogik. Quellen zur Naturgeschichte der bürgerlichen Erziehung*. Frankfurt am Main: Ullstein, 1977. A very useful anthology of early German texts on child-raising.

Ryan, William. *Blaming the Victim*. New York: Vintage, 1972. One of the great works of our time.

Saadawi, Nawal El. *The Hidden Face of Eve: Women in the Arab World*. Tr. and ed. by Dr. Sherif Hetata. Boston: Beacon Press, 1982.

Schaps, Regina. *Hysterie und Weiblichkeit: Wissenschaftsmythen über die Frau*. Frankfurt am Main: Campus, 1982.

Scherpf, L. "Zur Aetiologie und Symptomatologie kindlicher Seelenstörungen." *Jahrbuch für Kinderheilkunde*, 16 (1880): 167–323. On masturbation and "moral insanity."

Schmalfuss, G. "Zur Castration bei Neurosen." *Archiv für Gynaekologie*, 26: (1885) 1–57.

Schmuckler, J. K. "Die Onanie im Kindesalter." *Archiv für Kinderheilkunde*, 25 (1896): 241–45. On the importance of pediatricians being able to "diagnose" masturbation.

Schrag, Peter. *Mind Control*. New York: Random House, 1978.

——— and Diana Divoky. *The Myth of the Hyperactive Child and Other Means of Child Control*. New York: Random House, 1975.

Schultze, B. S. "Gynäkologische Behandlung und Geistesstörung." *Berliner klinische Wochenschrift*, 20 (1883): 340–43.

Scull, Andrew, ed. *Madhouses, Mad-Doctors, and Madmen: The Social History of Psychiatry in the Victorian Era*. Philadelphia: University of Pennsylvania Press, 1981. A useful anthology.

Scully, Diana and Pauline Bart. "A Funny Thing Happened on the Way to the Orifice: Women and Gynecology Textbooks." *American Journal of Sociology*, 78 (1973): 1045–50.

Sebbar, Leila. *On tue les petites filles*. Paris: Stock, 1978. One of the few books about sexual abuse of girls in France.

Seidenberg, Robert and Karen DeCrow. *Women Who Marry Houses: Panic and Protest in Agoraphobia*. New York: McGraw-Hill, 1983. A feminist account of agoraphobia.

Shorter, Edward. *A History of Women's Bodies*. New York: Basic Books, 1982.

Showalter, Elaine. "Victorian Women and Insanity." In Scull, pp. 313–39. An excellent account of the clitoridectomies performed by Baker-Brown in England.

———. *The Female Malady: Women, Madness and English Culture, 1830–1980*. New York: Pantheon, 1985.

Smith-Rosenberg, Carroll. *Disorderly Conduct: Visions of Gender in Victorian America*. New York: Alfred A. Knopf, 1985. A collection of essays by one of the foremost feminist historians in the U.S.

Snowden, Rich. "Working with Incest Offenders: Excuses, Excuses, Excuses." *Aegis* 35 (1982): 56–63.

Soldan, Wilhelm Gottlieb. *Geschichte der Hexenprozesse aus den Quellen dargestellt*, 1843. 2nd ed. (ed. Heinrich Heppe), Stuttgart, 1880; 3rd ed., Munich, 1912.

Spitz, Rene A. "Authority and Masturbation: Some Remarks on a Bibliographical Investigation." *Psychoanalytic Quarterly*, 21 (1952): 490–527. Includes a 317-item bibliography particularly useful for the German literature.

Stanko, Elizabeth A. *Intimate Intrusions: Women's Experience of Male Violence*. Boston: Routledge & Kegan Paul, 1985.

Stark, Evan, Anne Flitcraft and William Frazier. "Medicine and Patriarchal Violence: The Social Construction of a 'Private' Event." *International Journal of Health Services*, 9 (1979): 461–93.

Steiner, Ferdinand. "Beiträge zur Kenntniss der hysterischen Affectionen bei Kindern." *Jahrbuch für Kinderheilkunde*, 44 (1897): 187–221. Valuable for its long bibliography.

Sterz, Heinrich. "Ueber psychische Störungen im Pubertätsalter." *Jahrbücher für Psychiatrie*, 1 (1879): 94–119.

Sulloway, Frank. *Freud: Biologist of the Mind*. New York: Basic Books, 1979.

Summit, Roland. "Beyond Belief: The Reluctant Discovery of Incest." In M. Kirkpatrick, ed., *Women in Context*. New York: Plenum, 1981. One of the few works by a male psychiatrist recognizing the reality of incest.

——— and J. Kryso. "Sexual Abuse of Children: A Clinical Spectrum." *American Journal of Orthopsychiatry*, 48 (1978): 237–51.

Tanner, Thomas Hawkes. "On Excision of the Clitoris as a Cure for Hysteria."

Transactions of the Obstetrical Society of London, 8 (1867): 360–84. Supports Baker-Brown's operation.

Tauffer, Wilhelm. "Beiträge zur Lehre der Castration der Frauen, im Anschlusse an 12 Fälle." *Zeitschrift für Geburtshilfe und Gynäkologie*, 9 (1883): 38–65.

Trevor-Roper, H. R. *The European Witch-Craze of the Sixteenth and Seventeenth Centuries*. New York: Harper, 1965.

Trombley, Stephen. *All That Summer She Was Mad: Virginia Woolf, Female Victim of Male Medicine*. New York: Continuum, 1982.

Trube-Becker, Elisabeth. *Gewalt gegen das Kind: Vernachlässigung, Misshandlung, sexueller Missbrauch und Tötung von Kindern*. Heidelberg: Kriminalistik, 1982. A comprehensive overview of violence against children in modern Germany, including sexual assault.

Tuczek. "Zur Lehre von der Hysterie der Kinder." *Berliner klinische Wochenschrift*, 23 (1886): 511–14, 535–36. Chilling case history of a ten-year-old girl.

Veith, Ilza. *Hysteria: The History of a Disease*. Chicago: University of Chicago Press, 1975.

Virkkunen, Matti. "Victim-Precipitated Pedophilia Offences." *British Journal of Criminology* 15 (1975): 175–80.

Walker, Lenore E. *The Battered Woman*. New York: Harper Colophon, 1979.

Walters, Ronald G. *Primers for Prudery: Sexual Advice to Victorian America*. Englewood Cliffs: Prentice-Hall, 1974. Some good quotes on masturbation and nymphomania.

Ward, Elizabeth. *Father-Daughter Rape*. New York: Grove, 1985.

Wettley, Annemarie and W. Leibbrand. *Von der 'Psychopathia sexualis' zur Sexualwissenschaft*. Stuttgart: Ferdinand Enke, 1959.

Williams, Gertrude J. and John Money, eds. *Traumatic Abuse and Neglect of Children at Home*. Baltimore: Johns Hopkins University Press, 1980.

Young, Leontine. *Wednesday's Children: A Study of Child Neglect and Abuse*. New York: McGraw-Hill, 1964. One of the first books to address this topic.

Young, Wayland. *Eros Denied: Sex in Western Society*. New York: Grove, 1964.

Index